675 Reproducible Ways To Develop Yourself And Your People

Strategies, ideas, and activities for self-development and learning in the workplace

Laurel Alexander

HRD Press, Inc. • Amherst • Massachusetts

Published by: HRD Press, Inc.
22 Amherst Road
Amherst, Massachusetts 01002
1-800-822-2801 (U.S. and Canada)
1-413-253-3488
1-413-253-3490 (fax)
http://www.hrdpress.com

ISBN: 978-1-61014-387-5

Production services by Anctil Virtual Office
Cover design by Eileen Klockars
Editorial services by Sally M. Farnham

Contents

Introduction

Self-development is an organic process: you can start from any point and your journey unfolds from there. Defining self-development is a little like defining a painting; it can mean anything to anyone. Self-development is essentially a state of awareness. Imagine yourself as an onion, a cabbage, or a rose—self-development is about peeling back the layers of the self and bringing the real you into light and consciousness. As a rule, we muddle through life, reacting and responding: self-development is about purposefully traveling through life with a sense of will and awareness about our thoughts, feelings, and behaviors, and changing whatever we can through action.

Self-development is a rippling-out process. Awareness and changes ripple out from the center of the individual and affect their behavior that in turn affects those closest to them, out into the community and into the workplace. If we are each catalysts of rippling change, consider how much we must affect each other. Although self-development is a personal process, its organic unfolding impacts on others who, in turn, affect us.

The self-development of individuals affects the organization they work for, because their behavior impacts on organizational culture and delivery. The organization has a developmental process and growth plan of its own origin, which gives rise to developmental opportunities for individuals who in turn are developing themselves, which has an input into the organizational growth, and so on . . .

This resource is designed as a dip-in, dip-out aid to the self-development of yourself and your people. It can be used in a number of flexible ways. Each module starts with an overview of the subject and moves on to exercises categorized as follows:

◆ Individual Tasks and Reflections
◆ Working with Others (a peer, colleague, or partner)
◆ Working with a Mentor
◆ Developing Others (these exercises are for facilitators to use in groups)
◆ Useful Web Sites (live at the time of writing this resource)

The exercises can be used in isolation or in conjunction with other learning methods or as a base for other self-development work, including:

Job shadowing	Job rotation
Task-force work	Projects
Portfolio development	Action learning sets
Field work	Research
Assignments	Case studies
Workbooks	Using reference books
Learning log development	Assessments
Biography work	

Achieving Ambitions with Goal Setting

INTRODUCTION

Goal setting is a very powerful technique that can yield strong returns in all areas of your life. By knowing precisely what you want to achieve, you know what you have to concentrate on and improve, and what is merely a distraction. By setting goals, you can:

◆ Achieve more
◆ Improve performance
◆ Increase your motivation to achieve
◆ Increase your pride and satisfaction in your achievements
◆ Improve your self-confidence
◆ Plan to eliminate attitudes that hold you back

Research has shown that people who use goal setting effectively:

◆ Suffer less from stress and anxiety
◆ Concentrate better
◆ Show more self-confidence
◆ Perform better
◆ Are happier and more satisfied

The first step in setting personal goals is to consider what you want to achieve in your lifetime. Setting lifetime goals gives you the overall perspective that shapes all other aspects of your decision making. Try to set goals in all of the following categories:

Career	Learning
Creativity	Attitude
Physical fitness	Hobbies
Family	Finance
Community work	Social life

The way in which you set goals strongly influences their effectiveness. The following broad guidelines apply to setting effective goals:

◆ Express your goals positively.
◆ Set a precise goal, putting in dates, times, and amounts so that achievement can be measured.
◆ Where you have several goals, give each a priority. This not only helps you avoid feeling overwhelmed by too many goals, it also helps direct your attention to the most important ones.
◆ Write goals down to avoid confusion and give them more force.
◆ Keep the immediate goals you are working toward small and achievable. If a goal is too large, you may feel that you are not making progress toward it.

Set performance, not outcome, goals.

You should take care to set goals over which you have as much control as possible. Goals based on outcomes are vulnerable to failure because of circumstances and factors beyond your control. If you base your goals on personal performance, skills, or knowledge to be acquired, then you can keep control over the achievement of your goals and draw satisfaction from them. Another flawed approach is to have outcome goals based on the rewards of achieving something—for example, increased income or recognition by others.

Set specific, measurable goals.

If you achieve all the conditions of a measurable goal, then you can be confident and comfortable in its achievement. If you consistently fail to meet a measurable goal, then you can adjust it or analyze the reason for failure and take appropriate action to improve your skills. Goals may be set unrealistically high for the following reasons:

◆ Other people (parents, media, society) can set unrealistic goals for you, based on what they want.
◆ If you do not have a clear, realistic understanding of what you are trying to achieve and of the skills and knowledge to be mastered, it is difficult to set effective and realistic goals.
◆ Many people base their goals on their best performance, however long ago that took place. This ignores the inevitable backsliding that can occur for good reasons and the factors that led to that best performance. It is better to set goals that raise your average performance and make it more consistent.

Alternatively, goals can be set too low for the following reasons:

◆ **Fear of failure.** If you are frightened of failure, you will not take the risks needed for optimum performance. As you apply goal setting and achieve goals, your self-confidence should increase, helping you take bigger risks. Consider failure as positive, because it shows you areas in which you can improve your skills and performance.
◆ **Taking it too easy.** It is easy to use the reasons for not setting goals unrealistically high as an excuse to set them too low. If you're not prepared to stretch yourself and work hard, then you are extremely unlikely to achieve anything of any real worth.

Setting goals at the correct level is a skill that is acquired by practice. You should set goals so that they are slightly out of your immediate grasp, but not so far distant that there is no hope of achieving them.

When you are thinking about how to achieve goals, asking the following questions can help you focus on the sub-goals that lead to their achievement:

◆ What skills do I need to achieve this?
◆ What information and knowledge do I need?
◆ What help, assistance, or collaboration do I need?
◆ What resources do I need?
◆ What can block progress?

Goal setting can go wrong for a number of reasons:

◆ Goals can be so vague that they are useless. If achievement cannot be measured, goal setting will not increase your self-confidence, nor can you observe progress toward a greater goal. Set precise, quantitative goals.

◆ Goal setting can be unsystematic, sporadic, and disorganized. If this is the case, your goals will be forgotten, you will fail to measure the achievement of goals, and you will gain no feedback to put into new goals. Be organized and regular in the way in which you use goal setting.
◆ Too many unprioritized goals may be set, leading to a feeling of overload.

When you have achieved a goal, take time to enjoy the resulting satisfaction. Absorb the implications of the achievement and observe the progress you have made toward other goals.

If you have failed to reach a goal, ensure that you learn the lessons of the failure. These may be that:

◆ You didn't try hard enough
◆ Your technique, skills, or knowledge were faulty and need to be enhanced
◆ The goal you set was unrealistic

If you have achieved a goal, this should feed back into your next goals:

◆ If the goal was easily achieved, make your next goals harder.
◆ If the goal took a discouraging length of time to achieve, make your next goals a little easier.
◆ If, while achieving the goal you noticed a deficit in your skills, set goals to put this right.

Remember, too, that goals change as you mature; adjust them regularly to reflect this growth in your personality. If goals no longer hold any attraction, let them go. Goal setting is your servant, not your master; it should bring you real pleasure, satisfaction, and a sense of achievement.

INDIVIDUAL TASKS AND REFLECTIONS

·····························

1.1 Lifetime Goals

Consider the following areas of your life:

Career	Learning
Creativity	Attitude
Physical fitness	Hobbies
Family	Finance
Community work	Social life

◆ Decide your goals in these categories and assign a priority to them from A to D.
◆ Review the goals and reprioritize until you are satisfied that the goals and priorities you have set reflect the shape of the life that you want to lead. (Make sure that the goals you have set are those that you—not your parents, spouse, family, or people around you—want them to be.)
◆ Once you have set your lifetime goals, set a 25-year plan of smaller goals that should be achieved if you are to fulfill your lifetime plan.
◆ Then set a five-year plan, one-year plan, six-month plan, and one-month plan of progressively smaller goals that should be attained in order to achieve your lifetime goals.
◆ Set a daily "to do" list of things that you should do today to achieve your lifetime goals.
◆ Finally, review your plans, and make sure that they suit the way in which you want to live your life.
◆ Once you have decided your first goal plans, keep the process going by reviewing and updating your "to do" list daily. Periodically review your other plans, and modify them to reflect your changing priorities.

WORKING

WITH OTHERS

....

WORKING

WITH A MENTOR

....

DEVELOPING

OTHERS

....

RECOMMENDED

HRD PRESS TITLES

....

1.2 Peer Goals

Consider your peers. Do you share lifetime goals with them? What influences you and your peers in your department of lifetime goals? How do these goals change and why?

1.3 Career and Learning Goals

Consider the areas of career and learning in your life (you could include any other lifetime goals as well) and work through the following with your mentor.

◆ Decide your career goals and assign a priority to them from A to D.
◆ Review the goals and reprioritize until you have satisfied that the goals and priorities you have set reflect the shape of the life that you want to lead. (Make sure that the goals you have set are the goals that you—not your parents, spouse, family, or people around you—want to be.)
◆ Once you have set your lifetime goals, set a 25-year plan of smaller goals that should be achieved if you are to fulfill your lifetime plan.
◆ Then set a five-year plan, one-year plan, six-month plan, and one-month plan of progressively smaller goals that should be attained in order to achieve your lifetime goals.
◆ Set a daily "to do" list of things that you should do today to achieve your lifetime goals.
◆ Finally, review your plans, and make sure that they suit the way in which you want to live your life.
◆ Once you have decided your first goal plans, keep the process going by reviewing and updating your "to do" list on a daily basis. Periodically review your other plans, and modify them to reflect your changing priorities.

1.4 Personal Goal Setting

Introduce the subject of achieving ambitions with goal setting. Ask each learner to choose one area of lifetime goals and to identify a connected goal. Using an action plan, ask the learners to create a (timed) process for achieving this goal. Organize them into groups of three to discuss each goal and provide feedback. Go back into the larger group to discuss the benefits or otherwise of action plans and feedback.

SkillBuilders, 35 different titles, 12 pp. each.
Goal and Objective Setting Profile, 16 pp.

INTRODUCTION

Fact. There is more to life than work.

Fact. Eight-hour days are things of the past. You now spend 10 to 14 hours working. That doesn't leave much time for anything else, does it?

Is your life out of balance? Do you spend more time at work than you would like? Do you concentrate too much on meeting everyone else's needs? How do your own needs get met?

Finding and maintaining a comfortable balance in life is a challenge. Most probably, you direct so much time and attention on work that you sacrifice other areas of your life. Think of balance as paying attention to every aspect of your life on a regular basis. It's about attending to your multidimensional self so that you can make conscious choices about how you spend your time and energy at work and in life.

There are four aspects of living that need your attention: the *physical, mental, emotional,* and *spiritual* dimensions. Paying too little attention to any one of them will create the feeling of being out of sync with yourself. Appropriate attention to each dimension will give you the power to find the right mix of priorities and actions for creating a balance between life and work. When you're in balance, you are more creative and more productive. Listed below are some actions you can take in each of the dimensions that will assist you in creating more balance between work and life:

1. Your physical self at work:
   —Take frequent breaks.
   —If you find you are sitting down a lot, stand up and move around approximately every 15 minutes.
   —If you're on your feet, wear comfortable shoes, stretch your back and legs, and sit down periodically.
   —Invest in an ergonomically correct work area.
   —Take time for well-balanced meals.

2. Your *physical* self in life:
   —Exercise.
   —Rest and relax your body.
   —Get the appropriate amount of sleep you need.
   —Eat nutritious foods.
   —Refrain from smoking.
   —If you drink alcohol, do so in moderation.

3. Your *emotional* self at work:
   —Monitor the emotions you feel.
   —Take time to process what you observe.
   —Refrain from dumping your feelings on someone else, especially when you're feeling angry.
   —Take a break before dealing with an emotionally charged situation so that you can respond in an appropriate manner.
   —At the end of the working day, release all your concerns so that you can be ready for time outside of work.
   —Leave work at work.

4. Your *emotional* self in life:
   —Take time for yourself daily.
   —Meditate, commune with nature, or read inspirational material.
   —Sit and do nothing.
   —Become comfortable with who you are outside of your title and occupation.

5. Your *mental* self at work:
   —Plan your work and your time.
   —Look for ways to eliminate time-bandits by using technology, uncluttering your office, and saying "no" to requests that don't fit in with your master plan. Set reasonable schedules for project completion.
   —Delegate any work you don't really need to do yourself.

6. Your *mental* self in life:
   —Schedule family and personal activities.
   —Unclutter your home.
   —Let go of perfectionist tendencies about how things should be.
   —Set goals that allow you to discover yourself.
   —Pursue a variety of interests unrelated to work.

7. Your *spiritual* self at work:
   —Align yourself as truthfully as possible with the organizational direction.
   —Reflect daily on your personal goals and behavior.
   —Consider whether you're on the most appropriate path for you.
   —Determine whether your daily activity is aligned with what you truly want to accomplish.

How you live your life is much more important than what you do. Creating and maintaining balance in life is worth the effort because you'll enjoy the process of living while being true to your essential self.

INDIVIDUAL TASKS AND REFLECTIONS

2.1 A Mind Map of Your Life

Where are you now and are you satisfied with your position? Drawing a Mind Map* of your life can help identify areas of satisfaction and dissatisfaction. Take a large sheet of paper and write "MYSELF NOW" in the center. From this, draw branches representing different areas of your life. Next draw lines coming from the main branches, representing offshoots. Finally, add a star to show satisfaction and a black spot to show dissatisfaction. Parts of your life you might want to include are: ambitions, travel, work, health, hobbies, friends, lovers, family, money, retirement, education, creativity, spirituality, and so on.

2.2 Your Relationship With Your Work

◆ Do you see work as a means to an end—for example, your salary pays the bills you have to pay?
◆ Do you see work as an escape from being at home?
◆ How do you see work fitting in with your life?

2.3 Looking After Yourself

Rate yourself in the following questionnaire, using the scale "often," "sometimes," or "never."

---

*Buzan, T. (1974), *Use Your Head*, London: BBC Publications.

Physical	Rating
I eat balanced and regular meals including fresh foods and healthy snacks.	
I get enough sleep—six to eight hours a day on a regular basis.	
I feel safe in my relationships and in my environment.	
I take steps to protect myself in risky or unsafe situations.	
I do some form of physical activity at least three to four times a week.	
I take care of my health needs—physical, dental, eye check-ups.	
Emotional and Social	**Rating**
I give and receive in terms of warm touch, hugs, and/or sexual expression.	
I express my emotions—I frequently laugh, cry when I'm sad, and so on.	
I ask for, and accept, nurturing from others when I need it.	
I have opportunities to nurture and encourage others.	
I have friends with whom I can celebrate in good times and call when I am down.	
I take time for fun and leisure.	
Intellectual	**Rating**
I have opportunities to learn, to solve problems, to grow, and to change.	
I do things that give me a sense of purpose, joy, and fulfillment.	
I make my own choices and set goals for myself.	
Spiritual	**Rating**
I accept myself as unique and worthy, with strengths and weaknesses.	
I take time for solitude and to reflect on what is important to me.	
I have opportunities to live by the values I believe in.	

WORKING WITH OTHERS

....

2.4 How You Relate to Your Work Colleagues

◆ Do you have many friends at work?
◆ Do you socialize with your colleagues away from work?

2.5 Talking to Work Colleagues

Consider what you talk to work colleagues about—other than work issues!

2.6 Talking Outside of Work

Do you often talk about work outside of work?

2.7 Needs and Wants

Ask your mentor to ask you repeatedly "What do you need?" followed by "What do you want?" You can extend this exercise by sorting and prioritizing your answers under headings such as relationships, career, quality of life, and so on.

2.8 Life-Purpose Questions

Ask yourself the following questions:

◆ Does the work I'm currently doing express what I truly want to be doing? If not, how can I take steps toward discovering and doing work that would be personally fulfilling?
◆ Would I like to return to study and further my education and training? If so, how could I move in that direction?
◆ Do I have creative outlets? If not, what creative activities could I develop?
◆ Have I developed my spiritual nature? Would I like to explore this further?
◆ What would I like to have accomplished by the time I reach 70 in order to feel that my life has been meaningful and productive?
◆ What values give my life the greatest meaning—for example, happy family life, career achievement, good health, personal growth, and so on?
◆ What would be a summary of my most important life purposes?
◆ What are the obstacles to pursuing and realizing my life purposes?

2.9 Action Planning

Based on your answers to the above, set an action plan for: three months, six months, one year, and three years.

2.10 $1,000 for Nothing

Ask the learners to individually consider: "Suppose you were given a check for a $1,000 every week for doing absolutely nothing—would you still go to work? Why? If you didn't have to work, what would you do with your life?" Organize them into small groups to discuss, then reconvene the whole group for further discussion.

2.11 The Workaholic

Introduce the subject of balancing life and work. Brainstorm the characteristics and behavior of a workaholic.

2.12 Pie Chart of Life

Introduce the subject of balancing life and work. Ask the learners to identify the different areas of their life—for example, work, family, social interaction, special interests, and so on. Ask them to draw a pie chart or graph to show how much time, in their opinion, they give to each area. Do they want to change any emphasis? How might they do this?

RECOMMENDED HRD PRESS TITLES

The Complete Guide to Wellness, 600 pp.
Personal Stress and Well-being Assessment, 16 pp.

3

Basics of Transactional Analysis

Eric Berne, founder of transactional analysis (TA), made complex interpersonal transactions understandable. TA offers a concept explaining how our present life patterns originated in childhood and develops explanations of how we may continue to replay childhood strategies in adult life, even when these produce results that are self-defeating or painful.

TA is used in educational settings to help teachers and learners stay in clear communication and avoid setting up unproductive confrontation, in management and communications training, in organizational analysis, and by social workers, police, and religious clergy. In fact, TA can be used in any field in which there is a need for understanding individuals, relationships, and communication.

The Central Concepts of TA

The central concepts of TA are as follows:

1. **The ego state models.** An ego state is a set of related behaviors, thoughts, and feelings—a way in which we manifest a part of our personality at a given time. Transactional analysis portrays three ego states: Adult (behaving, thinking, and feeling in response to what is going on in the here and now), Parent (behaving, thinking, and feeling in ways that reflect one of your parents or other parent figures), and Child (behaving, thinking, and feeling as you used to when you were a child).

2. **Transactions, strokes.** We can address each other from any of our ego states, and reply in turn. This exchange is a transaction. The use of the ego state model to analyze sequences of transactions is true transactional analysis. When we transact with each other, I signal recognition of you and you return that recognition; any act of recognition is a stroke. People need strokes to maintain their psychical and psychological well-being.

3. **Life script.** Each of us in childhood writes a life story ourselves; most of it has been written by the age of seven, although we may revise it further during adolescence. As adults, we are usually no longer aware of the life story we have written, yet we are likely to live it out faithfully. This is our life script. In script analysis, we understand how people may set up problems for themselves, without being aware of this, and how they may begin to solve those problems.

4. **Discounting, redefining, symbiosis.** Sometimes we distort our perception of reality so that it fits our script; this is redefining. One way to ensure that the world seems to fit our script is to selectively ignore information without conscious intention; this is discounting. As adults, we may unconsciously enter into relationships that replay the childhood relationships we had with our parents. When this happens, and the two people function as though they had only two ego states between them instead of six, we refer to it as a symbiosis.

5. **Rackets, stamps, games.** As children we may notice that certain feelings are encouraged while others are prohibited. To get our strokes we may decide, without conscious awareness, to feel only permitted feelings. When, as adults, we continue to cover our authentic feelings with those that were permitted to us as children, these substitute feelings are known as racket feelings. If we experience a racket feeling and store it up instead of expressing it at the time, we are said to be saving a stamp. A game is a repetitive sequence of transactions in which both parties end up experiencing racket feelings.

6. **Autonomy.** To realize our full potential, we need to update the strategies for dealing with life that we decided on as infants. We need to move out of our script and gain autonomy. The tools of transactional analysis are designed to help people achieve that autonomy, the components of which are awareness, spontaneity, and the capacity for intimacy.

The philosophical assumptions of TA are:

◆ People or OK (I'm OK, you're OK).
◆ Everyone has the capacity to think
◆ People decide their own destiny, and these decisions can be changed.

We can have a fear of people in authority when there is an imbalance between "controlling parent" and "adopted child." This fear can be a result of our parents' unrealistic expectations of us. Their critical and blaming style may have had an influence on how we interact with others. We may see those in authority as having unrealistic expectations of us and fear that we can't meet them. As adults, we may misunderstand basic assertiveness from others as an attempt to control us. Our reaction might be to feel intimidated, to avoid confrontation or criticism, or to compromise our values to accommodate the authority figure. We may also tend to take things personally, become arrogant to conceal this, and feel incompetent. As we begin to feel more comfortable with authority/parent figures, we can place criticism in a more positive light and recognize that people in authority have their own fears and defenses. We come to realize that their behavior doesn't determine how we feel about ourselves, and we can start choosing our behavior rather than reacting to others. As we feel more comfortable with authority figures, we act with increased self-esteem and stand up for ourselves more.

Keywords for the Inner Parent

The nurturing parent:

◆ Is direct
◆ Is protective
◆ Nurtures
◆ Offers constructive criticism
◆ Encourages
◆ Is loving
◆ Loves unconditionally
◆ Shares power
◆ Supports
◆ Safeguards you against threat
◆ Is nonjudgmental
◆ Wants the best for you
◆ Is responsible
◆ Cares for you and others

◆ Is your own best friend
◆ Listens
◆ Looks after your health
◆ Is sympathetic
◆ Sees you have friends who care
◆ Has a built-in guide for survival
◆ Warns you of danger

The nurturing inner parent can also be overprotective and smothering.

The controlling parent:

◆ Tells you the do's and don'ts.
◆ Makes sure you do the right things.
◆ Deals only in "acceptable" behavior.

The controlling inner parent can also be hypercritical, demanding, conditional, judgmental, and manipulative.

Keywords for the Inner Child

Adopted Inner Child	Natural Inner Child
Powerless	Innocent
Helpless	Fun-loving
Demanding	Curious
Abandoned	Imaginative
Victim	Spontaneous
Lonely	Magical
Easily hurt	Energetic
Vulnerable	Open
Rejected	Loved
Dependent	Young
Manipulative	Warm
Compliant	Playful
"Good"	Fresh
Depressed	Sensitive
Withdrawn	Gregarious
Negative	Relaxed
Cynical	Into holidays, sports, jokes, travel
Avoids intimacy	Into nature, art, writing
Bears grudges	Into magic, acting, the spiritual
Doesn't know how to protect self	

An "adopted" or needy child can, as an adult, show the behavior and characteristics of a victim. Or they may ignore their own needs (as their needs were ignored in the past) and become a rescuer of others.

The Dynamics of the Inner Parent, Child, and Adult

Dialogue can take place between the Child and the Parent. This is where, in effect, we become our own parent. We are able to take responsibility and look after our own needs. The Adult part of our nature will encourage others to help themselves.

> **The Adult is . . .**
> an objective gatherer of information, adaptable, organized, intelligent, a tester of reality, thoughtful, a straight talker, objective.
>
> **Function**: to solve problems, to process data

> **The Inner Child**
> Recordings of early years, feelings, responses, experiences, and old behavior will show themselves via outward expression as an "adopted" child or a "natural" child.
>
> **Function**: to be admired and encouraged, to have fun and excitement, to experience creativity, spontaneity, and intimacy

> **The Inner Parent**
> Attitudes/behaviors from external sources (parent figures) become internalized and are then outwardly expressed.
>
> **Function**: to protect/ teach others, to make automatic decisions— for example, when to eat

◆ If you come from your **Adult only,** you are boring, robotic, and without compassion, and have relationship problems.
◆ If you come from your **Child only,** you can't think for yourself, and you need much support.
◆ If you come from your **Parent only,** you are not in touch with reality.

Parent, Child, and Adult Interpersonal Behaviors

| | Parent | | Child | | Adult |
	Critical	Nurturing	Adopted	Natural	
Voice tone/pitch	critical disgusted	loving concerned	whiney placating	free energetic	even
Words	bad should always	good splendid nice	can't wish try	want fun wow	practical why how
Gestures	arms folded frowning	smiling open arms	pouting helpless	loose uninhibited	alert open
Attitude	judgmental authoritarian	caring giving	demanding ashamed	curious changeable	evaluates

3.1 Mother

How did you experience your mother's parenting style in terms of "controlling parent" and "nurturing parent"?

3.2 Father

How did you experience your father's parenting style in terms of "controlling parent" and "nurturing parent"?

3.3 Your Parenting

If you are a parent, how would you assess your parenting style in terms of "controlling parent" and "nurturing parent"? How much of your parenting style is derived from your own parents?

3.4 Being Parented

Consider how others in your personal and professional life demonstrate their parenting style to you. How do you feel about their parenting style? How do you react?

3.5 You as a Child

Looking through the key words for "adopted child" and "natural child," what kind of child do you think you were?

3.6 Today's Child

How do you think you express the "adopted child" and "natural child" today?

WORKING WITH OTHERS

3.7 Parenting Others

Physical parenting isn't the only means through which we express our parenting styles; we also express it with intimate partners, friends, and work colleagues. How do you express your parenting style to intimate partners, friends, and work colleagues?

3.8 Positive Strokes

Today, give five people a positive stroke (a compliment).

3.9 Leading Others

How does your parenting style affect the way you lead or manage others?

WORKING WITH A MENTOR

3.10 Parenting and Work

Discuss with your mentor how your parenting style comes through in your work roles. How might you modify any unsuitable behaviors?

3.11 Child and Work

Discuss with your mentor how your inner child comes through in your work roles. How might you modify any unsuitable behaviors?

DEVELOPING

OTHERS

....

RECOMMENDED

HRD PRESS TITLES

....

3.12 Group Dynamics

Divide the learners into small groups of three. Ask each person to take turns being the Child (C), the Parent (P), and the Adult (A) in a role-play situation. In each role-play, two of the group interact while the third member observes.

Relating Styles Assessment and Workbook, 52 pp.

4
Building Positive Work Relationships

INTRODUCTION

Guidelines for building positive work relationships include the following:

◆ Be tolerant of others' weaknesses.

◆ Be tolerant of your own weaknesses. Don't be self-critical in front of another person, because, after a while, both of you will believe it.

◆ Be a good listener.

◆ Remember that physical warmth bonds people together. Try touching, a wink, eye-to-eye contact, a smile.

◆ Don't expect closeness through inappropriate behavior. Pouting, withdrawing, or being curt, negative, and whiney seldom draw people closer. Own up to your emotions and feelings and express them in an open, honest, clear, and direct way.

◆ Learn to give and accept praise. Compliment people on their character, not on their appearance. If you don't accept praise, people will eventually stop giving it.

◆ If you need to scream at someone, do it at the right person. Don't take it out on your spouse, children, or yourself.

◆ Learn to say "no" to yourself and others when, after objective self-assessment, it seems the appropriate thing to do. Rescuers and do-gooders are often resentful because they expect, but receive, little in return.

◆ When confronted, listen to what the other person has to say without expressing the typical defensive, reactive self that resides in each of us. No one likes to be criticized, but change cannot occur without self-awareness, which in turn cannot develop without feedback. Learn to ask for feedback. Be honest with your feelings to yourself and others.

◆ Learn to be direct, open, and clear in giving messages. Don't be afraid to express your negative emotions. The key to self-expression is how you state your feelings. Most relationships are strengthened through the creative use of conflict.

◆ Make time for yourself. Learn to look after yourself without always feeling selfish or guilty.

◆ Make time for others. Time is a matter of priorities. If you want to do something badly enough for yourself or another, you will make the time.

◆ Remember that 70 percent of your communication is nonverbal. Be in touch with the messages conveyed by your body language, voice inflection, posture, and facial expressions.

◆ Avoid "winning" situations. If you "win" a discussion, it is at the expense of someone else, and you have to deal with that person's feelings. No one is right all the time. Nor can you be all things to all people at all times.

◆ Tackle life's problems systematically. People who are stressed try to undo their "mistakes" in a hurry. Set realistic personal and other-directed goals. If you don't succeed, don't give up. You might need to adjust your goals or simply keep trying.

◆ Come to accept the fact that not all life's conflicts, including your own, may be resolvable, now or in the future. Some people and situations simply can't or don't want to change. Don't expect yourself or another to alter behavior without proper know-how and motivation.

◆ Learn to set limits with yourself and others. Avoid being the rescuer or doormat. Failing to set limits leads to resentment.

◆ You don't have to justify your every move in life. An honest response is appropriate, but avoid feeling the need to make excuses for your actions. Also, don't cop out of any responsibility when someone else is depending on you. If the world becomes angry with you, it might be because you have become undependable.

◆ Finish unfinished business. Whenever you suppress a feeling, it will eventually manifest itself magnified many times over. Beware of depression, illness, or emotional outbursts as expressions of suppression.

◆ Offer your point of view when it is asked for.

> If you can say "no" in a relationship, you don't have to say "no" to the relationship.

Trust within relationships is critical, particularly with today's emphasis on team management. Friendships, families, and organizations need trust to operate effectively. When people trust each other, everything works better. But trust doesn't come automatically; it must be earned. Strong trust-builders:

◆ Sincerely regret doing wrong to others and are quick to apologize when they do something wrong

◆ Are good listeners

◆ Look out for other people's interests as well as their own

◆ Are fair in their dealings with everyone

◆ Clarify their intentions so that others will understand their actions

◆ Seek input on issues from the people who will be affected by their decisions or actions

◆ Generously praise people

◆ Willingly cooperate with their colleagues and are more interested in achieving good results than in who will get the credit

◆ Strive to understand how others feel and are sensitive and empathetic to others' feelings

◆ Keep promises—you can rely on them to do what they said they would do

◆ Tell the truth, even when it might be painful or to their disadvantage

◆ Are genuinely interested in other people and have a high relationship orientation

◆ Care about others and treat others the way in which they would want to be treated themselves

INDIVIDUAL TASKS AND REFLECTIONS

4.1 Relationship Patterns

Take a large sheet of paper and write "ME" in the center. Using the key for relationship patterns as outlined below, create your relationship chart.

Relationships that are linked	
Family by birth, marriage, or agreement	~~~~~~~~~~~~~~
Problems that need working on	★
Others	
Would like the relationship to get closer	◄──────────►
Would like to end the relationship	-------------------------

4.2 Trusting Others

Consider the people in your personal and professional life who you would trust. Identify their trust-building characteristics and behavior.

4.3 Not Trusting Others

Consider the people in your personal and professional life who you do not trust. Identify the characteristics and behaviors that inhibit your trust of them.

WORKING WITH OTHERS
....

4.4 Relationship Self-Assessment

Complete the following self-assessment and then give the sheet to a colleague to complete. Use the responses "rarely," "sometimes," or "often" to indicate the extent to which you or your colleague use the skill.

Relationship Skills	Self	
1 Understanding yourself ◆ Identifying your feelings accurately ◆ Understanding the influence of your background		
	Self	**Colleague**
2 Talking about yourself ◆ Communicating well using nonverbal language ◆ Ability to "own" your thoughts and feelings ◆ Expressing feelings appropriately ◆ Sharing personal information		
3 Developing relationships ◆ Revealing strengths and weaknesses ◆ Giving feedback ◆ Receiving feedback ◆ Identifying and overcoming barriers to trust ◆ Discussing your relationships constructively		
4 Defining yourself ◆ Overcoming mental barriers to assertion ◆ Expressing wants ◆ Taking the initiative ◆ Coping with others' negative behavior ◆ Not allowing others to define you on their terms		
5 Disciplined listening ◆ Awareness of your barriers to listening ◆ Being a safe person to talk to ◆ Understanding verbal and nonverbal language ◆ Tuning in to the feelings of others ◆ Actively showing attentivenes ◆ Being able to step into another's world		
6 Helpful responding ◆ Communicating understanding of another's words ◆ Communicating understanding of another's feelings ◆ Ability to help another clarify a problem ◆ Helping another generate solutions		

(continued)

(continued)

Relationship Skills	Self	Colleague
7 Managing anger and conflict		
◆ Awareness of when you feel angry		
◆ Expressing your anger constructively		
◆ Handling criticism constructively		
◆ Showing a problem-solving orientation		
◆ Being collaborative rather than competitive		
◆ Assuming responsibility for managing conflict		

WORKING WITH A MENTOR

4.5 Strong and Weak Relationship Skills

Identify your strong and weak relationship skills. Note whether there are any differences in relationship styles between your personal and professional life. Discuss with your mentor. How does your mentor see your relationship skills? Create an action plan to improve your weak relationship skills.

4.6 The Mentor Relationship

What are the dynamics of the relationship between you and your mentor?

DEVELOPING OTHERS

4.7 Talking About Yourself

Introduce the subject of building positive relationships and talking about yourself, as detailed above. Brainstorm the necessary skills. Put the learners into pairs to discuss their skills and give each other feedback. Reconvene the larger group to discuss the outcomes and experience.

4.8 Developing Relationships

Introduce the subject of building positive relationships and developing relationships, as detailed above. Brainstorm the necessary skills. Put the learners into pairs to discuss their skills and give each other feedback. Reconvene the larger group to discuss the outcomes and experience.

4.9 Defining Yourself

Introduce the subject of building positive relationships and defining yourself, as detailed above. Brainstorm the necessary skills. Put the learners into pairs to discuss their skills and give each other feedback. Reconvene the larger group to discuss the outcomes and experience.

4.10 Disciplined Listening

Introduce the subject of building positive relationships and disciplined listening, as detailed above. Brainstorm the necessary skills. Put the learners into pairs to discuss their skills and give each other feedback. Reconvene the larger group to discuss the outcomes and experience.

4.11 Helpful Responding

Introduce the subject of building positive relationships and helpful responding, as detailed above. Brainstorm the necessary skills. Put the learners into pairs to discuss their skills and give each other feedback. Reconvene the larger group to discuss the outcomes and experience.

4.12 Managing Anger and Conflict

Introduce the subject of building positive relationships and managing anger and conflict, as detailed above. Brainstorm the necessary skills. Put the learners into pairs to discuss their skills and give each other feedback. Reconvene the larger group to discuss the outcomes and experience.

RECOMMENDED HRD PRESS TITLES

Relating Styles Assessment and Workbook, 52 pp.

INTRODUCTION

Nowadays, each one of us has the opportunity to be in charge of our own working life. It is up to each person to plan their career and reskill when appropriate. Are you aware of the following facts?

◆ The skills most commonly thought to be lacking are IT skills, communication skills, and personal skills.

◆ According to the Department for Education and Employment, growth in demand in the higher skilled occupations is predicted to the year 2005 and beyond and there is a growing emphasis on multiskilling and quality.

◆ Core workers are expected to have a wide range of skills including leadership, managerial, development, professional, and technical abilities.

◆ If you want to get the maximum return from your networking, you need to give a high profile to your transferable skills.

◆ You need to be able to work without a clear job description and to prepare yourself for short-term employment.

◆ To stay in work you will need to constantly demonstrate your value to the organization in each new situation.

◆ Your place within a new company is as the supplier, fulfilling a need to the customer (the employer).

Stages of Working Life		
Life-Stage	**Age**	**Events**
Pulling up roots	18–22	Leaving the nest, flexing the wings to express individuality.
Early adulthood	22–28	First commitments to adult responsibilities, trying out parental rules in the world.
Transition	28–32	Re-examination of parental rules, reassessment of current relationships and career, challenges to our old ways of thinking, more long-term planning beginning to occur.
Consolidation	32–39	Seeking to become established, the beginning of feeling pressured by time, making long-term goals based on our true individuality and not family expectations.
Metamorphosis	39–45	Facing the chasm between ideals and reality, new career, new relationships, breaking away.
Stabilization	45–55	Increased stability, following changes.
Mellowing	55–	Achievement losing potency in the face of increased self-satisfaction and inner peace with self.

Having located potential work, you then need to market yourself and negotiate terms. Once in the job, you will be required to work on many levels, possibly handling a variety of tasks simultaneously. Learn to see every potential work situation as a market. Find new ways to exploit your skills, knowledge, and experience, and learn how to take advantage of opportunities to sell yourself.

Because full-time, permanent work will become harder to obtain, the trend will be toward having two or three part-time jobs or doing contract work (being self-employed and contracted to do occasional specialist work, and likely to work for more than one organization). Rather than the traditional 9 to 5 job, you are likely to have a composite career that has several strands running at the same time, starting and finishing ad hoc.

Other ways in which you might work include telecommuting (working at home for an employer or freelancing using computers, fax machine, modem, and telephone) or interim management (a temporary manager for only the duration of a project). Alternatively, you might be a core worker. A core worker is someone who is probably between 25 and 45 years old. They are likely to be career-minded and will work in the central part of an organization, probably in management or project development. A core worker is full-time and will have an intense and heavy workload. Their career progression is likely to be a series of high-powered jobs, not necessarily with the same organization.

> In order to maintain a productive and financially rewarding working life, you will need job-specific skills plus job-search skills—**and you are responsible for acquiring them.**

INDIVIDUAL TASKS AND REFLECTIONS

5.1 Why Do You Work?

On a scale from 1 to 5 (1 being the most true), write the number that indicates how true you think each of the following statements is. Work:

◆ Is something I do for money   _____

◆ Helps me get up in the morning   _____

◆ Takes me away from the family   _____

◆ Gives my life structure   _____

◆ Gives me an identity   _____

◆ Gives me a social life   _____

◆ Provides me with a sense of purpose   _____

◆ Provides me with interesting challenges   _____

◆ Makes me feel needed   _____

◆ Gives me status   _____

◆ Is unenjoyable   _____

◆ Is boring   _____

5.2 Job Analysis

Take your last or current job and analyze what you have learned from your responsibilities and experiences.

5.3 Different Ways to Work

How do you want to work?

◆ Part time	Do you want to job-share?
◆ Temporary	Do you want casual work you can drop in and out of?
◆ Core	Are you career-minded?
◆ Contract	Are you a specialist?

5.4 Updating Skills

Consider the following:

- ◆ How might learning improve your work prospects?
- ◆ Do you want a vocational qualification? Why?
- ◆ Do you know how you like to learn—for example, self-study, classroom, one-to-one coaching?
- ◆ How might you pay for your learning?

5.5 Transferable Skills

Which of your current skills could be transferred to other occupations?

5.6 Local Labor Knowledge

- ◆ Which are the ten biggest factories in your area?
- ◆ Which are the two biggest factories in your town?
- ◆ Which are the ten biggest office firms in your area?
- ◆ Which are the two biggest office firms in your town?
- ◆ Which firms in your town have announced layoffs within the past six months?
- ◆ Which new firms have moved into your town within the past six months?
- ◆ Consider the key companies in your town and area. Would you consider working for them and why?

5.7 Values

Go through the list below, checking those values that are important to you:

❑ Sense of community	❑ Sense of accomplishment
❑ Autonomy	❑ Being a success
❑ Being a team member	❑ Being appreciated
❑ Being seen as an expert	❑ Being of service
❑ Creativity	❑ Developing new skills
❑ Financial security	❑ Gaining knowledge
❑ Having authority	❑ Having feedback
❑ Having responsibility	❑ Helping society
❑ Sense of identity	❑ Having influence
❑ Working under pressure	❑ Overcoming challenges
❑ Public contact	❑ Respect from others
❑ Opportunities for self-development	❑ Self-respect
❑ Sense of purpose	❑ Social interaction
❑ Status	❑ Supervising others
❑ Supporting others	❑ Taking risks
❑ Being proactive	❑ Sense of usefulness

5.8 Occupational Awareness

Are you aware of the amount of demand for your area of expertise? Is your work seasonal—for example, lecturing and tutoring during the academic year? Do you need to upgrade your skills to keep abreast of current trends? Do you keep yourself up-to-date so that you have a head start in terms of new trends within your profession?

5.9 Progression

What is the progression route through the organization you work for? How have work colleagues progressed in or out of the organization?

5.10 I Am a Person

Who are you? Who or what we believe ourselves to be is relevant to how we perceive ourselves out in the world. Write down, without thinking, who or what you believe yourself to be at this point in time. Discuss with your mentor.

5.11 Life Check

Reflect on this current period in your life and ask yourself, "Where am I at in my life right now?" Think about what kind of time this is for you. Consider the event or events that marked the beginning of this period and think about the chief characteristics of this period. Is it a hectic time? A time of crisis? A period of transition? A stagnant period? Draw any images, colors, or forms, or write down any words or statements that reflect where you are in your life at this particular time. Discuss with your mentor.

5.12 Wants and Needs

What we need and want in our work may be one and the same. What we want is desirable, but is not essential to our well-being. What we need is vital to our sense of self. Discuss the following with your mentor and find out what the difference is for you.

◆ I want . . . *(for example, stimulation, a stable income for emotional security, to create something of substance and for a reason, to be challenged, a higher income, sense of belonging)*
◆ I need . . . *(for example, to contribute to household expenses, to be doing something useful, to be more independent, to be needed, to develop new skills)*
◆ What will happen if I don't have it? *(For example, I will feel trapped/useless/bored/frustrated)*
◆ What could I do to remedy the situation? *(For example, retrain, consider more permanent positions offering autonomy)*

5.13 Self-Discovery

Discuss with your mentor how you might begin taking steps toward discovering and doing work that would be personally meaningful, including asking yourself:

◆ What are my career goals for the next 6 months?
◆ What are my career goals for the next 12 months?
◆ Why are these goals important to me?
◆ Who can I get to help myself achieve these goals?
◆ How can they help me achieve these goals?
◆ How will I know when I have achieved them?

WORKING
WITH OTHERS
....
WORKING
WITH A MENTOR
....

DEVELOPING

OTHERS

. . . .

5.14 Fantasy Career

Introduce the subject of career planning. Say to your group, "You are to imagine that there are no constraints of time, money, age, health, status, ties, and so on. Identify details such as job specification, the lifestyle that accompanies it, with whom you would work, in what kind of surroundings, with what kind of authority and responsibilities, with what kind of working day. Detail career progression, status and income sought, opportunities for using your present skills and developing others, and integration of your career development with other life roles." Now ask them the following questions:

◆ What does the fantasy indicate about what you would value and aspire to?
◆ What are the differences between your fantasy and reality?
◆ How much of your fantasy is achievable either now or in the future?
◆ What are the barriers to your achieving some of your fantasy and how might these be overcome?
◆ What would be the consequences of your working to achieve some of the features of your fantasy, for yourself and for other people?
◆ What objectives would you like to set yourself on the basis of this exercise?

RECOMMENDED

HRD PRESS TITLES

. . . .

SkillBuilders, 35 different titles, 12 pp. each.

6 Changing Interpersonal Behavior

Are you happy with how you relate to other people? Would you like to be more outgoing or less dominant in a group? Would you like to be able to start up a conversation with anyone or do you need to take a step back?

Let's take a typical interpersonal behavioral problem: for example, you're unhappy with your tendency to dominate conversations at social gatherings or meetings. You end up crowding other people out and, as a result, you often alienate them. To rectify the problem, you could take the following steps:

◆ Set a goal (for example, "I'll stop talking so much when in groups").

◆ Identify an action you take to alert yourself in typical situations (for example, decide to keep your mouth shut for a while, instead of always jumping into the conversation). However, also consider whether there is a positive action you might be able to take to achieve your goal more fully, such as focusing on listening more to the other person.

◆ Devise a reminder for when you feel yourself slipping into the behavior you want to avoid. For example, if listening is not your natural response when you're socially stimulated, you need to be reminded of exactly what you should do. However, this reminder will have to be motivational. Because you typically become so stimulated when you're in the company of others, you conclude that, unless a reminder makes you *want* to listen, you'll have trouble doing it. So you decide on a combination reminder. In trying to identify an important reason for taking the trouble to listen when you'd rather talk, it occurs to you that the word *friends* helps convey what you really want to accomplish—and what you've been losing. Therefore, you decide that the reminder "Listen to your friends" will give you both the instruction and the inspiration to carry out your action. You then mentally attach the reminder to the stimulus. Subsequently, in social situations, you monitor and adjust by thinking "Listen to your friends" whenever you feel the urge to jump into the conversation.

Changing interpersonal behavior can be daunting, but your ability to change your behavior is not a matter of willpower. Your willpower will be there when you admit your fears and identify whether other people or your organization is complicating matters with its own fears. The following situations can cause interpersonal difficulties in the work environment:

◆ **Communication.** Fears that "it won't come out right" are often mis-identified and are, more accurately, fears of embarrassment, rejection, or failure.

◆ **Rejection.** These are fears of not getting something we already don't have.

◆ **Embarrassment.** Most of us have had fears of looking foolish, of seeming incompetent, of being taken for granted, of needing help. When our solution to these anxieties is to avoid the problem, we often find ourselves in a victim role.

◆ **Conflict.** The fear of conflict, or of strong emotional reaction, is widespread and particularly insidious.

◆ **Failure.** Most fears of failure are actually about being exposed. Are you assuming that a failure in outcome means you are a failure as a person?

> You can change your behavior.

Positive action in changing interpersonal behavior is effective for two reasons. First, positive action yields objective information, which helps distinguish exaggerated from real risk. Second, positive action separates having fear from being driven by fear. When you begin changing fundamental habits, successful behavior comes naturally.

INDIVIDUAL TASKS AND REFLECTIONS

6.1 Improving Your Body Language Through Postural Exercise

Practicing T'ai Chi, the Alexander Technique, yoga, and other forms of postural exercise and meditation can give you an upright, relaxed, and balanced posture, which will then give you internal confidence with your body language when relating to others. You might want to explore the possibilities.

6.2 Learning Interpersonal Behavior

Interpersonal skills are learned from childhood onward. Who influenced your style of interpersonal behavior? How have you modified what you learned for better or worse?

6.3 Going By Appearance

What image of yourself do you want to convey to others?

- ◆ Mother Earth?
- ◆ Mad professor?
- ◆ Designer-label?
- ◆ Cool?
- ◆ Something else?

- ◆ Harassed executive?
- ◆ Macho?
- ◆ Dippy hippy?
- ◆ Iron lady?

6.4 Self-Assessment

Use the following checklist to assess your interpersonal behaviors.

Behavior	Good (✓)	Needs Improving (✓)
Using questions		
Using touch		
Maintaining the appropriate physical distance		
Dealing with conflict		
Problem solving		
Thinking skills		
Awareness of feelings		
Giving criticism		

(continued)

(continued)

Behavior	Good (✓)	Needs Improving (✓)
Mirroring another's gestures		
Using hand gestures		
Listening skills		
Body stance		
Eye contact		
Facial expressions		
Voice pace		
Voice tone		
Voice volume		

6.5 Choosing Change

What interpersonal behaviors would you like to change in yourself? Why?

WORKING WITH OTHERS

....

WORKING WITH A MENTOR

....

DEVELOPING OTHERS

....

6.6 Colleague Assessment

Give the assessment in task 6.4 to a colleague to complete on your own interpersonal skills. Discuss.

6.7 Mentor Assessment

Give the assessment in task 6.4 to your mentor to complete on your own interpersonal skills. Discuss.

6.8 Different Style

Define and discuss with your mentor the different ways in which you communicate with the various people in your life.

6.9 Group Interpersonal Skills

Introduce the subject of changing interpersonal behavior. Divide the learners into groups of four to brainstorm elements of interpersonal behavior. Reconvene the whole group in order to compile a central list. Ask the learners to rate themselves for each element (good, needs improving). Keeping the learners in their groups, ask them to rate each other.

6.10 Rating for Change

Introduce the subject of changing interpersonal behavior. Brainstorm elements of interpersonal behavior. Ask the learners to rate themselves on these elements (good, needs improving). Ask them what behaviors they would like to change and why. Ask them to choose one behavior to change and to devise two strategies to change it. Divide them into groups of three to discuss. Reconvene the whole group to share their ideas on behavior and strategies.

RECOMMENDED HRD PRESS TITLES
....

50 Activities for Interpersonal Skills Training, 430 pp.
Communication Effectiveness Profile, 16 pp.

7 Coaching Others

A good coach encourages others to think for themselves. In other words, good coaches teach others to fish for themselves, rather than feeding them fish. Coaching is a form of leading—you lead people to think differently. Coaching means asking questions that lead others to new insights, and helping people solve their own problems. One of the challenges in coaching is to resist offering people your own answers and thereby metaphorically feeding them fish; it is an accepted fact that people commit themselves most fully to their own solutions.

Coaches help people carry out any occupational task more effectively and aim to help high performers reach greater heights.

Managers who use coaches are committed to self-improvement, and it is becoming increasingly evident that managers develop more effectively with the help of a coach rather than just relying on ad hoc experience or courses.

> Coaching is not complete until the other person has a concrete action plan to do something different.

Advice can be helpful, but it is only short term; it is no substitute for helping others to think for themselves. This means asking open-ended, nonjudgmental questions to stimulate broader thinking on their part. When the individual you are coaching gets off track, ask them to consider certain implications of their preferred course of action rather than telling them your answers. As a last resort, when you need to give someone the answer, pose it as a question: "How do you think this approach would work for you?" Avoid closing down too quickly on a solution—strive to dig deeper into how the other person thinks by probing with further open questions, such as "I wonder what leads you to that view?" or "Can you help me understand your reasoning there?" Acknowledge any insights gained and good points made. Ask what they will do differently and by when. Strive always in coaching to maintain and enhance the other person's self-esteem.

Your team can grow much faster if you assume a coaching role. Team members need training and support to help them gain their full power to perform the team's work as well as to perform work as a team. If you are going to help your team develop necessary skills, you must cultivate a set of coaching skills, including listening, communicating, advocating, team building, facilitating decision making, training, educating, and mentoring.

INDIVIDUAL TASKS AND REFLECTIONS

7.1 Good Coaching by Another

Consider a recent situation where someone has coached you well. How did you feel? Why was the coaching good? What made it work well? What were the outcomes for you?

7.2 Bad Coaching by Another

Consider a recent situation where another has coached you badly. How did you feel? Why was the coaching bad? Why didn't it work? What were the outcomes for you? What might you have done differently if you had been the coach?

7.3 Good Coaching by You

Consider a recent situation where you coached another well. How did you feel? Why was the coaching good? What made it work well? What were the outcomes for the other person?

7.4 Bad Coaching by You

Consider a recent situation where you have coached another badly. How did you feel? Why was the coaching bad? Why didn't it work? What were the outcomes for the other person? What could you have done differently?

7.5 Self-Assessment of Coaching Skills

Use the following scale to rate yourself on each statement:

Never = 1   Sometimes = 2   Usually = 3   Always = 4

Coaching Skill	Rating
I listen to my team members actively, empathetically, respectfully, and without passing judgment.	
I communicate with a clear, consistent message to my team members.	
I act as a strong advocate for my team with others in the organization.	
I work hard on team building with my team members.	
I support my team members in making their own decisions.	
I provide continuing training to team members in participatory management.	
I provide education so that team members understand the theory behind what they're doing.	
As a mentor, I help my team members develop their skills and the confidence to use those skills.	

Take a look at those areas you've rated a 1 or 2. Try to move those up to the 3 or 4 range. By developing your skills as a coach, you will develop a more effective and efficient team.

WORKING WITH OTHERS

7.6 Coaching Assessment

Identify a situation where another person will coach you. Create an assessment form for you to use upon completion. After the session, you could also give this sheet to the person who coached you to use as feedback.

7.7 Coaching Self-Assessment

Identify a situation where you are coaching another. Create a self-assessment form for you to use upon completion. After the session, you could also give this sheet to the person you are coaching to use for feedback.

WORKING

WITH A MENTOR
....

7.8 Mentoring Coaching Skills

Ask your mentor to sit in on a session when you are coaching another person. Complete a self-assessment sheet, and your mentor can make notes. Discuss both sets of observations. Create an action plan to develop identified skills.

DEVELOPING

OTHERS
....

7.9 The Best Coach

Introduce the subject of coaching others. Brainstorm ideal coaching skills and strengths.

7.10 Role Play Coaching

Introduce the subject of coaching others. Using a volunteer from the learners, role play, with you as the coach, good coaching skills. Then role play bad coaching skills. Ask the observers to list the good skills (and how they might be improved) and the bad skills (and how they might be improved). Armed with this list, divide the learners into groups of three: two to role play and one to observe. Feedback comes from the learner being coached, the observer, and from the coach's own self-assessment.

RECOMMENDED

HRD PRESS TITLES
....

The Manager's Pocket Guide to Workplace Coaching, 140 pp.
The Manager's Pocket Guide to Effective Mentoring, 128 pp.
50 Activities for Coaching and Mentoring, 306 pp.
Coaching Effectiveness Profile, 16 pp.

8

Conducting Interviews

INTRODUCTION

Interviews are particularly useful for discovering the story behind a respondent's experiences and to pursue in-depth information around a topic. Before you start to design your interview questions and process, clearly identify the purpose of each interview. This helps you keep a clear focus on the intent of each question.

Types of Interviews

◆ **Informal, conversational, general interview.** Here, predetermined questions are asked. This approach is intended to ensure that the same general areas of information are collected from each interviewee.
◆ **Standardized, open-ended interview.** Here, the same open-ended questions are put to all interviewees. This approach facilitates faster interviews that can be more easily analyzed and compared.
◆ **Closed, fixed-response interview.** Here, all interviewees are asked the same questions and are asked to choose answers from the same set of alternatives.

Preparing the Sequence of Questions

◆ Get the respondents involved in the interview as soon as possible.
◆ Before asking about controversial matters (such as feelings and opinions), first ask about some facts. With this approach, respondents can more easily engage in the interview before warming up to more personal matters.
◆ Intersperse fact-based questions throughout the interview to avoid a long sequence of fact-based questions, which tends to leave respondents disengaged.
◆ Ask questions about the present before asking questions about the past or future. It's usually easier for respondents to talk about the present and then work into the past or future.
◆ The final questions might be formulated to allow respondents to provide any other information they wish to add and their impressions of the interview.

Wording Your Questions

◆ Wording should be open ended. Respondents should be able to choose their own terms when answering questions.
◆ Questions should be as neutral as possible. Avoid wording that might influence answers—for example, evocative wording.
◆ Questions should be asked one at a time.
◆ Be careful about asking "Why?" questions, because these imply a cause-effect relationship that might not truly exist. Such questions might also cause respondents to feel defensive—for example, that they have to justify their response—which might inhibit their responses to this and future questions.

Preparing for the Interview

◆ Choose a setting with little distraction. Avoid bright lights or loud noises, make sure that the interviewee is comfortable, and so on.
◆ Explain the purpose of the interview.
◆ Address terms of confidentiality. Explain who will be allowed access to the respondent's answers and how their answers will be analyzed.
◆ Explain the format of the interview. Explain the type of interview you are conducting and its nature. If you want the respondent to ask questions, specify whether they are to do so as the questions occur to them or wait until the end of the interview.
◆ Indicate how long the interview will take.
◆ Tell the respondent how to get in touch with you later if they want to.
◆ Ask the respondent if they have any questions before the start of the interview.
◆ Don't rely on your memory to recall the respondent's answers. Ask for permission to record the interview or have someone else present to take notes, or take notes yourself.

Carrying Out the Interview

◆ From time to time, check that the tape recorder (if used) is working.
◆ Ask one question at a time.
◆ Attempt to remain as neutral as possible—don't display strong emotional reactions to their responses.
◆ Encourage responses with occasional nods of the head, "uh huhs," and so on.
◆ Be careful about the impression conveyed when taking notes. If you jump to take a note, it might seem as if you're surprised or very pleased about an answer, which might influence answers to future questions.
◆ Provide a transition between major topics—for example, "We've been talking about . . . and now I'd like to move on to. . . ."
◆ Don't lose control of the interview. This can occur when a respondent strays to another topic, takes so long to answer a question that time begins to run out, or even begins asking the interviewer questions.

Immediately After the Interview

◆ Check that the tape recorder (if used) worked throughout the interview.
◆ Go over your written notes—for example, clarify any semi-illegible words, ensure that the pages are numbered, fill out any notes that don't make sense, and so on.
◆ Write down any observations made during the interview. For example, where did the interview take place and when? Was the respondent particularly nervous at any point? Were there any surprises during the interview?

Guidelines for Conducting and Analyzing Interviews

To be a good interviewer, you need good self-awareness. If you are self-aware, you will be able to read in others what you have learned to read in yourself. Here are a few principles for conducting and analyzing interviews:

1. Observe contact reaction as the candidate walks into your office or the interviewing space. Remember that 70 percent of all communication is nonverbal.

2. Do not hasten to put the candidate at ease. The mental and emotional state of candidates as they enter into the interviewing process is important information. It can tell you a great deal about how they relate to new people and what their self-concept is. If the candidate continues to be nervous, then you can use some techniques to put the person at ease.

3. Develop a set of questions and ask the same questions of each candidate. If you want to distinguish one person from another, you have to get a range of responses. The way to do this is to ask the exact same questions of each candidate, and then compare their answers.

4. Start with stereotypical interview questions, but be aware that your purpose in doing so is to make the subject comfortable. Then take off from there and go deeper. Your objective is to get the subject talking, in as much of a discursive, narrative fashion as possible.

5. Sample all relevant areas of the candidate's life, such as work, education, competencies, and personality. In each category, however, start the candidate talking about something they are totally familiar with. Proceed from the impersonal to the personal, from the familiar to the unfamiliar, and from the intellect to the emotions.

6. Take notes on, or tape record (with their permission), the interview.

7. Maintain a steady presence from one interview to the next. Do not behave one way toward one candidate, and in an entirely different way toward another. If you unduly influence one candidate toward a negative, or defensive, reaction and another candidate toward a positive reaction you, again, compromise your interview data.

8. Consider the interview as a real-life or on-the-job process. In effect, the ideal way to look upon an interview is as a laboratory to sample projected workplace behavior by the candidates. Within the bounds of necessary time limits, you as the interviewer should set up interactions and experiments that will represent possible scenarios on the job.

9. Note the emotional flavor of the interview. If you keep yourself steady as a measuring instrument, you will observe that different candidates will bring into the interview a type of emotional atmosphere. Some interviews will feel warm and open to you; others might feel cold and closed. This should be an indication of the kind of atmosphere a subject will help generate in the workplace.

10. Do not err on the side of being afraid to ask penetrating questions. Be professional, be courteous, and demonstrate a genuine interest in the person you are interviewing. This is the way to build trust, and trust is critical to success in gaining insight into each candidate.

11. Be aware that the toughest challenge in the interview process is interpreting the data. Many interviewers see the discussion process as the most important aspect of interviewing. In reality, the true meaning of the interview will only emerge with skillful interpretation of the data you have gathered. Proper interpretation of data involves matching a given candidate with a given job in such a way that the organization is assured that the tasks assigned to that job will be carried out well, and that the person will mesh well with others in the organizational culture.

INDIVIDUAL TASKS

AND REFLECTIONS
....

8.1 A Bad Interview

Consider an interview you have attended as an interviewee that you felt went badly. What happened? How did the interviewer's behavior or questions affect your performance? How might they have conducted the interview better?

8.2 A Good Interview

Consider an interview you have attended as an interviewee that you felt went well. What happened? How did the interviewer's behavior or questions affect your performance?

8.3 A Good Interviewer

Consider an interview you conducted that you think went well. How did you experience it? Consider the interviewee's response. What did you do or say that made the interview work?

8.4 A Bad Interviewer

Consider an interview you conducted that you think went badly. How did you experience it? Consider the interviewee's response. What did you do or say that made the interview go badly? How might you have conducted the interview better?

8.5 Interviewer Skills

What, in your opinion, are the essential skills of an effective interviewer?

WORKING

WITH OTHERS
....

8.6 Self-Assessment

Identify an interview situation that you will be conducting. Create a self-assessment form and complete it at the end of the interview.

8.7 Interview Assessment

Identify an interview situation where you will be interviewed. Create an assessment form and complete it at the end of the interview.

WORKING

WITH A MENTOR
....

8.8 Joint Assessment

Ask your mentor to sit in on an interview you will be conducting (with the interviewee's permission). Using a self-assessment form, assess yourself at the end of the interview and ask your mentor also to assess your performance. Compare and discuss. Based on this, identify skills you need to develop and an action plan to do so.

DEVELOPING

OTHERS
....

8.9 Group Interviews

Divide the learners into small groups of three. Each takes a turn to be the interviewer, the interviewee, and to provide feedback.

8.10 Role Play

Introduce the subject of conducting interviews. Brainstorm the skills necessary for a good interviewer. Choose a volunteer and role play an interview with you as the interviewee. You can videotape the session. The group will offer feedback on both performances. The performers are to assess themselves and each other as well. Ask for another two volunteers and repeat the exercise.

RECOMMENDED

HRD PRESS TITLES

....

The Manager's Pocket Guide to Interviewing and Hiring Top Performers,
    180 pp.
The Manager's Pocket Guide to Recruiting the Workforce of the Future,
    105 pp.
25 Role Plays for Interview Training, 280 pp.

9 Counseling in the Workplace

There are basically four types of strategy for helping others in the workplace:

◆ **Giving advice:** making suggestions about courses of action another person can, and possibly should, take, looking at the situation from your perspective.
◆ **Direct action:** taking action yourself to provide for someone else's needs—for example, stopping a fight.
◆ **Counseling:** helping someone explore a problem so that they can decide what to do about it.
◆ **Teaching:** helping someone acquire knowledge and skills you think they will need.

Counseling in the workplace can be used for:

◆ Participants in work-related courses who wish to do personal work on a related matter
◆ People who wish to talk over personal or work-related problems in complete confidence with someone
◆ People who are facing redundancy or career changes
◆ People who have suffered trauma

Counseling has a powerful, long-term impact on people and organizational effectiveness. It involves talking with a person in a way that helps that person solve a problem or helps create conditions that will cause the person to improve their behavior. It involves thinking, implementing, and knowing human nature, timing, sincerity, compassion, and kindness. It is much more than simply telling someone what to do about a problem.

Leaders must demonstrate the following qualities in order to counsel effectively:

◆ **Respect for employees.** This quality includes the belief that individuals are responsible for their own actions and ideas. It also includes an awareness of a person's individuality in terms of unique values, attributes, and skills.
◆ **Self-awareness.** This quality is an understanding of you as a leader. The more you are aware of your own values, needs, and biases, the less likely you will be to project your feelings onto your employees.
◆ **Credibility.** This quality is achieved through both honesty and consistency between your statements and actions. Credible leaders are straightforward with their people and behave in such a manner that their people respect and trust their words.
◆ **Empathy.** This quality entails understanding an employer's situation. Empathetic leaders will be better able to help people identify the situation and develop a plan to improve the situation.

The purpose of counseling is to help employees develop in order to achieve organizational or individual goals. At times, the counseling is directed by policy and, at other times, you, as a leader, should choose to counsel to develop employees. Regardless of the nature of the counseling, you should demonstrate the qualities of an effective counselor (respect, self-awareness, credibility, and empathy) and employ the skills of communication. While the purpose of counseling is to develop their people, leaders often categorize counseling based on the topic of the session. The main counseling categories include performance counseling, problem counseling, and individual growth counseling. While these categories can help organize and focus counseling sessions, they must not be viewed as separate and distinct types of counseling. For example, a counseling session that focuses on resolving a problem may also have a great impact on improving job performance, and a counseling session focused on performance may also include a discussion of opportunities for growth. Regardless of the topic of the counseling session, you should follow the same basic format to prepare for, and conduct, counseling.

There are six steps of effective counseling:

1. Identify the problem. Make sure that you really know the problem. Analyze the forces influencing the behavior. Determine which of these forces you have control over and which of the forces the employee has control over. Determine if the force has to be modified, eliminated, or enforced.
2. Plan, coordinate, and organize the session. Determine the best time to conduct the session.
3. Conduct the session using sincerity, compassion, and kindness. This does not mean you cannot be firm or in control.
4. During the session, determine what the employee believes causes the counterproductive behavior and what will be required to change it.
5. Try to maintain a sense of timing as to when to use directive or non-directive counseling. (See below for definitions.)
6. Using all the facts, make a decision and/or a plan of action to correct the problem. If more counseling is needed, set a firm date and time for the next session.

After the session, and throughout a sufficient time period, evaluate the employee's progress to ensure that the problem has been solved.

There are also two types of counseling—directive and non-directive. In directive counseling, the counselor identifies the problem and tells the person being counseled what to do about it. In non-directive counseling, the person being counseled identifies the problem and determines the solution with the help of the counselor. The counselor has to determine which of the two types, or some appropriate combination, to apply to each situation. Whichever approach is chosen, a workplace counseling session will be most effective if you keep in mind the following guidelines:

◆ Move the individual being counseled toward an action outcome.
◆ Know when to refer the person to someone else—for example, the Human Resource Department.
◆ Avoid becoming personally involved.
◆ Avoid being judgmental.
◆ Keep asking questions.
◆ Make sure that you use active listening techniques.

INDIVIDUAL TASKS AND REFLECTIONS

9.1 Counseling or Helping

What, in your opinion, is the difference between counseling and helping?

WORKING

WITH OTHERS

....

WORKING

WITH A MENTOR

....

DEVELOPING

OTHERS

....

9.2 Reflecting on a Counseling Experience

When were you last counseled in a work situation? What did it feel like for you? Were the outcomes satisfactory for you? What made the session work or not work?

9.3 Case Studies

If it is within your role to counsel others at work, select two examples of recent counseling and reflect on:

◆ Your attitude toward counseling (for example, does it vary from person to person?)
◆ Your body language (for example, is it open and positive or closed and discouraging?)
◆ Your verbal style (for example, does it encourage the other person to talk?)
◆ Outcomes of when you counsel others (for example, does the other person change positively as a result?)

9.4 Shadowing a Colleague

Shadow a colleague who does work-related counseling for an agreed-upon amount of time (and with the agreement of the person being counseled). Reflect on your observations.

9.5 Mentoring and Counseling

What counseling skills does your mentor use? Discuss.

9.6 Role Play I

Set up a role-play situation with a colleague who has a work-related problem. Ask your mentor to be present and provide feedback on your performance. Ask the person being counseled for feedback as well. Assess your own performance.

9.7 Role Play 2

Ask your mentor to set up a role-play situation for you with someone who has a work-related problem and provide feedback on your performance. Ask the person being counseled for feedback as well. Assess your own performance.

9.8 Conducting a Performance Counseling Session

Organize the learners into groups of three. Each group of learners will rotate the following roles:

◆ The supervisor performing the counseling session
◆ An employee with a behavioral problem
◆ A facilitator to provide feedback and coaching to the supervisor

Ask each learner within a group to practice each role in every exercise. For example, in exercise 1, the first learner will be the supervisor, the second learner will be the employee, and the third learner will be the facilitator or coach. After completing the exercise, they will then rotate roles and repeat exercise 1. This process will be repeated a third time so that they all get to role play the supervisor, employee, and facilitator in exercise 1. Once each learner has played all three roles in exercise 1, the group will then move on to exercise 2, and repeat the process. They will then continue on to exercises 3 and 4 using the same procedure.

◆ **Exercise 1.** The employee is persistently late for work and takes longer-than-normal breaks.
◆ **Exercise 2.** The employee occasionally goes to a bar during their lunch break. They aren't exactly drunk, but their behavior suggests that drinking alcohol has affected their efficiency.
◆ **Exercise 3.** The employee is a good worker, but can get irritable and snappy when under pressure. Because their work involves dealing with the public in person and on the telephone, their customer service skills sometimes suffer as a result of stress.
◆ **Exercise 4.** The employee is a good worker and is ready to handle more responsibility, which will involve participation in meetings and giving presentations. Their problem is that they tend to clam up in meetings and are scared of giving presentations due to a lack of confidence.

Allowing each learner to perform all three roles has several advantages. Each learner gets to:

◆ Practice it
◆ Coach it
◆ Be on the receiving end of it

At a very minimum, each learner should perform the role of supervisor in each exercise as they build on each other.

9.9 Role Play and Group Feedback

Set up a role play with a colleague. One of you is the counselor, the other is the counselee with a work-related issue to work through. The counselee should be reasonably difficult and the counselor should make several errors—some more subtle than others. Video the sessions. During the training session, ask the learners to comment on the behavior and performance of the counselor. Using the same script plus the learners' modifications, ask for two volunteers to role play the new version. Follow this up with group feedback and discussion.

RECOMMENDED HRD PRESS TITLES

....

50 Activities for Developing Counseling Skills in Managers, 296 pp.

10 Creating a Wellness Program

Why create a wellness program? For the good of the company or the good of the individual? We can see company health and individual health here as two sides of the same coin. The company can only be a healthy working entity when the parts are working well, both individually and together. The physical and psychological well-being of employees contributes to their effectiveness and motivation both in and out of the workplace. That is not say that a healthy person will necessarily be a good worker, but if a company can encourage a good health program, this will be a positive investment in the employees who are any company's most valuable asset.

Stress and Nutrition

When life becomes busy, it's tempting to forget about a balanced diet by skipping meals or eating while on the run. However, when your body doesn't get the balance of nutrients it needs, you may end up trying to do more with less energy. Even healthy low-fat foods don't constitute a high-energy diet on their own. Below are some hints to remedy this.

◆ Eat quickly prepared foods if you need to, but aim for a combination of grain products (like bread and pasta) and vegetables or fruit, along with a modest amount of protein (dairy, meat, or bean) at least three times a day. It can be as easy as choosing a turkey sandwich with some fresh fruit or having vegetable chili and whole-grain bread for dinner.

◆ Set aside time to eat meals at a pace that allows you to taste and enjoy them. The 15 or 20 minutes it takes to put aside work and other distractions will be more than compensated by a noticeable energy boost.

◆ Stress can also increase desire for extra snacks and high-fat comfort foods. Snacks can be an important part of good eating, so don't force yourself to starve if you're hungry. But snacking when you're not really hungry doesn't give you more energy.

◆ Sweets and caffeine-containing products may be enjoyed occasionally if you like, but avoid using them throughout the day, or you may experience huge dips and surges in your energy levels.

◆ A 15-minute catnap, a walk around the block, or a stretching session will most probably give you renewed energy.

◆ Review your priorities and set aside enough time to get adequate sleep for the most dramatic effect on your energy levels.

◆ Set priorities to make the most of your time and let go of the rest. And when pressures in your life increase, simplify eating routines to save time if need be, but don't give up on the good nutrition that can help you through stressful times.

Easy Ways to Boost Your Activity Levels

◆ Walk as much as possible by parking the car a few blocks away from where you're headed or walk to an appointment instead of driving. Whenever you're walking, try to focus on long strides and a quicker than normal pace. This gets the heart rate going a bit faster than if you were just strolling along.

◆ Use the stairs instead of the elevator. Walk up the stairs as quickly as you can. For variation, try slowing down and taking two stairs at a time to further strengthen your legs.

◆ During breaks at work, walk up and down the stairs or around the building. Find any type of activity that keeps you moving during your break (you can sit at your desk and relax afterward).

◆ Whenever you're walking somewhere, take the long way around.

◆ At the supermarket, carry your groceries back to the car without using the shopping cart. And park the car in a spot farthest from the store entrance.

◆ Whenever possible, stand instead of sit. Even standing will burn more calories than sitting down.

◆ Lose the remote control. When was the last time you actually got up from your seat, engaged all your leg muscles, and walked over to change the channel on the TV?

◆ Unless it's urgent, always opt for the restroom that's farthest from you. Better yet, use the restroom upstairs!

◆ When cleaning your house, exaggerate your movements and make them big. Wash windows with a rag and make big arm circles and up and down movements. When vacuuming, switch hands every so often to give your arms and torso equal time on each side. Make long, rhythmic movements with the vacuum cleaner to increase your heart rate and deep clean the carpet at the same time!

◆ Plant a garden and work in it during the spring and summer. Gardening will take your body through a whole range of movements.

◆ Get rid of the riding lawn mower. Get back to basics with a push mower.

◆ Whenever possible, do your own home improvements or repairs.

◆ If you use a fireplace to help heat your home in the winter, chop and/or stack the wood yourself. Feeling more aggressive? Load and haul the wood home yourself instead of having it delivered to your doorstep.

◆ If you have children, or grandchildren, spend some quality time playing with them. Few things can jump-start your heart as quickly as trying to keep up with a child!

◆ Make a date with your partner to go out dancing once or twice a month. The longer and harder you dance, the better!

◆ Take lessons to learn how to play tennis, ski, golf, or any other activity you think you might enjoy.

◆ When spending the day at the beach, don't just sunbathe. Swim, rent a row boat, or go water skiing, and get active in the water.

◆ Join the local hiking, walking, or cycling club.

> Always exercise safely and within your fitness level.

A Weight Management Plan for Success

Whether you have tried to lose weight on your own or with the help of an organized program, the focus is too often on restrictive diets and unrealistic goals. Not being able to reach these goals can set you up for an endless cycle of failure and discouragement. Also, limited food choices may trigger binge eating, which can undermine your efforts. Weight management involves adopting a lifestyle that includes a healthy eating plan and regular physical activity. The key to managing weight throughout life is a positive attitude and the right kind of motivation. Here are four strategies for holistic weight management:

◆ **Strategy 1.** Make health, not appearance, your weight management priority. A realistic goal is to achieve a healthy weight—not necessarily the lowest weight you can reach or an ideal weight from a chart.

◆ **Strategy 2.** Focus on a healthy eating style, not on dieting. Dieting is usually short term and rarely produces long-term success.

◆ **Strategy 3.** Eating for good health and eating to control weight are virtually the same. Choosing a healthy eating plan that includes a variety of foods can accomplish both objectives.

◆ **Strategy 4.** People who keep physically active are more successful at losing and keeping off extra pounds. A physically active lifestyle offers many rewards in addition to weight management, such as heart health, strong bones, and stress relief. For weight management, experts recommend a combined total of 30 minutes of moderate activity on most days. Smaller amounts are OK, but try to accumulate at least 30 minutes a day. If you haven't been physically active for a while, build up the time gradually.

Focus on increasing daily physical activity, rather than setting unrealistic exercise goals. Pick an activity that you enjoy and are likely to continue, such as a brisk walk in the morning or a swim after work. Before beginning any exercise program, however, be sure to consult your doctor.

To make sure that your weight management plan is safe and effective, ask yourself a few questions before you begin. Does your plan:

◆ Include a variety of high-fiber, low-fat foods with a balance of protein and carbohydrate?

◆ Include appealing foods you will enjoy eating for the rest of your life, not just for a few weeks or months?

◆ Allow you to eat your favorite foods in moderation?

◆ Include regular physical activity?

If you can answer "yes" to all these questions, chances are your weight-loss program will yield long-term success.

INDIVIDUAL TASKS AND REFLECTIONS

10.1 Nutrition

Do you know whether you are eating a balanced and nutritious diet (high-fiber, low-fat, moderate carbohydrate, and a limited amount of animal protein)? Do you know whether you suffer from food allergies? (Food can be linked to physical symptoms and mood swings.) Are you eating at the right times for your metabolism—for example, do you suffer from dips in blood sugar?

10.2 Weight Management

Are you happy with your weight management? There is no ideal weight—only the weight that suits your particular shape, size, age, and lifestyle. Do you want to lose or gain weight?

10.3 Exercise

When was the last time you formally exercised—for example visited the gym? When was the last time you informally exercised—for example, walked to work or did some gardening?

10.4 Stopping Smoking

Do you want to stop smoking? Have you tried to stop smoking and failed? What possibilities have you explored for stopping smoking?

10.5 Stress Management

Do you suffer from psychological or physical stress symptoms? Do you need to manage your stress levels more effectively? How might you do this?

WORKING

WITH OTHERS
....

10.6 Lunchtime Good Health Program

Consider starting up a lunchtime Employee Good Health Program with your colleagues, holding weekly or monthly meetings with guest speakers.

10.7 Workplace Mini-Gym

Why not get together with your colleagues to see if there is an unused area in your building that could be turned into a mini-gym?

WORKING

WITH A MENTOR
....

DEVELOPING

OTHERS
....

10.8 Creating a Personal Wellness Program

Discuss with your mentor ways in which you might create a personal wellness program.

10.9 Individual Wellness Program

Introduce the subject of creating an individual wellness program. Brainstorm the different areas of good health, covering mind, body, and spirit. Ask the learners to identify areas that they would like to develop for themselves. Discuss the types of resources that are available—for example, complementary health therapists, stress management courses, and so on. Organize them into groups of four to discuss ways of accessing and using health resources to create a personal wellness program. Reconvene the larger group to discuss ideas.

10.10 Organizational Wellness Program

Introduce the subject of creating a wellness program as an organization. Brainstorm the different areas of good health, covering mind, body, and spirit. Ask the learners to identify areas that they would like to see developed within the organization. Discuss the types of resources that are available—for example, complementary health therapists, stress management courses, and so on. Organize them into groups of four to discuss ways of accessing and using health resources to create an organizational wellness program. Reconvene the larger group to share ideas.

RECOMMENDED

HRD PRESS TITLES
....

Complete Guide to Wellness, 600 pp.

50 Activities for Managing Stress, 300 pp.

INTRODUCTION

Critical thinking is the art of thinking about your thinking while you are thinking in order to make your thinking better.

Sounds like quite a juggling act? The key to understanding critical thinking involves recognizing and working with the basic building blocks that construct and color our thought processes. These are:

◆ Point of view (our perception)
◆ Purpose (the reason for the thought process)
◆ Information (the raw material for the process)
◆ Assumption (any pre-established criteria we might be using)
◆ Implications (the consequences of the process)
◆ Interpretation (the meaning of the process)
◆ Concepts (any ideas buried within the information)

If you are aware of these building blocks and can reflect on their relevance, accuracy, and logic, you can then judge what influence they are having on any decisions or conclusions you reach.

Critical thinking—and the self-awareness that accompanies it—is a skill that you can master with time and practice. The starting point involves developing a series of reflective questions that you can use to question your ideas. These questions can be categorized into four basic types:

◆ **Summary/definition questions:** getting your head around the shape of the idea
◆ **Analysis questions:** breaking down the idea and looking at it from a number of angles
◆ **Hypothesis questions:** exploring "what ifs" to understand how the idea might work
◆ **Evaluation questions:** making a judgment about the idea

Listed below are some example question frames from each of the four question categories:

◆ Summary and definition questions:
—What is . . .?
—When . . .?
—Who . . .?
—What is an example of . . .?

◆ Analysis questions:
—How . . .?
—What are the reasons for . . .?
—What other examples of . . .?
—What is the relationship between . . . and . . .?
—What is (are) the problem(s) /conflict(s)/issue(s) . . .?
—What are possible solutions/resolutions to these problems/conflicts/
issues . . .?
—Why . . .?
—What are the functions of . . .?
—What are the causes/results of . . .?

◆ Hypothesis questions:
  —If . . . occurs, then what happens . . .?
  —If . . . had happened, then what would be different . . .?
  —What does theory x predict will happen . . .?

◆ Evaluation questions:
  —Is your idea/thought process/conclusion . . .
    · Good or bad?
    · Effective or ineffective?
    · Applicable or not applicable?
    · Correct or incorrect?
    · Relevant or irrelevant?
    · Proven or not proven?
  —What are the advantages/disadvantages of . . .?
  —What is the best solution to . . .?
  —What should or should not happen . . .?
  —What is my opinion of . . .?
  —What is my support for my opinion of . . .?

Additional skills that are useful for developing critical thinking include:

◆ **Creativity.** The ability to generate lots of ideas and think in new directions can help give you a totally fresh perspective on an idea.
◆ **Decision making.** The skills involved in gathering data, evaluating them, and then acting on them offer a useful way of structuring your thought processes.
◆ **Mindpower (for example, memorizing).** Using techniques such as memorizing help expand your capacity to hold a number of ideas in your mind at any one time and consequently allow you to think in more depth.
◆ **Planning.** The skills of goal setting, making and testing assumptions, and establishing parameters are a useful aid to managing your initial approach to a problem.
◆ **Problem solving.** The ability to analyze different alternatives without leaping on the first solution that presents itself will give your thought processes a degree of objectivity and rigor.
◆ **Understanding how we learn.** If you are conscious of the environment and conditions under which your mind is most receptive to new ideas and learning, you can recreate those environments in which to do your thinking.

INDIVIDUAL TASKS AND REFLECTIONS

11.1 Exploring Thoughts Underlying Feelings and Feelings Underlying Thoughts

Take the time to sit and focus on your feelings right at this moment. What are the thoughts underlying your feelings?

11.2 Exploring Feelings Underlying Thoughts

Take the time to sit and focus on your thoughts right at this moment. What are the feelings underlying your thoughts?

11.3 Developing Criteria for Evaluation: Clarifying Values and Standards

Identify an issue that requires a decision from you. How are you going to develop the criteria in order to evaluate the outcome? By what values and standards are you developing that criteria?

11.4 Analyzing or Evaluating Actions or Policies

Identify and analyze an action or a policy you have recently initiated.

11.5 Examining or Evaluating Assumptions

Consider a recent assumption you have made. Examine the reasons why you made it. Evaluate your process and any consequences.

11.6 Thinking Independently

Consider a situation where a group decision was necessary and analyze your thought processes and contribution.

11.7 Exercising Fairmindedness

How do you exercise fairmindedness in your interpersonal relationships?

11.8 Developing Intellectual Humility and Suspending Judgment

Observe your processes involving judgment for a week. To what extent do you judge others (and is this related to the extent you judge yourself?). How might you develop intellectual humility in your relationships with others?

11.9 Listening Critically: The Art of Silent Dialogue

Observe yourself when listening to others. How do you listen?

11.10 Evaluating the Credibility of Sources of Information

Identify a situation, of which you are part, involving a source (or several sources) of information from others. How are you going to evaluate the credibility of the source(s) of information?

11.11 Critical-Thinking Analysis

Using the assessment below, evaluate your own performance in the following critical-thinking criteria. Ask your mentor to comment on your rating and discuss together. Move on to a discussion of the process you went through in this self-evaluation.

WORKING WITH OTHERS

WORKING WITH A MENTOR

Critical-Thinking Criteria	Good (✓)	Needs Improving (✓)
Thinking independently		
Exercising fairmindedness		
Exploring thoughts underlying feelings and feelings underlying thoughts		
Developing intellectual integrity		
Developing confidence in your reasoning ability		

(continued)

(continued)

Critical-Thinking Criteria	Good (✓)	Needs Improving (✓)
Developing your perspective		
Developing criteria for evaluation		
Questioning deeply		
Analyzing or evaluating arguments, interpretations, beliefs, or theories		
Generating or assessing solutions		
Analyzing or evaluating actions or policies		
Reading critically		
Listening critically		
Comparing and contrasting ideals with actual practice		
Thinking precisely about thinking		
Examining or evaluating assumptions		
Distinguishing relevant from irrelevant facts		
Evaluating evidence and alleged facts		

11.12 Developing Intellectual Courage

Identify a problem that requires you to change your perspective. Discuss with your mentor.

11.13 Questioning Deeply: Raising and Pursuing Root or Significant Questions

Consider a fundamental issue in your life that, although not presenting any major problems at the moment, is of ongoing concern to you. Discuss with your mentor, with your mentor constantly questioning you.

11.14 Reading Critically: Clarifying or Critiquing Texts

Ask your mentor to suggest for you a challenging piece of reading related to one of your areas of interest. Write a critique. Discuss.

11.15 Comparing and Contrasting Ideals with Actual Practice

Identify a situation that requires you to adapt or create a new process. Consider your ideas for solving the problem. Initiate the solution and evaluate. Compare and contrast your ideas with the actual practice of reality. Discuss with your mentor.

DEVELOPING

OTHERS
....

11.16 Exploring Critical Thinking

Introduce the subject of critical thinking. Taking the seven points below, either divide the learners into small discussion groups and ask them to come up with key bullet point summaries or discuss the points within the larger group. The points are as follows:

1. Exploring thoughts underlying feelings and feelings underlying thoughts
2. Developing intellectual humility and suspending judgment
3. Comparing analogous situations: transferring insights to new contexts
4. Developing one's perspective: creating or exploring beliefs, arguments, or theories
5. Questioning deeply: raising and pursuing root or significant questions
6. Analyzing or evaluating arguments, interpretations, beliefs, or theories
7. Thinking precisely about thinking: using critical vocabulary

RECOMMENDED

HRD PRESS TITLES
....

Polarity Management, 288 pp.
Quick Wits: A Compendium of Critical Thinking Skills, 250 pp.

12
Delegating

Delegation is:

◆ The process of effectively using group members by sharing authority and entrusting them with responsibility
◆ The process of empowering group members or individuals through task completion in an effort to reach the organization's goals and objectives

Some signs that you might need help with delegation skills include:

◆ Constantly taking work home with you and/or working overtime
◆ Not receiving work you assign on time
◆ Finding a pile of work waiting for you when you return from an absence
◆ Making decisions without staff input, thus causing resentment

So how do you delegate? First decide which tasks to delegate using the following guidelines.

◆ Identify tasks with sensitive implications and keep them for yourself.
◆ Identify tasks that might impact outside of your department—across the organization—and keep them for yourself.
◆ Identify tasks that others might be more skillful at completing and give them to others.
◆ Identify tasks that others might enjoy more than yourself and give them to others.

Then plan the delegation as follows:

◆ Further review the details of each task.
◆ Establish performance standards.
◆ Provide a training support or a back-up person.
◆ Clarify appropriate limits of authority.

Select a member of staff:

◆ Match the task to their interests and skills.
◆ Balance challenge with support.
◆ Be sure not to overload them.
◆ Consider the staff member's developmental needs.

Assign the task:

◆ Spell out the specifics of the task.
◆ Identify priorities within the task.
◆ Clarify the degree of authority.
◆ Identify any constraints.
◆ State deadlines for completion.

Finally, follow up:

◆ Maintain opportunities for communication during the process.
◆ Insist on updates from staff members.
◆ Initiate contact for further direction/support.
◆ Encourage different styles of task management.
◆ Record performance and offer appropriate feedback.
◆ Allow for mistakes.

When you delegate, you distribute responsibility and authority to others while holding them accountable for their performance. The ultimate accountability, however, still lies with you. That is why you must establish appropriate controls and checkpoints to monitor progress. Your role is to set clear goals and expectations for the assignment without telling the employee how to do it. In this way, you allow others to discover for themselves the best way to follow through.

Here are some key steps in becoming a master at delegation:

◆ **Avoid perfection.** Instead of striving for perfection, establish a standard of quality and provide a timeframe for reaching it. Then let your team choose any reasonable means to reach that goal.
◆ **Give effective instruction.** Make sure that your employee has enough information to complete the job successfully.
◆ **Support your employees.** Communicate your expectations before work begins, then tell your team what you expect from them and what support they can expect from you.
◆ **Follow up on progress.** Once you have delegated a task to an employee, leave them to do the work, but check on their progress.
◆ **Praise the efforts of your team.** A few words of praise, a brief note, or a handshake goes a long way in expressing to your employees how much you appreciate their skills and talents.
◆ **Recognize that others have ability.** Sometimes managers believe that only they can do something the right way. This belief often develops because an employee handles an assignment differently from a supervisor.
◆ **Know your true interests.** Delegation is difficult for some people who actually prefer doing the work themselves rather than managing it. Ironically, people are often promoted to management as a result of their technical excellence rather than their ability to manage.
◆ **Trust your team.** If you do not trust members of your team, take time to consider why. Ask yourself if your own actions may be the root cause for your lack of trust—for example, have you delegated authority as well as responsibility?
◆ **Delegation isn't all or nothing.** Because of your team's various skills and confidence levels, tasks often need to be delegated gradually. As an employee becomes more competent and confident, you can give them more authority and accountability.
◆ **Treat delegation as teaching.** People are reluctant to accept a delegated responsibility when mistakes are more frequently punished than accepted as part of the learning process. Your willingness to accept mistakes will encourage your team to accept assignments.

You can develop the right attitude to delegation by:

◆ Maintaining enough personal security in your own position so that you don't feel threatened by delegation
◆ Becoming willing to take risks
◆ Trusting your team members
◆ Becoming task oriented with your current relationships

Communicate responsibilities to team members by:

◆ Setting SMART (Specific, Measurable, Attainable, Relevant, Time-bound) goals
◆ Developing a clear understanding of goals with team members
◆ Defining the relative importance of the goals and task to the team members
◆ Explaining the potential complications
◆ Staying results-oriented, not procedure-oriented
◆ Setting performance standards for the task
◆ Communicating the consequences of superior, good, and poor performance

Grant the appropriate level of authority by:

◆ Determining which level of authority the team member is capable of handling
◆ Notifying others of the authority granted
◆ Communicating the level of authority to the team member

Provide the appropriate level of support by:

◆ Letting team members know what resources are available
◆ Giving notice to others of the team member's new responsibilities
◆ Communicating the extent of your availability to help

Monitor the delegation by:

◆ Recording current performance information
◆ Providing sufficient levels of coaching to the team member
◆ Enforcing predetermined performance standards and communicating how the team member is meeting those standards
◆ Maintaining open, objective communication with the team member
◆ Giving the team member opportunities to provide feedback on your delegation abilities during the task

Evaluate the delegation by:

◆ Comparing results of the task with the initial goals—why was or wasn't the delegation successful?
◆ Evaluating the team member's role during the delegation
◆ Assessing the team member on efficiency, timing, creativity, and cooperation
◆ Discussing your evaluation with team members
◆ Providing team members with constructive criticism—both positive and negative feedback

INDIVIDUAL TASKS AND REFLECTIONS

12.1 Delegation Skills

Try out the following questionnaire to reflect on your skills:

Delegation Skills	Yes (✓)	No (✓)
Do you allow your people to make mistakes?		
Do your people get promotions at least as frequently as other people with equivalent responsibility in the organization?		
Do you frequently take work home or work late at the office?		

(continued)

(continued)

Delegation Skills	Yes (✓)	No (✓)
Does your operation function smoothly when you're absent?		
Do you spend more time working on details than you do on planning and supervision?		
Do your people feel that they have sufficient authority over Human Resources, finances, facilities, and other resources?		
Is your follow-up procedure adequate?		
Do you overrule or reverse decisions made by your subordinates?		
Do you bypass your subordinates by making decisions that are part of their jobs?		
Do you do several things that your subordinates could, and should, be doing?		
If you were incapacitated for six months, is there someone who could take your place?		
Do your key people delegate well to their own subordinates?		
Do your subordinates take the initiative in expanding their authority with delegated projects without waiting for you to initiate all assignments?		
When you delegate, do you specify:		
◆ The results you expect?		
◆ The tasks or activities to be carried out?		
◆ All of these?		

Self-Assessment	Yes (✓)	No (✓)
Do you think you are:		
◆ A doer rather than a manager?		
◆ Unsure of others' ability?		
◆ Unwilling to take risks?		
◆ A perfectionist?		
◆ Fearful of being resented?		
◆ Concerned that others could take the credit for your work?		
◆ Unsure of how to delegate?		

(continued)

(continued)

Attitude Toward Delegation	Yes (✔)	No (✔)
Do you regard others as unsuitable for delegation because they are:		
◆ Inexperienced?		
◆ Disorganized?		
◆ Under pressure?		
◆ Lacking sufficient information or resources?		
◆ Lacking confidence?		
◆ Unwilling to accept responsibility?		
Do you tend to see tasks as unsuitable for delegation because they are:		
◆ Too important?		
◆ Of a sensitive or confidential nature?		
◆ Urgent?		

WORKING

WITH OTHERS

....

12.2 Delegation Checklist

Create a delegation checklist for yourself. Identify three tasks that could be delegated to others and work through the checklist to complete.

12.3 Delegating to You

How do others delegate to you? How do you respond?

WORKING

WITH A MENTOR

....

DEVELOPING

OTHERS

....

12.4 Delegation Skills and Weaknesses

Analyze your delegation skills and weaknesses. Discuss and create an action plan to improve your skills. Review regularly with your mentor.

12.5 Brainstorming Delegation

Introduce the subject of delegation. Brainstorm the reasons for delegating. Brainstorm the skills necessary for delegating.

12.6 Failed Delegation

Introduce the subject of delegating. Brainstorm the reasons why delegating fails. Ask each learner to identify a situation where they could have delegated or did delegate and it didn't work. Organize the learners into groups of four to discuss and come up with ways in which each learner could have dealt with their own delegation problem more effectively.

12.7 Current Delegation

Introduce the subject of delegation. Ask each learner to identify a current situation in which they need to delegate. Organize the learners into groups of four to discuss and come up with ways in which each learner can deal with their specific delegation effectively.

RECOMMENDED HRD PRESS TITLES

50 Activities for Developing People Skills, 250 pp.

13 Developing Emotional Intelligence

INTRODUCTION

Emotional intelligence—a concept originally coined by Daniel Soleman, author of Emotional Intelligence (1996) and Working with Emotional Intelligence (2000)—involves balancing our thoughts and feelings. Sometimes in order to avoid feeling, we rationalize or intellectualize our feelings. Equally, we can sometimes immerse ourselves to an unhealthy extent in our feelings, without any logical thought processes.

Imagine that someone you know says to you, "Can't you do anything right—you fool!" What would you think? How would you feel? What would you do?

Now, imagine that the voice talking is your own and that you are thinking such thoughts about yourself. You might recognize a similar kind of negative self-talk dominating your own thoughts. This self-critical voice works by:

◆ Emphasizing past failures
◆ Ignoring anything good that happens
◆ Setting impossible standards of perfection
◆ Assuming others' thoughts about you are negative
◆ Calling you names

There is a relationship between thoughts, feelings, and behavior. Our thoughts give rise to our feelings. This combination gives rise to behavior and action. If we think, "Yes, I can get through this exam," we feel positive, upbeat, and confident, and we have more chance of sailing through the exam successfully. If we think, "I'll never do it," we feel insecure, powerless, and anxious, and have more chance of failing the exam.

Negative thinking may be a sign that you have uncomfortable feelings such as sadness, hurt, or anger that need to be acknowledged and released. When thoughts are mostly negative due to low self-esteem, more often feelings of anxiety, anger, and sadness are experienced. As a result of negative thinking, actions are more likely to include withdrawing from people and avoiding new situations, or perhaps acting out our hostility with sarcasm or blame. Yet, believe it or not, these negative thoughts serve a purpose. That critical voice protects you in a backward kind of way from fear of failure and rejection. However, negative thinking can become automatic and so ingrained in your self-image that you end up living your life that way.

Encouraging interactions during childhood go a long way toward promoting positive self-talk when we are adults. But if that was not the case, it doesn't mean you can't work to develop positive self-talk now. Tuning in to your personal thoughts is the first step in doing something about negative self-talk. Once you become aware of how your self-talk sounds, imagine what a kind, supportive voice would say. This could be a parent, a grandparent, a favorite teacher, or a friend. Here's what an encouraging person might say:

◆ "Go ahead. Give it a try. You do have the skills required to do the job. You deserve this promotion!"
◆ "You're good!"
◆ "Good for you! You did very well!"

The Interaction Between Thoughts, Feelings, and Actions

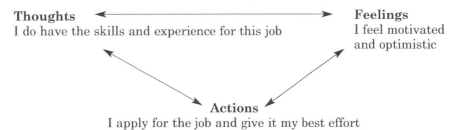

Thoughts
I do have the skills and experience for this job

Feelings
I feel motivated and optimistic

Actions
I apply for the job and give it my best effort

Imagine that someone you know says to you, "Wow. You're a star!" What would you think? How would you feel? What would you do? See the difference that positive thoughts make on your thoughts, feelings, and behavior!

Many of us have difficulty admitting we have feelings, let alone expressing them. If as children our feelings were met with disapproval or anger, we learn to hide them. As adults, we carry stored feelings of shame, rage, or guilt deep within ourselves—we only allow ourselves to experience "acceptable" feelings. This means that the way in which we respond to life is distorted in order to protect ourselves from what we are actually feeling.

When we repress our feelings, we might be unaware of them, distort them, experience depression, have only superficial relationships, or develop a physical illness. As we get in touch with our feelings and learn to express them honestly, our stress levels decrease. As we learn to share our feelings with others, so we will find others sharing theirs with us. As we allow our feelings to surface, the pain diminishes and we find ourselves less overwhelmed by them. As we experience and express our feelings, we begin to identify the feelings, openly express them, and increase our intimacy levels.

We may avoid taking responsibility for our feelings in the following ways:

◆ Denial (I'm fine)
◆ Projection (taking it out on the cat when you've had a bad day at the office)
◆ Collusion (controlling the behavior of others through manipulation)
◆ Rationalization (thinking your way out of feelings)
◆ Avoidance (excessive drinking or becoming a workaholic rather than facing, say, a marriage break-up)

Ultimately, you must create your own kind and supportive thoughts. Use positive self-talk and affirmations regularly to reinforce your self-image and sense of worth. Affirmations are positive self-talk statements that:

◆ Start with *I*
◆ Are clear and brief
◆ Are set in the present
◆ Become more effective with repetition

More often than not, we tend to use the "you" message—for example, "You stop that!" or "You shouldn't do that!" Other words that we use to disown our thoughts and feelings include *people, we, that, there,* and *it*. By using *I*, as in "I don't feel like going for a drink" or "I feel frustrated when people keep interrupting me," we own our thoughts and feelings. Use *I*:

◆ When disclosing feelings and thoughts
◆ To show responsibility for owning your feelings, thoughts, and actions
◆ To acknowledge your separateness to others
◆ To engender less defensiveness in another

Examples of Affirmations	
I have unique abilities and talents.	I take care of myself.
I feel safe and confident.	I can make a difference.
I am willing to take risks to grow and change.	When something goes wrong, I handle it.
I am a good person, mistakes and all.	I am worthy and capable.

In order to balance our thoughts with our feelings, we need to understand ways in which we can sabotage our processes. These are as follows:

◆ **Overestimating.** This refers to overestimating the odds of a negative outcome to a situation. This state creates anxiety by causing you to imagine greater danger than is really likely.

◆ **"Should" statements.** These are the mark of your inner perfectionist. Imposing "shoulds" on yourself will keep you anxious and will lower confidence and self-esteem. Once your inner perfectionist has told you what you should do, your inner critic comes in to tell you how far you fall short.

◆ **Catastrophizing.** This is a distorted mode of thinking in which you inaccurately view a situation as catastrophic or insufferable. It often follows overestimating.

◆ **Emotional reasoning.** This is a tendency to judge something illogically, based on feelings.

◆ **Overgeneralizing.** To overgeneralize is to falsely assume that because you have had one bad experience, your bad experience will always repeat itself in a similar situation. This manifests itself by jumping from one instance in the present to all instances in the future. If you use words such as *always, every,* and *everyone,* then you are overgeneralizing.

Examples of Irrational Beliefs	Rational Thinking
I must be upset by other people's problems.	I'm not helping others in trouble by making myself miserable over them.
I must be competent, never make mistakes, and achieve all the time.	I want to do things well, but it's OK to make the occasional mistake.
I need to depend on someone stronger than myself.	The only person I really need to rely on is myself.
My bad feelings are caused by things outside my control.	Problems may be influenced by factors outside my control, but my reaction to them is under my control.
It's easier to put off difficult things than face up to them.	Putting off problems doesn't make them easier to face up to.

INDIVIDUAL TASKS AND REFLECTIONS

13.1 Disarming the Inner Critic

Make a list of mental messages your inner critic (your negative inner dialogue) uses to sabotage you. Take each message and check it against the following:

◆ Has your critic made a general rule from one isolated example?
◆ Does your critic insist that you are either completely responsible for everything or that you have no responsibility at all?
◆ Does your critic use exaggerated positive or negative descriptions rather than accurate ones?
◆ Does your critic insist that everything you do has to be perfect, otherwise it is garbage?

13.2 Criticizing Yourself

Observe yourself over the next week and become more aware of how often you have critical thoughts of yourself.

13.3 Activity Anxiety

Identify an activity that causes you anxiety. What are your irrational beliefs about it? How do you sabotage your thought processes?

13.4 Irrational Beliefs

Identify four of your negative or irrational beliefs (about anything) and write them down on the left-hand side of a sheet of paper. Now create four positive affirmations in response on the right-hand side of the sheet. Try actively using them and notice whether any change occurs in your thought processes.

13.5 Feelings

Generally, how aware are you of your feelings? Can you normally identify and express them appropriately?

13.6 Learning How to Deal with Feelings

How did your parents and other role models teach you to deal with your feelings?

WORKING WITH OTHERS

13.7 The "I" Word

Notice how many times you use (or avoid using) the "I" word in your daily conversations.

13.8 Daily Interactions

Become more aware of your daily interactions with people. Notice your responses to them. What are your thoughts and feelings? How do these influence your behaviors? Discuss with your mentor.

WORKING WITH A MENTOR

13.9 Observe and Assess

Identify how your thoughts affect your feelings. Identify situations that you can observe and in which you can assess yourself. Discuss your observations and assessments with your mentor. Create a development plan to help you develop emotional intelligence.

DEVELOPING

OTHERS

....

13.10 Avoiding Feelings

Introduce the subject of developing emotional intelligence. Develop the theme into ways in which we may avoid taking responsibility for our feelings. Brainstorm to include denial, projection, collusion, rationalization, and avoidance. Put the learners into groups of four to discuss. Reconvene the larger group to share further thoughts.

13.11 Sabotage

Introduce the subject of developing emotional intelligence. Develop the theme into ways in which we sabotage our processes. Organize the learners into groups of four to discuss. Reconvene the larger group to share further thoughts.

RECOMMENDED

HRD PRESS TITLES

....

The Manager's Pocket Guide to Emotional Intelligence, 140 pp.
50 Activities for Developing Emotional Intelligence, 300 pp.
Emotional Intelligence Style Profile, 16 pp.

14

Developing Leadership

INTRODUCTION

Leadership is the ability to enable ordinary people to do extraordinary things.
—Sir John Harvey Jones

Leadership can be a lonely role, and a key to being an effective leader is coming to terms with the responsibility it entails. Since you are the pivot for providing vision and support to others, you need a network of support yourself such as mentors, colleagues, family, and friends. It is also important to understand that you may be a leader in a particular sphere, but this doesn't necessarily make you a suitable leader in all spheres.

Effective leaders:

◆ Have a strong belief in their own and other people's capabilities and set out to release this latent power in themselves and others
◆ Respect others and believe that they, given the opportunity, will contribute to the success of the organization through their own inner conviction and drive
◆ Personalize rather than generalize their leadership approach, in that they do not seek or use a single best-practice approach, but set out to create an empathetic relationship in which leader behavior matches the needs of those being led
◆ Democratize hierarchical work environments by using the structures, processes, and procedures to strengthen and enable people rather than control them
◆ Inspire their followers and put enthusiasm into everything they do
◆ Act as protectors of others by supporting their people from attack from outside interests
◆ Through a process of tutoring and mentoring, develop their people's self-esteem so that they have the potential to become effective achievers themselves
◆ Release the latent self-leadership capability of their people so that they behave in ways that encourage them to take charge of their environment and take responsibility for their own actions
◆ Manage by using an effective combination of direction, delegation, and listening
◆ Enhance the worth of their people by ensuring that they are in tune with the environment and are producing effective outcomes

> Do you have a mission and vision?
> Do you have a mission and vision for your team?

Effective leadership is a balancing act. The pivot is the task that needs to be completed, while the balancing act lies in the facilitation of personnel needed for completion. A leader may need to balance one individual, several apparently unconnected individuals, or a specific team of individuals while focusing throughout on the task.

The critical leadership key skills and qualities have been defined as follows:

Developmental skills	Enthusiasm
Empathy	Stability
Creativity	Effective thinking skills
Innovation	Ability to lead by example
Responsibility	Integrity
Inspires trust	Drive
Interpersonal skills	Confidence
People focus	Self-awareness
Commitment	Courage
Experience and knowledge of the job	Emotional intelligence
Foresight	

Robert Tannenbaum and Warren Schmidt (1973) have identified the following six leadership styles:

1. **Tell.** The leader tells the team what to do, and they have no say in the matter.
2. **Sell.** The leader tells the team what to do and gives reasons for the action, and they have no say in the matter.
3. **Test.** The leader puts forward their solution or decision and asks for the team's agreement.
4. **Consult.** The leader explains the situation, suggests a solution, and asks the team for their solutions.
5. **Join.** The leader explains the situation and then joins the team to explore and discuss possible solutions.
6. **Delegate.** The leader explains the situation and asks the team to come up with possible solutions, but takes no part in the discussion, agreeing only to accept the team's conclusions.

> A leader is best when people rarely know he exists; not so good when people serve and acclaim him; worst when they despise him. Fail to honor people, and they fail to honor you. But of a good leader, who talks little, when his work is done, his aim fulfilled, they will all say, "We did this ourselves."
>
> —Lao Tzu

Meredith Belbin (1996) has produced some excellent research on team leadership (and team roles). Examples of leadership styles are given below:

Examples of Leadership Styles	
The Motivator	**The Supporter**
Enthusiastic	Likeable
Sympathetic	Team player
Influential	Predictable

(continued)

(continued)

The Motivator	The Supporter
Charismatic	Deliberate
Social	Loyal
Dramatic	Patient
Friendly	Low risk-taker
Generous	Easy-going
Fatal flaw: Talks too much	**Fatal flaw:** Agrees too much
The Perfectionist	**The Director**
Conscientious	Ambitious
Orderly	Risk-taker
Self-disciplined	Forceful
Mature	Powerful
High standards	Responsible
Fretful	Energizing
Accurate	Organizer
Systematic	Self-confident
Fatal flaw: Questions too much	**Fatal flaw:** Directs too much

INDIVIDUAL TASKS AND REFLECTIONS

14.1 Self-Assessment

Go through the following checklist and assess your leadership skills and strengths:

Leadership Skills	Good (✔)	Needs improving (✔)
Motivating others		
Planning and organizing		
Team building		
Confronting		
Dealing with problems		

(continued)

(continued)

Leadership Skills	Good (✔)	Needs improving (✔)
Balancing priorities		
Making decisions		
Delegating		
Encouraging initiative in others		
Demonstrating fairness		
Sensitivity to the feelings of others		
Demonstrating tenacity		
Demonstrating self-belief		
Actively showing belief in others		
Encouraging others to collaborate		
Supporting and encouraging others		
Showing enthusiasm		
Monitoring progress		
Keeping people informed		
Practicing what you preach		
Actively encouraging feedback		
Minimizing anxiety in others		
Not apportioning blame		
Reviewing the team's performance		
Communicating an inspired view of the future		
Clarifying the values of the team		
Promoting understanding		
Seeking to understand before making judgments		
Valuing and building on individual differences		
Being approachable		
Emphasizing the importance of learning		

(continued)

(continued)

Leadership Skills	Good (✔)	Needs improving (✔)
Providing direction and focus		
Setting objectives and agreeing on targets		
Encouraging new ways of doing things		
Developing other people		
Standing up for other people's interests		
Treating mistakes as learning opportunities		
Promoting other people's self-esteem		
Recognizing individual effort		
Listening to people's ideas and problems		
Admitting when you're wrong		
Showing commitment		
Being positive		
Taking risks		
Being proactive		
Managing change		
Managing resources		
Taking responsibility		
Communicating empathy		
Communicating respect		
Acting honestly in accordance with your own feelings		
Making use of specific examples rather than talking in theoretical generalizations		
Demonstrating positive verbal and nonverbal language		

14.2 Qualities of a Leader

What do you think are the most important qualities for a leader to possess?

14.3 Past Leader

Consider a good leader you have known in the past. What was it that made them a good boss? Consider their leadership behaviors.

WORKING
WITH OTHERS

14.4 Peer Assessment

Give the self-assessment checklist in task 1 to a colleague and ask them to assess your skills and strengths.

14.5 Subordinate Assessment

Give the self-assessment checklist in task 1 to a subordinate and ask them to assess your skills and strengths.

WORKING
WITH A MENTOR

14.6 Action Planning

Discuss what you do to demonstrate your leadership ability and how you can develop your leadership qualities.

14.7 Mentor Assessment

Give the self-assessment checklist in task 1 to your mentor and ask them to assess your skills and strengths.

14.8 Mentor Leadership

What is your mentor's leadership style?

DEVELOPING
OTHERS

14.9 Famous Leaders

Introduce the subject of developing leadership and brainstorm ideal skills and strengths. Organize the learners into small groups and ask them to consider examples of leadership—for example, Microsoft founder Bill Gates, former New York Mayor Rudolf Giuliani, and so forth. Reconvene the larger group and draw out the advantages and disadvantages of good and bad leadership.

14.10 Key Skills Improvement

Ask the group to individually consider their roles as leaders using the checklist for leadership skills and strengths, and to identify two key skills they need to improve upon. Organize the learners into groups of three. Give each person a set time to discuss their two key skills and to receive feedback from the rest of the group in formulating an action plan.

RECOMMENDED
HRD PRESS TITLES

Leadership Effectiveness Profile, 16 pp.
The Manager's Pocket Guide to Leadership Skills, 200 pp.
50 Activities for Developing Leaders, Volumes 1 and 2; 300 pp. each.

INTRODUCTION

Empowerment is a little like delegation—responsibility and power that managers grant employees. The reality today is that many front-line employees already have a great deal of power. The key is to recognize their power and motivate them to channel it in the interests of the business. For example:

◆ Employees who serve both internal and external customers and suppliers, and whose innovations are crucial, have the power to make or break your business. You cannot empower them; you just need to acknowledge how important and powerful they already are.

◆ Employees are now recognized as those who carry out the most critical jobs, and managers are increasingly seen as facilitators or coaches who simply need to stand back and let their people do their jobs. Nevertheless, it is difficult for people to fully exploit their power because managers still have the power to promote or fire them. Both sides have their own sort of power and, today, the balance is more equal than it used to be.

◆ An equal balance of power implies partnership, not empowerment—the catch is that partners expect an equal balance of reward distribution as well. The key here is not so much to empower employees who are already powerful, but to motivate them to channel their power to maximize business results.

So how do you empower people? First your organizational culture has to adjust, and then people have to be developed to overcome their fear of acting without your approval. Many employees are already more than able to take all the responsibility you can give them. The solution is to encourage them to realize how much power they already have by virtue of specialist skills and knowledge.

The most difficult aspect of empowerment is changing old habits—your unwillingness to let go and employees' inabilities to abandon their fears. Trust takes time to build: regular feedback, both to the manager and to the empowered, will build their confidence.

> Empowerment entails a more fundamental change than mere delegation.
>
> Empowerment is about the natural shift of power to knowledge, away from position.

What would you empower your people to do?

◆ Handle customers?
◆ Participate in major decisions?
◆ Make strategic contributions?
◆ Demonstrate creativity?
◆ Handle urgent problems?

Empower people when:

◆ Employees are close to customers
◆ Innovation is critical
◆ Technology is complex
◆ Processes are changing rapidly
◆ The environment is uncertain
◆ Employees demand personal growth, responsibility, and development
◆ Initiative has a high payoff value
◆ People need motivating
◆ The individuals concerned are ready
◆ Close supervision is impossible
◆ The manager can genuinely let go
◆ The manager is supportive and a good coach

Consider not empowering when:

◆ Consistency and uniformity across employees is essential
◆ Costs need to be minimized and tightly controlled
◆ Operations need to be standardized
◆ Errors are too costly
◆ People are untrained or otherwise not ready
◆ Employees are too dependent and lack confidence
◆ Individual initiative may be too costly
◆ Motivation is already strong with the way things are
◆ Close supervision is essential
◆ The organization's culture is not supportive
◆ The managers are not ready to let go

Empowerment may fail for any one of several reasons:

◆ The manager's fear of losing power
◆ Pressure from the manager's boss to be knowledgeable about all details
◆ The rationalization that employees are not ready
◆ Fear of losing control
◆ The feeling that "Only I can make the right decisions"
◆ Fear of having nothing to do—being redundant or having no purpose
◆ Fear of losing face or status
◆ Not accepting that subordinates are more knowledgeable or better placed to make some decisions
◆ Lack of support from the organization's culture—demands for more centralized decision making
◆ Preaching the educational value of making mistakes while still punishing them

---

Guidelines to Empowerment

◆ We create our own reality by what we believe to be true.
◆ We always have a choice.
◆ Change the inner, and the outer will follow.
◆ The more we learn to support ourselves, the more in control of our lives we feel.

A Three-Stage Skills Model of Empowering Others		
Stage	**Definition**	**Skills for A to Use**
1 Exploration	A enables B to explore the problem from B's perspective and to focus on specific concerns.	◆ Giving attention ◆ Listening
2 Understanding	B is helped to see themselves in a new perspective and to focus on what they might do to cope more effectively. They are helped to see what strengths and resources they might use.	◆ Giving attention ◆ Listening ◆ Empathy ◆ Information sharing ◆ Staying in the present ◆ Goal setting
3 Action	B is helped to consider possible ways to act, look at consequences, plan action, implement it, and evaluate.	◆ Giving attention ◆ Listening ◆ Empathy ◆ Information sharing ◆ Staying in the present ◆ Goal setting ◆ Creative thinking ◆ Problem solving ◆ Evaluating

INDIVIDUAL TASKS AND REFLECTIONS

15.1 Being Empowered

Consider a situation in which someone has empowered you. What happened? What does it feel like to be empowered? What happened as a result?

15.2 Being Disempowered

Consider a situation in which someone has disempowered you. What happened? How did you feel? What did you do?

WORKING WITH OTHERS

15.3 Disempowering Others

Consider a situation in which you have disempowered someone else. How did you disempower them? Why did you disempower them? How do you think they might have felt? With hindsight, how might you have empowered them?

15.4 Empowering Others

Consider a situation in which you have empowered someone else. How did you empower them? How do you think they might have felt? What did it feel like to have empowered someone?

15.5 Disempowering People

Complete the following checklist:

Do you . . .	Yes (✔)	No (✔)
◆ Make sure you handle the important issues?		
◆ Insist on approving actions that your people could take on their own?		
◆ Criticize your people for not consulting you on decisions they could make?		
◆ Offer your answers instead of drawing solutions from your people?		
◆ Occupy most of the spotlight most of the time?		
◆ Lead all your meetings and cross-functional exchanges?		
◆ See your role as making decisions and having the answers?		
◆ Feel you need to look after or protect your subordinates?		
◆ Show discomfort or disapproval when your people disagree with you?		
◆ Jump on your people for mistakes but forget to praise their successes?		
◆ Ridicule your people's ideas as unworkable?		
◆ Generally like to see things done your way?		

If you answered "yes" to more than half of these questions, the chances are that you disempower at least some of the people who work for you.

WORKING WITH A MENTOR

15.6 Attitudes to Empowerment

Analyze and discuss, with your mentor, attitudes to empowerment.

15.7 Empowering Culture

Analyze and discuss, with your mentor, whether your organization encourages an empowering culture. If appropriate, how might such a culture be encouraged?

DEVELOPING OTHERS

15.8 Facilitating Empowerment in Others

Introduce the subject of empowering others and the three-style skills model. Divide the learners into groups of three—two role-players, one of whom empowers the other using the three-style model, plus an observer to give feedback. The learner who is empowered can also provide feedback to the person facilitating the empowerment. Reconvene the large group to share experiences and discuss.

15.9 Facilitator Empowerment

This exercise needs to be done near the end of a training session. Ask the learners to analyze how the facilitator has facilitated learner empowerment in the group and with individuals.

15.10 When and When Not to Empower

Introduce the subject of empowering others. Brainstorm the reasons for empowering people. Ask the learners to consider their position in empowering others and to suggest when it is and is not appropriate to empower. Share ideas and discuss.

15.11 Why Empowerment Fails and Succeeds

Introduce the subject of empowering others. Brainstorm why empowerment fails and why it succeeds. Ask each learner to provide one example of giving empowerment that failed and one where it succeeded (and the reasons for each). Organize the learners into pairs to discuss and to identify ways in which they might improve their empowerment skills. Reconvene the larger group to share and discuss empowerment strategies.

Developing Employee Capital, 200 pp.

RECOMMENDED HRD PRESS TITLES
....

16
Facilitating Learning

Facilitation is the art of guiding others in self-discovery. Facilitation isn't about leading, teaching, or training. It's about providing a safe environment or arena for people to make discoveries for themselves. It's almost like self-directed learning, but there is a coordinator (facilitator) to hold it together and to guide it along. The facilitator could be seen as the chair, if you like.

Effective facilitators:

◆ Adapt their small-group activities to suit the participants, the environment, and the desired outcomes

◆ Are proactive (before using a small-group activity, they modify it on the basis of the characteristics of the participants and the purpose of the activity)

◆ Are responsive and make modifications during the small-group activity to keep the different tensions within acceptable ranges

◆ Are resilient (they accept whatever happens during the small-group activity as valuable data and continue with the activity)

Within any small-group activity, there are six stress areas that can enhance or destroy its effectiveness. These revolve around:

◆ **Structure.** How is the session structured? How is each activity structured? A session needs to have a beginning, middle, and end that makes sense and moves forward so that participants feel that there is a constructive reason for being there. Furthermore, each activity needs to have the same structure, but also needs to address individual motivation and achievement. It's a bit like the microcosm and macrocosm philosophy. The world (session) is a larger representation of the individual (activity)—both having the same structure on different scales.

◆ **Timing and pace.** This refers to the timing of the session and the pace of activities. When pacing activities, do you take account of what has happened in the previous one? You may want to proceed rapidly, but the participants may want to go slower—and rushing them could lead to fragmentation of discovery and learning. Usually, groups like to know how much time they have for a task.

◆ **Interaction.** Here we look at interaction between participants and interaction between facilitator and participants. Competition and cooperation are both beneficial. What you don't want is for the participants to develop a sense of competition with you, as the facilitator. They need to know you have the authority, but not the control.

◆ **Focus (individual and group).** By this, we mean how well (or badly) the participants are focusing on the sessions and the activities. Some activities can press personal buttons that can lead to a shift in individual and group focus. If appropriate, you can use the change in dynamics to make a more in-depth explanation. Some individuals, although they may be interested in the subject, feel uncomfortable in a group work situation, leading to difficulties in productivity.

◆ **Needs (individual and group).** Although you will be aware of group needs prior to the session, some unforeseen needs could emerge during it. Equally (though less likely), you may be aware of individual needs prior to the session, but these will probably manifest themselves during an activity. Up to a point, individual needs should be observed and (if possible) quietly worked on with the individual concerned at the time. It might be necessary to remove the individual from the activity and to one side, or to talk to them after the session. It is helpful to respond to group needs immediately, as this may well tease out areas for further discovery.

◆ **Control and authority.** Who has control? A facilitator has ultimate authority in terms of holding the session/activity together. The participants have control because the session must work toward fulfilling their needs.

The number and type of participants, and the structure and purpose of the activity, influence how these stresses manifest themselves. The secret of effective facilitation is to maintain a balance between any two extremes of stresses. Beyond that, you may use a variety of tactics to increase or decrease the elements in each stress area:

◆ **Structure**

To *increase* the stress element, start with a detailed explanation of the activity rules and emphasize the importance of sticking to the rules. Every so often, refer to the objectives of the session or activity.

To *decrease* the stress element, reassure the participants that it is not absolutely necessary to stick to the rules. Reaffirm the rules when and if required. As the session develops, add impromptu activities.

◆ **Timing and Pace**

To *increase* the stress element, begin the activity promptly and move it along quickly. Announce intermediate time limits. Intermittently summarize, and move on quickly.

To *slow down,* intercept the activity with further activity ideas. If a participant or the team finishes the activity before time is up, ask them to review and revise.

◆ **Interaction**

To *increase* participation interaction, compare the results of individuals/ teams. Ask provocative questions and use the names of participants to help facilitator-learner and learner-facilitator familiarity.

To *reduce* participant interaction, increase the conflict between participants and external constraints—for example, outcomes. Make sure that you move around the participants or groups.

◆ **Focus**

To *increase* focus on the *process,* introduce game elements, regularly check on progress, or let the participants suggest changes to the activity. Keep referring to the individual outcomes for the activity.

To *increase* focus on the *outcomes,* use a performance reward system for individuals/teams. Instigate a subtle air of competition.

◆ **Needs**

To *increase* focus on *individual needs,* organize the participants into groups of equal strength. You can encourage shy people to participate by giving them achievable responsibilities.

To *increase* focus on *group needs,* identify the dominant participants and give them additional roles—for example, taking notes. Encourage the group to make regular progress checks to ensure that everyone's needs are being met.

◆ **Control**

To *increase* control *between you and the participants,* work with "user-friendly" participants to ensure external control.

To *increase participant control,* explain that your role is that of facilitator as opposed to leader or trainer. When the participants ask you a procedural question—for example, "What do we do next?"—reframe it to the group as "What would you like to do next?"

◆ **Authority**

To *increase your authority,* scatter your wisdom periodically while encouraging participants to develop your thoughts and ideas.

To *decrease your authority* (and encourage participant development), set the task and boundaries and then withdraw physically (to the back of the room or outside it).

Further Hints for Facilitating Learning

◆ Flexible facilitation means that you should be aware of your biases about group experiences (as a member and a facilitator) and how they influence you in your current role as a facilitator.
◆ Before planning a small-group activity, you need to collect information on the likely preferences of your participants along each of the six stress areas. The best strategy for collecting this information is to interview the participants and possibly cross-check your information with other facilitators who are familiar with the group.
◆ Whether you are designing a new activity or using an existing one, integrate your understanding of the participants' preferences into design and implementation.
◆ As your participants work through the activity, continuously monitor the levels of various stresses. If the six stresses are at optimum levels, do not interfere with the flow of the activity. However, some tensions are likely from time to time. Wait to see if the group makes its own adjustments. With inexperienced groups, you may need to intervene with appropriate adjustments.
◆ Conduct a debriefing session with the participants to collect information on their perceptions of the different stress levels. This can be done by asking the participants questions such as "When did you feel the activity was too tightly structured?" or "When did you feel the facilitator interrupted you too often?"

INDIVIDUAL TASKS AND REFLECTIONS

16.1 A Positive Group Experience

Consider a positive group experience in which you were involved. Consider the methods of the facilitator. What did they do well? How did you respond? How did other group members respond?

16.2 A Negative Group Experience

Consider a negative group experience in which you were involved. Consider the methods of the facilitator. What did they do? How did you respond? How did other group members respond? What might you have done differently if you had been the facilitator?

16.3 Facilitating Well

Consider a positive group experience that you facilitated. Consider the methods you used. What did you do well? How did you feel? How did group members respond? What was the outcome of the group activity?

16.4 Facilitating Badly

Consider a negative group experience that you facilitated. Consider the methods you used. What did you do that didn't work? How did you feel? How did group members respond? What was the outcome of the group activity? With hindsight, what could you have done to improve your facilitation?

WORKING WITH OTHERS

16.5 Self-Assessment

When you next facilitate a group, create a self-assessment sheet to complete when you have finished. You could ask key group members, or the entire group, to complete it as well.

16.6 Assessing a Facilitator

Create a facilitator assessment sheet. The next time you are part of a facilitated group, assess the facilitator's skills. You might like to share your findings with the facilitator afterward.

WORKING WITH A MENTOR

16.7 Facilitating with Your Mentor

Ask your mentor to come and observe you facilitating a group. When you have finished, you and your mentor both complete an assessment of your performance and discuss it. Work toward an action plan for improving your facilitation skills.

16.8 Mentor Facilitation

Observe your mentor facilitating a group. Afterward, you and your mentor both complete an assessment of their performance and discuss what you could learn from it.

DEVELOPING OTHERS

16.9 The Roles and Skills of a Facilitator

Introduce the subject of facilitation skills. Brainstorm the role of a facilitator. Brainstorm the kinds of skills necessary.

16.10 Being Facilitated and Being the Facilitator

Introduce the subject of facilitation skills. Divide the learners into groups of four to discuss positive and negative experiences of being facilitated. Reconvene the larger group to draw out comments. Organize the learners back into the groups to discuss positive and negative experiences of being a facilitator. Again, reconvene the larger group to draw out comments.

16.11 The Facilitator on the Line

This exercise should be done near the end of a session. Using yourself as a resource, ask the group to identify the positive and negative facilitation skills you have demonstrated.

16.12 The Learner as Facilitator

Introduce the subject of facilitation skills. Give each learner the opportunity to be the group facilitator. They are to facilitate a group discussion for 5 or 10 minutes depending on how many learners there are in the group. Allow time for group feedback between each facilitation.

RECOMMENDED

HRD PRESS TITLES

....

Interacting with Others Assessment and Workbook, 52 pp.
The Complete Guide to Facilitation, 673 pp.

··

INTRODUCTION

······························

If you can develop your creative abilities, you are better placed to find solutions to problems. Also, the more you can blend creativity with your logical planning and evaluation skills, the more effective you will be and the more you can produce. Channeling creativity in productivity involves going through a number of processes, such as:

◆ **Gathering data:** concerned with analyzing tasks, gathering data, and trying out ideas
◆ **Frustration:** when we doubt our ability and become bored or irritated
◆ **Gestation:** when we put the issue on hold and it sinks into the unconscious
◆ **Birth:** the moment of inspiration from the unconscious as promoted by the right side of the brain
◆ **Reality testing:** living and testing out the reality

Hemispheres in the Brain

Did you know that the left hemisphere of the brain is almost always larger than the right hemisphere, and that there is a difference in the function of each hemisphere?

One of the most important advances in the study of the brain occurred in the 1960s when Roger Sperry of the California Institute of Technology led a team of researchers to a new understanding that the two hemispheres of the brain each control different processes.

The left hemisphere is responsible for the understanding and production of speech, the written word, and language, and can also perform complicated logical activities and mathematical computations. By contrast, the right hemisphere can only comprehend very simple language, but does have a highly developed sense of space and pattern and is superior to the left hemisphere in constructing geometric and perspective drawings.

It is now widely accepted that the left side of the brain is viewed as our logic and language side, while the right side is seen as the seat of creativity and imagination.

Left Brain Characteristics	Right Brain Characteristics
◆ Linear thought—one idea follows another	◆ Holistic thought—ability to see patterns linking ideas
◆ Uses verbal ideas and words to describe things	◆ Uses gestures or pictures to describe things
◆ Logical	◆ Intuitive
◆ Analyzes—breaks things down into separate parts	◆ Synthesizes—puts parts together to form a whole

(continued)

(continued)

Left Brain Characteristics	Right Brain Characteristics
◆ Poor spatial sense	◆ Good spatial sense
◆ Uses symbols in representation	◆ Sees things as they are
◆ Good numerical sense	◆ Poor numerical sense
◆ Good sense of time	◆ Poor sense of time
◆ Relies on fact	◆ Relies on instinct

Inner Creativity

To understand and develop inner creativity, we first need to understand the psyche. Beneath the conscious ego is the essential Self that guides and directs the body through the subconscious mind. We all know that something keeps our heart pumping, lungs breathing, and so on, all without conscious intent. This has been called the subconscious. Our subconscious also houses the fullest potential of the psyche. When we can tap this inner realm—raise the subconscious intent to conscious awareness—we get in touch with and use our inner creativity. There are many ways to reach this inner creative potential. First, we need to put the ego to rest temporarily. The chattering personality needs to be set aside for a time so that the fullness of the entire psyche can see the light of the mind. Some good methods of quietening our thoughts in order to access inner creativity are meditation, soft focus, and self-awareness.

◆ **Meditation.** There are many forms of meditation. Fruitful meditation involves closing the eyes, stilling the mind, and focusing on a specific thought or sound (mantra). Meditation puts your brain into an alpha or, when you become proficient, a wakeful theta state. In this altered state, the gap will open and the creative mind will emerge.

◆ **Soft focus.** This is an excellent way to stop the thinking process in a busy environment. Just allow the eyes to maintain a soft focus on a neutral surface—for example, a wall or ceiling—and be aware of everything around you without focusing on any one thing. You will notice that your peripheral vision is increased and your sensitivity to your entire environment is enhanced, while your mind is calmed. When you create a soft focus, the ego is temporarily set aside and the subconscious mind, where inner creativity abounds, can come to the surface.

◆ **Self-awareness.** The practice of self-awareness runs through all the great religious and philosophical disciplines. Buddhists, Zen Buddhists, Sufi mystics, Christian mystics, Hindu yogis, and Taoists all practice the art of mindful self-awareness. This is a non-judgmental form of watching one's daily actions and thoughts in the present moment in a detached frame of mind. When learned and applied, this can create the necessary gap between the ego and the Self, and great clarity of mind unfolds.

Creative Triggers

One valuable way to access the creative mind is to use state-dependent memory. This form of memory offers the recall of a vivid past event during which you had a great insight. In the recall, you revisit the same feelings and mood that were present in the original event. The easiest way to summon a particular event is to devise a personal trigger that, when pushed, will immediately evoke identical feelings. This technique is a combination of biofeedback and memory of the "moment of discovery" experience. This is how it works:

◆ Choose a personal trigger. Put your index finger and thumb together, or touch your forehead as a physical way of initializing the memory recall.

◆ Sit back, close your eyes, relax, and remember a time when you had a difficult problem to solve.

◆ Remember the room you were in, the time of day, the surroundings, and the nature of the problem that you needed to resolve.

◆ Now, remember the moment the solution came to you. As you remember this exact moment of revelation, concentrate on the feeling. Immerse yourself in the feeling of elation and relief you felt when the insight appeared and the problem was solved.

◆ Now use the personal trigger. For example, as soon as you remember the moment of resolve, put your index finger and thumb together and hold that feeling. As you repeat this exercise a few times each day, the act of putting your index finger and thumb together should elicit an exact feeling of resolved insight.

Henceforth, when you use the specific physical trigger, the AHA experience will be immediately recalled. The trigger will take you out of associated memory and circular thought patterns and into the ideal mental state for creativity. This works particularly well in the workplace when creative solutions are needed immediately.

Intuitive Insight

Intuition, if practiced daily, will accelerate your creativity. Intuition taps into that source of knowledge and wisdom that lies just below the surface of conscious awareness. This level of mind has been given various names. Jung called it the collective unconscious. Formal science has yet to give it a specific name, except to refer to it as the subconscious or unconscious mind. This is the same level of mind that, without our conscious thought, keeps our heart beating and our lungs breathing, and generates our bodily homeostasis.

How do you access this wisdom on demand? Whenever you are completely at a loss about something, just stop and go into a "mindless, non-thinking" state for as long as you're comfortable with it. Looking at anything neutral, such as a white wall or the ceiling, will do. You will return to conscious "thinking" within a few minutes and will have a fresh thought or approach to whatever you were working on.

Creative Breath

Controlling your breathing greatly aids clarity of mind, and creativity is a product of a clear unobstructed mind. One effective way to achieve a creative solution quickly is by controlled breathing. When we need a creative solution to a problem, we need as much inspiration as we can acquire. The word *inspire* is derived from the Latin roots *in* and *spirare* or, literally, to breathe in. To be inspired is to be full of the breath of life. Yogic disciplines teach that the air we breathe is full of *prana* or the spirit of life. The Chinese call this energy *chi*.

From a scientific standpoint, oxygen levels in the brain are tied to levels of the neurotransmitter serotonin, the hormone that controls states of consciousness and mood. You can regulate your levels of serotonin by controlling your breathing. Too much serotonin in the brain causes irritation and stress. When you need to produce a more heightened state of awareness for immediate problem solving, you can control your breathing and decrease the levels of serotonin that can result in greater relaxation and allow the brain's intuitive, non-linear activities to flow more smoothly. Here are two methods for increasing brain hormonal and hemispherical balance:

◆ The first method is slow deep breathing, holding the breath momentarily between breaths. Holding the breath oxygenates the brain and facilitates clarity. Deep breathing promotes alpha brain waves and relaxes the body and mind.

◆ Another method is to breathe through alternating nostrils. The Chinese believe that the nostrils are an indication of hemispherical dominance. Whichever nostril you habitually breathe through can tell you which side of the brain you favor. Pinch your nostrils together across the bridge of your nose and release the right nostril. Inhale through your right nostril for a count of four. Pinch both nostrils again for a count of four. Release the left nostril and exhale for a count of four. Inhale through your left nostril for a count of four. Pinch for a count of four. Release the right nostril and exhale for a count of four. Repeat the cycle four times. If you practice this for about ten minutes you will improve your mental clarity. You will also slow down your brain waves from beta to alpha, thus facilitating intuitive thought.

INDIVIDUAL TASKS AND REFLECTIONS

17.1 Creative People

Who would you consider to be a creative person (dead or alive, real or fantasy)? Why?

17.2 Creative You

Would you consider yourself to be a creative person? If you do, why? If not, why?

17.3 Your Creative Qualities

Although there is no rigid formula for a creative person, the following qualities do seem to mark many creative people. Rate your creative qualities as follows: 1 = very good; 2 = good; 3 = not so good.

Creative Qualities			
Independence	☐	Inquisitiveness	☐
Non-conformist attitude	☐	Confidence	☐
Determination	☐	Learning attitude	☐
Intuitiveness	☐	Openmindedness	☐

17.4 Left or Right Brain?

Do you identify more with the qualities of the left or right side of the brain?

WORKING WITH OTHERS

17.5 Creative Buzz Group

Set up a creative buzz group with some colleagues to solve problems and find solutions.

17.6 Generating Creativity

Consider your approach to creativity and discuss with your mentor in what areas of your life and how you could improve the generation of creative solutions.

17.7 Meditation

Introduce the subject of generating creative solutions. Explain the basics of meditation. Guide the learners through a relaxation exercise followed by a ten-minute meditation using guided imagery (for example, a beach or country scene) or a word (for example, *calm* or *creative*).

17.8 Soft Focus

Introduce the subject of generating creative solutions. Explain the basics of soft focus. Guide the learners through a relaxation exercise followed by a ten-minute soft focus exercise.

17.9 Creative Trigger

Introduce the subject of generating creative solutions. Explain the basics of the creative trigger. Guide the learners through a relaxation exercise followed by the creative trigger exercise (p. 80).

17.10 Intuitive Insight

Introduce the subject of generating creative solutions. Discuss the role of intuition in daily life by asking such questions as:

◆ What is intuition?
◆ Give examples of how intuition has worked for you.
◆ What encourages intuition?
◆ What blocks intuition?
◆ How might we use intuition in daily life?

17.11 The Cabbage

Introduce the subject of generating creative solutions. Give the learners five minutes to each come up with 20 creative uses for a cabbage. Discuss.

17.12 Defining Creativity

Introduce the subject of generating creative solutions. Discuss the role of creativity in daily life by asking such questions as:

◆ What is creativity?
◆ How has creativity worked for you?
◆ What encourages creativity?
◆ What blocks creativity?
◆ How might we use creativity in daily life?

Problem Solving and Decision Making Toolkit, 150 pp.
50 Activities for Creativity and Problem Solving, 240 pp.
Problem Solving and Decision Making Profile, 16 pp.

18
Giving and Receiving Feedback

Criticism or feedback? Our initial response to criticism is likely to be negative. By contrast, the word *feedback* sounds as though we have a role in deciding whether or not it is appropriate.

Feedback is most useful when it is . . .	Feedback is least useful when it is . . .
◆ Specific	◆ Vague
◆ Focused on behavior	◆ Impossible to change the situation
◆ Positive	◆ Negative
◆ Useful	◆ Given in front of others
◆ Supportive	◆ Based on hearsay and speculation
◆ Given privately	◆ Based on one incident
◆ Based on first-hand information	◆ Used to protect feelings/egos
◆ Fair	◆ A personality attack
◆ Given with care	◆ Given thoughtlessly
◆ Expressed directly	◆ Expressed indirectly or to someone else
◆ Easily acted on	◆ Difficult to act on
◆ Uncluttered by evaluative judgments	◆ Judgmental
◆ Well timed	◆ Delayed

Handling Negative Feedback

When you feel under attack, your first instincts are to focus on that feeling, making it more intense. You are more likely to react, rather than choose how you want to act. In responding to negative feedback, the momentum of defensive emotions builds rapidly because we mentally focus on the "right" things we are doing, while obsessing about the "wrong" things the other person is doing. This tendency leads us to take a righteous position and listen less as the negative feedback continues.

Here's a three-step process to follow when responding to negative feedback:

1. Acknowledge that you heard the person, with a pause, nod, or verbal acknowledgment. Whether or not the negative feedback is justified, if

you try to avoid discussing it, it will loom larger in everyone's minds as you attempt to move on. Do not disagree or counterattack. Avoid blaming or bad labeling language such as "You don't know what you are talking about."

2. Ask for more information so that you both can cool off and stay focused on the issue, rather than the feelings or personalities.

3. If you believe the comments are accurate, then say so. If an apology is appropriate, give it sooner rather than later. Then say what you plan to do differently to respond to the negative feedback. Ask for their response to your comments. The sooner you verbally agree, if you find truth in the negative feedback, the more likely you are to engender respect from the other person and any others who witness the interaction. If, on the other hand, you disagree with the comments, say "May I tell you my perspective?" This maneuvers the other person to giving you permission to state your view, as you have been willing to listen to theirs.

Further ways to respond to negative feedback are as follows:

◆ You can agree with the true criticism of negative qualities—for example, your response to "You haven't called me lately" could be "I agree. I haven't called you in the past two weeks."
◆ You can actively prompt criticism of your behavior—for example, "I would like your opinion on how I spoke in that presentation."
◆ Note the comment and, if you realize it doesn't apply to you, let the speaker know you register their remark, but don't respond to it.
◆ If someone is verbally dumping on you, do not interrupt or counter-attack in midstream. Doing this will only prolong their comments. When they have finished, ask, "Is there anything else you want to add?" followed by something like, "What would make this situation better?"
◆ Ask them to propose a solution to the issue they have raised. If they continue to complain or attack, acknowledge that you heard them each time and, like a broken record, repeat, "What will make this situation better?" Then state your view and what you would like from them so that the other person moves from a criticizing to a problem-solving mode. If the other person continues on the downward track of criticism, say "I want to find a way to resolve your concern. When do you want to talk about it next?" In this way, you can disassociate yourself from the tone of that discussion and put the other person in the position of initiating follow-up.
◆ Whenever you have reason to believe someone is lying or not making sense, you will not build rapport by pointing it out to them. Instead, you might say, "How does that relate to the . . ." (then state the apparently conflicting information). This allows two possible outcomes: you might find out that you were wrong, and you can thus avoid embarrassment; or, by continuing to use nonthreatening questions, you can edge the other person into self-correcting, which protects your future relationship.
◆ Divide the negative feedback into its parts and respond to the unspoken assumption without playing the victim—for example, you could respond to "If you had company loyalty, you would do unpaid overtime," by saying, "What do you mean by company loyalty?"
◆ You can diffuse negative comments with comebacks such as "Are you aware of how that remark might sound to other people?"
◆ Ask the other person to clarify or expand their statement.
◆ When criticized, you are more likely to find resolutions sooner when the other person comes to trust your positive intent. Demonstrate your willingness to find a compromise.

◆ Especially in the beginning, listen more and talk less, keep your motions and voice lower and slower. These behaviors increase the chances that others will feel more safe and comfortable around you.

◆ Highlight commonalties more frequently than differences. Whatever you refer to most and most intensely will be the center of your relationship. Keep referring to the aspects of them and their points that you can support and want to expand upon.

◆ If the other person does not initially accept your response, consider making the same suggestion later on and in a different way. Try rearranging the same elements of a suggestion or offer to find a more mutually attractive compromise.

◆ You can acknowledge that there may be some truth in what is being said—for example, your response to "You never make the coffee" could be "I often make the coffee, but this week I haven't."

◆ Check out what you heard by reframing it in your own words.

> If we are aware of our own shortcomings and are either prepared to tolerate them or take steps to correct them, negative feedback from others is easier to take and we will be more able to give fair negative feedback to others.

A few pointers when giving negative feedback are as follows:

◆ Keep calm.

◆ Avoid labels, such as "typical woman."

◆ Be specific. For example, say "Red doesn't work in that design" as opposed to "You've got no idea about how colors work" or mention the specifics of the action done that you want to criticize.

◆ Keep to the point and don't introduce irrelevancies.

◆ Acknowledge the positive.

◆ Empathize with the other person's situation or feelings.

◆ Clarify your feelings about the action, take responsibility for your part in the interaction, and avoid laying blame on the other person.

◆ State what you want the other person to do differently in the future.

◆ Explain why you want what you're asking for or the reason you think the other person should change—for example, "When you do A [observation], I feel B [emotion]: I want you to do C [requested change] because of D [purpose]."

◆ Be descriptive, rather than evaluative or judgmental.

◆ Take into account the needs of both the receiver and giver.

◆ Let the criticism be well timed—as near the trigger event as possible.

◆ Give criticism within a situation that you can both relate to.

◆ Focus on behavior rather than the person and refer to behavior that can be changed.

◆ Own the criticism.

> **Giving Positive Feedback**
> To give others praise for their work makes them feel good and will encourage them to perform to their full potential. Always remember to give praise whenever you can.
>
> **Receiving Positive Feedback**
> Treat a compliment as a verbal gift. Accept graciously with a "thank you"—and don't put yourself down in the process!

INDIVIDUAL TASKS
AND REFLECTIONS
....

18.1 Criticism When Young

What do you remember about the way in which you were criticized when you were younger? Consider how parents, teachers, and significant others criticized you. How did it make you feel?

18.2 How do you react to negative feedback today?

How do you tend to react when you receive negative feedback now? Do you feel like a child again? Does negative feedback from certain people or in certain situations make you feel different—for example, worse?

WORKING
WITH OTHERS
....

18.3 Providing Feedback to Others (A)

Become more aware of how often you have critical thoughts of others. Do you tend to keep them to yourself? Do you tell a third party? Do you tell the person concerned? Are you more critical of some people than others? Do you know why?

18.4 Providing Feedback to Others (B)

How do you give feedback to other people? How do they react?

18.5 Offering Feedback

Set yourself a task to offer feedback to a colleague. Afterward, reflect on your thoughts, your behavior, and the outcome.

WORKING
WITH A MENTOR
....

18.6 Being on the End of Feedback

Discuss with your mentor how you feel when you are given feedback within your working environment. Then discuss how you feel when you give feedback within your working environment.

18.7 Role Play

Ask your mentor to criticize your ability to give and receive feedback. Discuss. You might then move on to criticize your mentor's ability to give and receive feedback and discuss.

DEVELOPING
OTHERS
....

18.8 Giving and Receiving Feedback

Introduce the subject of giving and receiving feedback. Ask the learners how they feel when (a) receiving feedback and (b) giving feedback. Discuss.

18.9 Improving Skills

Introduce the subject of giving and receiving feedback. Brainstorm the skills necessary to receive feedback. Then brainstorm the skills necessary to give feedback. In the whole group, create two checklists for learners to assess their own feedback skills. Now, organize them into groups of four to discuss ways of improving their feedback skills. Reconvene the whole group to share ideas.

18.10 Individual and Group Feedback

Introduce the subject of giving and receiving feedback. Based on the already completed checklist of feedback skills (see task 9 above), organize the learners into groups of three. One learner shares how they might improve their skills while another partner provides feedback. The third person observes and provides feedback to both learners. Each group member takes a turn at each role. Reconvene the whole group for group feedback.

RECOMMENDED HRD PRESS TITLES

Giving and Receiving Performance Feedback, 200 pp.

INTRODUCTION

Self-esteem is the value you place on yourself. Healthy self-esteem gives you energy to cope with the many challenges you face day-to-day. Sometimes, identity and sense of worth are totally dependent on having a job or being in a relationship. If these end, self-esteem might take a nose dive. When we experience low self-esteem, it doesn't mean we are failures—many successful people experience self-doubt from time to time. Whatever the reasons for self-esteem being low, people tell us that when they learn to give themselves approval from within, and develop new coping skills, their stress levels go down and their energy goes up—leading to greater self-esteem.

Self-esteem is about understanding yourself, believing in yourself, becoming your own power source, and taking responsibility—making your own choices. The following guidelines are keys to improving self-esteem:

◆ **Accept yourself.** Accepting yourself as you are now makes it possible for you to grow and develop. When you feel OK about yourself now, you are able to risk change.

◆ **Stop comparing.** You can't win in a comparison: usually you will evaluate yourself lower than the person you compare yourself to. If you do win in the comparison, you will tend to devalue the winning trait— for example, "I'm a better manager than Bob is, but so what! It takes computer skills to get ahead here." Instead of comparing yourself to others, celebrate the differences.

◆ **Make learning mistakes.** A mistake does not make you a failure. It's a sign that you're alive and developing. Treat a mistake as an opportunity to learn. Don't fall into the low self-esteem traps of blaming others, denying your mistakes, defending your behavior, or criticizing yourself for not being perfect.

◆ **Prune relationships.** Surround yourself with people who are positive and affirming. Sometimes this means that you need to let go of a relationship—or at least limit the amount of time you spend with that person.

◆ **Stop improving, start developing.** When you try to improve yourself, you start from a belief that there is something wrong with you that needs to be fixed. Instead, start with your strengths and talents and develop these. In this way, you can grow from a foundation of strength instead of a foundation of weakness.

◆ **Stop value judging.** Most people spend a great deal of time on "shoulds"—"I should do this. I shouldn't do that." All these "shoulds" are value judgments that lower your self-esteem. Try accepting yourself and others. Replace your "shoulds" with non-judgmental words such as *want, choose* or *prefer.*

◆ **Affirm yourself.** Each night before you go to bed, jot down five things you feel good about from the day. They don't need to be big things. They could be kindnesses you showed, feelings you expressed, or commitments you honored.

Our Beliefs Affect Our Self-Esteem

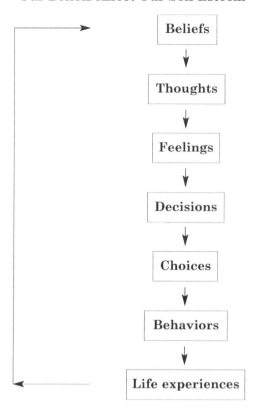

Our beliefs are principally stored in our subconscious. If we believe that we are inadequate, then our subconscious mind is compelled to create the conditions of that belief, thus making that belief a reality of our life. The energy of any belief we have gives us thoughts and feelings that are in harmony with that belief.

However, we are not born with our beliefs: they are a result of other people's beliefs combined with the circumstances of our past. To survive, we had to adopt the beliefs of our family and society, including the rigid rules and negative messages that we learned. These then become incorporated into our view of others and ourselves. For example, during childhood, we may not have been encouraged to believe in our own abilities or, as a result of constant criticism, we believed we were always wrong. To feel accepted, we tried harder to please. The harder we tried, the more frustrated we became because we never seemed to be able to please the grown-ups.

Consequently, as adults, we hold ourselves in low esteem, affecting our ability to achieve our goals. Fearful of making mistakes, we avoid taking risks. We feel responsible when things go wrong and can't accept credit when something goes right. When we experience low self-esteem, we may have a need to be perfect, have a negative self-image, be non-assertive, and fear failure and rejection. As we learn to see ourselves more realistically, our self-esteem increases. We interact with others more confidently and value our strengths, as well as our limitations. We become more willing to take risks. We recognize that we can learn from our mistakes. Relationships become healthier because we are able to validate ourselves and no longer need to look to others for validation. As our self-esteem increases, we begin to openly express feelings, care for ourselves, act more assertively, and become more confident.

So what are the causes of low self-esteem? Some of these are listed below:

◆ **Parental overprotectiveness.** The child didn't learn to trust outside the family, leading to an insecure adult fearful to venture far.

◆ **Parental neglect.** The child fails to receive adequate attention and nurturing, leading to an adult who neglects their own needs.

◆ **Overcritical parents.** The child left home with the feeling of never being good enough, leading to an adult with a longstanding sense of inferiority and a tendency to self-criticism.

◆ **Significant childhood loss.** Either divorce or death has made the child insecure, leading to adult overdependency on actions or people.

◆ **Parental rejection.** The child received an overt or covert message that they were unwanted, leading to an adult with tendencies toward self-rejection.

◆ **Parental overindulgence.** The child was given insufficient exposure to appropriate limits, leading to an adult lacking in persistence.

Balancing Your Inner Doubter and Reinforcer

Your doubter is that part of you that can hold you back from taking risks, but it also protects you—for example, by preventing you from crossing the road when it is not safe. The doubter can also plant guilt if you're not being productive and it can question bad relationships. So we should not aim to get rid of the doubter altogether, we just want to curb its negativity when it holds us back. Your doubter can keep you safe, but only in proportion to how safe you want to be. It's as if our personal power is really the controlling force. By using this energy, we can control the doubting part of our personality so that it works with, and not against, us. In order to do this, you need to be willing to have your doubter play a less significant part in your life (or else your doubter will find some excuse for you not to change).

To remedy this, imagine another part of your self—the reinforcer—as a positive energy that says, "Yes I can" and lets you take risks. Your reinforcer can give you positive messages when doubts begin to surface. So when you feel your doubting side emerging enough to negatively affect your thoughts, feelings, and actions, you need to call on the reinforcer for positive input. The reinforcer needs to work with, and not against, the doubter. Let your reinforcer take charge in situations where you feel overwhelmed by doubt.

There are many steps you can take to feel more positive:

1. **Tune in to your thoughts.** Pay particular attention to the negative ones. Hear your fears and anxieties. It's only when you become conscious of the negative words churning round in your head that you can then begin to find the positive words to balance yourself.
2. **Isolate destructive words.** Words such as *only, just,* or *should* are damaging to self-esteem. Eliminate them.
3. **Stop the thoughts.** Short-circuit negative messages as soon as they enter your mind. Although it's perfectly OK to acknowledge fear, you don't want to be overwhelmed by it, so picture yourself drowning out the inner voice of fear.
4. **Accentuate the positive.** Replace negative thoughts with happy ones.
5. **Reorientate yourself.** Move from painful anxiety to an active and problem-solving frame of mind.
6. **Emphasize opportunities.** Learn to recognize opportunities. Create opportunities. Observe how others find opportunities.
7. **Live now.** Make it a habit to reflect on at least one thing in each day that was enjoyable.
8. **Make your choice.** It's up to you to live your life as fully and as enjoyably as possible. Nobody owes you anything. You can decide to make the best of what life offers you or you can choose to ignore opportunities. Is your glass of life half full or half empty?

9. **Make friends with you.** Stop criticizing yourself and learn to like who you are—warts and all.
10. **Put less emphasis on perfection.** A photographer put together the perfect features from the faces of several well-known beautiful women and handsome men. The result was utterly bland and lacking in character. So when you strive toward perfection—and just whose idea of perfection is it anyway?—remember it is the oddity or the imperfection that adds interest and character.
11. **Find your sense of humor.** Laugh at yourself a little more.

INDIVIDUAL TASKS AND REFLECTIONS

19.1 Ask Yourself

Do you:

◆ Criticize yourself for mistakes?
◆ Overlook your accomplishments and doubt compliments?
◆ Worry about what others think?
◆ Find feelings difficult to express and handle?
◆ Feel anxious in social situations?
◆ Think about everyone else's needs before your own?
◆ Blame yourself when someone is unfair or hurtful?
◆ Think that anything less than perfect is not good enough?
◆ Avoid trying new things?
◆ Worry about your appearance?

If you've said "yes" to some or all of these ten questions, it's time to recharge or strengthen your self-esteem. It's normal for self-esteem to fluctuate depending on the challenges you are facing at the time, but if you're down more than up, there are solutions.

19.2 Compliments of the Season

For a period of one week, note how may compliments you have given, taken, or rejected each day. When we can gracefully accept a compliment, we are acknowledging our self-worth. Equally, when we give compliments, we are acknowledging the worth of someone else.

19.3 Past Doubts, Future Fears

Consider how past doubts are affecting you today. Ask yourself:

◆ Am I seeking approval today for something "bad" I did when I was younger?
◆ Did something embarrassing or frightening happen when I was younger that makes me fearful of doing similar things now?

19.4 Current Doubt, Past Fear

Identify a current doubt and the thoughts, feelings, and actions concerned with it. Recall an earlier experience when you felt the same anxious feeling that your present doubt is creating. How did you deal with them then? How are you dealing with those similar feelings now?

19.5 Didn't I Do Well?

Reflect upon:

◆ Times when you have been thanked or congratulated
◆ Qualities you like about yourself
◆ Responsibilities you have shouldered successfully
◆ Difficulties you have handled well

WORKING WITH OTHERS

19.6 Situations and Self-Esteem

Become aware of situations involving others that increase (and decrease) your self-esteem. What kind of situations are they? What happens? How do you feel?

19.7 Through the Eyes of Others

How much of how you feel about yourself is dependent on the reactions of others?

WORKING WITH A MENTOR

19.8 Editing the Past

Discuss with your mentor how past experiences may have affected your sense of self-worth. Identify the negative messages and let your reinforcer help you develop positive ones.

19.9 The Mentoring Relationship

How does your mentor make you feel about your self-worth? How might they help you increase your self-esteem through your relationship?

19.10 Mentor Role Model

Discuss with your mentor how they have developed their sense of self-esteem. What can you learn from this?

19.11 Conditioning in Self-Esteem

Introduce the idea of how our past conditioning can affect our sense of self-esteem. Brainstorm half a dozen ways this might happen. Ask the learners to split into smaller groups of three to discuss one of the brainstormed ways (let each group choose their own and try to make each one different). Reconvene the whole group to discuss.

19.12 Raising Self-Esteem

First, ask each learner to identify a situation in which their sense of self-esteem is low. Organize them into small groups of no more than four people so that each person has a chance to discuss their situation. The objective of the small-group exercise is to disclose, provide feedback, give compliments, and find possible solutions.

19.13 Positive Comments

Sit, with the group, in a large circle, and start off by saying something like 'The thing I like best about John [the person on your right] is his sense of humor." The named person on your right then picks up and says something positive about the person on their right until everyone in the group has had a turn.

Holding Meetings

Any meeting gives you a great opportunity to increase your visibility as a powerful and knowledgeable communicator. Reasons for having meetings are to:

◆ Share information
◆ Get members' views and proposals
◆ Discuss what the group needs to be doing
◆ Carry out legal business
◆ Develop networks
◆ Exchange ideas and experience
◆ Review whether a decision in action is working
◆ Decide on a proposal
◆ Discuss a decision made elsewhere
◆ Develop teamwork
◆ Support a team
◆ Learn

There are also several types of meetings:

◆ **Informative/advisory:** to give and receive information; to keep in touch; to coordinate activities; to record progress toward goals
◆ **Consultative:** to resolve differences; to involve people; to get to know people
◆ **Problem solving:** to create ideas; to identify alternative action; to initiate action
◆ **Decision making:** to generate commitment; to make decisions; to share responsibilities; to initiate action
◆ **Negotiating:** to create an agreement; to find a solution

Not all meetings are successful. Indeed, they often have a reputation for being a waste of time, a forum for a just one person's point of view, unclear in terms of their objectives or outcomes, and so on. Listed below are some reasons why meetings fail and what might be done about them.

Why Meetings Fail	Remedies
The meeting is unnecessary.	Share information by telephone, fax, letter, or e-mail.
The purpose of the meeting is unclear.	Define goals.
The meeting is poorly planned.	Plan and distribute the agenda before the meeting.
The meeting is held in an unsuitable or inappropriate environment.	Check the venue beforehand.

(continued)

(continued)

Why Meetings Fail	Remedies
The meeting is disrupted.	Check for likely disruptions and delegate urgent business.
The wrong people are present and the right people are absent.	Identify and invite the key decision makers.
The chairperson isn't adequate.	The chairperson needs to improve their skills.
Nothing is decided.	The chairperson needs to improve their skills.

When holding a meeting, it is a good idea to give some consideration to where people will be seated. Some strategic seating arrangements are illustrated below. They are designed to minimize disruption and maximize the chances of reaching the meeting's objectives.

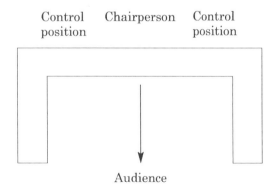

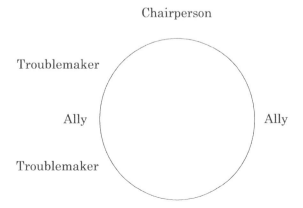

Participating in Meetings

If you are invited to a meeting, when you have found what the objectives of the meeting are, prepare to be supportive and encouraging. Aim to earn authority as a leader among equals. Be resourceful and collaborate on objectives. Participate and become involved. Good participation involves:

◆ Learning about issues
◆ Thinking before you speak
◆ Being reasonable
◆ Listening to others
◆ Speaking clearly and to the point
◆ Having confidence in yourself

To gain recognition, sit within good eye contact of the decision makers. If presenting, arrive early and select your vantage point. If it is a long table, choose the middle of one side; if it is an oval table, choose one of the narrow curved ends. To mitigate a confrontation, sit next to the challenger. To avoid attention, sit in a blind spot for the chairperson and wear a neutral outfit with no accessories.

Good communication isn't only about what you say, but also about your nonverbal signals. Undermining signals include:

◆ Slouching in your chair
◆ Looking down at your notes or out of the window
◆ Looking up at the ceiling
◆ Turning away
◆ Folding your arms across the body
◆ Using closed, threatening gestures
◆ A deadpan or cynical expression

Positive signals include:

◆ Sitting upright and alert
◆ Sitting forward
◆ Keeping your eyes on the speaker
◆ Taking notes on key points
◆ Turning your body to the speaker
◆ Opening your body language
◆ Smiling

Key Words to Use in Meetings		
able	advantage	brilliant
confidence	controlled	detail
economical	effective	emphasis
now	outstanding	professional
volume	tremendous	top
today	money-making	lowest cost
latest	key	instant

(continued)

(continued)

Key Words to Use in Meetings		
impelling	immediate	help
quality	quickly	results
satisfaction	smart	solved
special	successful	expert
excited	fair	new
save	safety	evaluate
proven	discover	guarantee
results	you	update
complete	endorsed	maximize
image	value	inform
sure	quality	personal
affect	best	venture
customer	future	empower
practical	skills	facilitate
knowledge	valid	reliable
original	fast	measure
motivate	involve	

Listed below are 18 guidelines for successful participation in meetings:

1. If attending a meeting for the first time, introduce yourself.
2. Make an impression by preparing ideas for agenda items that interest you.
3. Speak up at least once during every meeting you attend.
4. Familiarize yourself with the group dynamics of any new meeting you attend.
5. Study the agenda prior to the meeting.
6. Arrive early so that you can get to know others.
7. Know who's who.
8. Use powerful body language and verbal language.
9. Speak slowly and clearly and with authority.
10. Take credit for your ideas.
11. If you are aware that conflict may arise, plan for it and prepare to compromise.
12. Don't allow an argument to turn into a free-for-all.
13. Sit where you can be seen and heard (near to the head or to the right of someone with power).

14. If you anticipate conflict, sit on that person's dominant side (indicated by whether they are right- or left-handed) so that they will feel less threatened.
15. Don't allow an argument to turn into a battle.
16. If you want to exert an influence, speak early in a discussion.
17. Maintain eye contact.
18. Use your hands to express your point.

Chairing a Meeting

The agenda should contain:

◆ The organization's name
◆ Committee/group name
◆ Date, time, and place of meeting
◆ Finishing time
◆ Apologies
◆ Welcome
◆ Minutes of last meeting
◆ Matters arising
◆ Specifics
◆ Any other business
◆ Future meeting details

Minutes are used to record what is being decided, why it was decided, what action is to be taken, when and by whom, and what else was discussed. They should include:

◆ The organization's name
◆ The date, time, and place of the meeting
◆ Meeting description
◆ People present
◆ Apologies for absence
◆ Who chaired
◆ Corrections to the previous minutes
◆ Matters arising from the previous meeting
◆ Minutes for topics for this meeting (making specific reference to any decisions made and action to be taken, by whom and by when)
◆ The date, time, and place of the next meeting
◆ The time this meeting finished

Successful meetings depend on a strong chairperson, who follows the guidelines below:

◆ Encourage people to participate.
◆ At decision-making meetings, place the emphasis on whether the decision is the right one as opposed to whether members are happy with the outcome.
◆ Don't be afraid to sometimes ignore the feelings of others in order to reach a group decision.
◆ Remember that your attitude, as chairperson, will be reflected in the attitudes of the group members to each other during the meeting.
◆ Impose a firm discipline on proceedings.

When chairing a meeting, you also need to be able to deal with difficult people—those who want to argue, won't listen, talk too much, or hold fixed views. In such situations, you need to move the issue away from them and back into the wider group. Sometimes you can do this by simply restating the issue; alternatively, the best way of moving the meeting forward might be to allow controlled discussion. Other techniques you could use include intervention, asking for clarification, acknowledging strong feelings, summarizing, and then moving the topic on, injecting a little humor, asking direct questions, and using people's names.

As the chair, you want to extend your role to that of facilitator, enabling individuals in a meeting to interact with each other, even to the extent of using conflict as a tool for discovery and growth. A facilitator will create an atmosphere of support and openness, and they will encourage group members to express their feelings and contribute their ideas.

There are 15 guidelines for successful chairing:

1. When setting the agenda, consider your objectives and enclose any papers relevant to the meeting. Send out at least a week in advance.
2. Hold meetings in the morning, because they tend to be more productive at this time of day.
3. Organize supporting materials, anticipate problems, and be ready with solutions.
4. Remember that chairing a meeting is more about listening than talking.
5. Assign someone to take the minutes.
6. Open the meeting on a positive note.
7. Introduce each agenda subject via a brief overview.
8. Keep the meeting moving by staying focused on the current agenda subject. Keep your pre-set timescales for each area in mind.
9. Summarize occasionally and call for a decision when appropriate.
10. Make people feel positive and important. Acknowledge their contributions and use their names when you do so.
11. Encourage controlled discussion.
12. Remain impartial when emotions run high. Separate facts from opinion and clarify points.
13. Focus the meeting on problem solving.
14. Finish the meeting with a summary of the main points, action to be taken and by whom, as well as any decisions made.
15. Follow up the action to be taken via smaller meetings or individual sessions.

INDIVIDUAL TASKS AND REFLECTIONS

20.1 Meeting Roles

Why do you attend meetings and what are your roles?

20.2 Meeting Participant Analysis (A)

Identify a past meeting that you attended as a participant and that you felt went poorly. What were your thoughts, feelings, and observations (of your behavior, the behavior of others, the chairperson, and the outcomes of the meeting)? What could have been done to improve the meeting?

20.3 Meeting Participant Analysis (B)

Identify a past meeting that you attended as a participant and that you felt went well. What were your thoughts, feelings, and observations (of your behavior, the behavior of others, the chairperson, and the outcomes of the meeting)?

20.4 Chaired Meeting Analysis (A)

Identify a past meeting that you chaired and that you felt went poorly. What were your thoughts, feelings, and observations (of your behavior, the behavior of others, and the outcomes of the meeting)? What could have been done to improve the meeting?

20.5 Chaired Meeting Analysis (B)

Identify a past meeting that you chaired and that you felt went well. What were your thoughts, feelings, and observations (of your behavior, the behavior of others, and the outcomes of the meeting)?

WORKING WITH OTHERS

20.6 Colleague Role Play

Set up a role play (this could be a pure role-play situation or one with an additional objective in mind) with between four and six colleagues that has the key objective of improving meeting skills for you all. Agree on a common topic. Preprepare an assessment sheet for each participant to complete when the meeting is over. Meet again to discuss.

20.7 Post-Meeting Assessment

Use the following assessment checklist to analyze a recent meeting in which you played a key role.

Meeting Criteria	Yes (✔)	No (✔)
Was the meeting necessary?		
Did we meet at the right time?		
Did the right people attend?		
Did we have effective decision-making procedures?		
Did we use appropriate aids?		
Was the meeting useful?		
Was the meeting the right length?		
Was the agenda appropriate?		
Was the meeting room adequate?		
Did we keep appropriate records?		
Was timekeeping satisfactory?		
Were refreshments adequate?		
Do we plan to take action as a result of the meeting?		
Were interruptions handled well?		
Was the room laid out correctly?		

20.8 Post-Chair Assessment

If you are chairing a meeting (your mentor could be present), write up a post-meeting report, together with an assessment of your own performance including a breakdown of how you dealt with any problems. Make a diagram of the room layout. Discuss with your mentor and, together, create an action plan for identified skills development.

20.9 Participant Meeting Assessment

If you are a participant at a meeting (your mentor could be present), write up a post-meeting report, together with an assessment of your own performance including when you spoke. Discuss with your mentor and, together, create an action plan for identified skills development.

DEVELOPING

OTHERS

···················

20.10 Discussion of Meetings

Introduce the subject of increasing your power at meetings. Then facilitate a group discussion on:

◆ The reasons for having a meeting
◆ Why meetings fail
◆ Good participation and communication

20.11 Strategic Seating

Introduce the subject of increasing your power at meetings and move on to strategic seating. Encourage the learners to play around with different seating arrangements and roles.

20.12 Role Play a Meeting

Ask the group to agree among themselves on a reason for a meeting with an objective with which all the participants can identify. Then ask them to nominate a chairperson and secretary. The chairperson is to set up strategic seating and set out a short agenda. The learners then role play the meeting within a time-limit set by yourself. You can either participate in the meeting and provide feedback, or be an observer and provide feedback.

RECOMMENDED

HRD PRESS TITLES

······························

The Manager's Pocket Guide to Effective Meetings, 130 pp.
The Highly Effective Meeting Profile, 40 pp.

21
Introduction to Neuro-Linguistic Programming

Neuro-Linguistic Programming (NLP) is one of the most effective tools for transforming people and thereby organizations, because it provides models that are useful descriptions of how people interact with the world. These models are useful because, once the system involved is understood, NLP techniques can be used to alter people's subjective experience and thus change their behavior, beliefs, and values.

In the mid-1970s, Tom Peters was looking for the strategies for excellence in organizations. At about the same time, John Grinder and Richard Bandler were looking for the strategies for excellence at the individual level. Under the influence of the British thinker Gregory Bateson, John and Richard modeled the skills of some of the leading masters of communication and personal change. They called what they were doing Neuro-Linguistic Programming:

◆ **Neuro** refers to the neurological processes of seeing, hearing, feeling, smelling, and tasting, which form the basic building blocks of our experience.
◆ **Linguistic** refers to the ways in which we use language to represent our experience and communicate with others.
◆ **Programming** refers not to programming, as in computers, but rather to the strategies we use to organize these inner processes to produce results.

What are the foundations of NLP, and how do they relate to business? There are four principles:

1. **Rapport.** This is the relationship of trust and mutual influence that is at the heart of successful management. It is a comfortable, non-judgmental, mutually accepting relationship between people. Rapport develops when the person you are relating to believes that you are really listening to them and responding to their words and signals.
2. **Knowing your outcome.** NLP gives the skills not only to clarify business goals, but also to relate individual goals to organizational ones.
3. **Openness to feedback.** This refers to an individual's sensory openness to what they see, hear, and feel from others, in order to achieve greater understanding and appropriate responsiveness.
4. **Flexibility.** This refers to the ability to change what you are doing based on the feedback you are getting.

We all use a systematic coding structure to make sense of the world—some sort of internal coding system to distinguish between what we like and what we don't like. The same applies to beliefs and values. Your brain systematically distinguishes between things you believe and things you don't, and between things you value highly and things you value less highly.

The real use of NLP is that it shows you how to apply this knowledge deliberately. For example, take someone who is a highly successful manager in your organization. With NLP, it is possible to identify which aspects of their internal experience make them most effective. This would probably be a mixture of specific skills and behaviors, combined with attitudes, beliefs, and values that support those behaviors. Suppose that one belief is that "I am great at motivating my people." Now, imagine that another manager had all the skills and seemed to have the right behaviors, but held a different belief that "I am terrible at motivating my people." It is likely that, however good the second manager's skills are, they will not be used properly. With NLP, it is possible to change the second manager's belief to a more empowering one. This offers the possibility that all your managers can be the best.

At the heart of NLP is understanding how people do what they do well. This is called competency modeling. When a person does something exceptionally well, they will be conscious of some of the thoughts and moves they make, and can pass on tips to others. However, some aspects of excellence will typically be unconscious. NLP modeling identifies and defines the thought processes and mind patterns used by top performers. It enables us to discover the difference between competence and excellence in any given area of human activity and is used in training, business, management, sales, coaching, and counseling.

NLP identifies and defines how our minds work. Put simply, the world we perceive is not the real world. We each construct a unique model of the world in our heads at an unconscious level and then live in the model as though it was real. Most human problems derive from the models in our heads rather than from the world as it really is. As you develop your practical understanding of how these inner models work, so you can learn to replace unhelpful habits, thoughts, feelings and beliefs with more useful ones. NLP skills offer specific and practical ways of making desired changes in your own and others' behavior. So now you can ask yourself, "How would I like to redesign my life?" and "What would I want to achieve in both my personal and professional life if I knew how?" and actually go ahead and do these things.

NLP provides the tools and techniques for developing individuals, teams, and organizations to achieve success. It relates employees' skills and values to the business goals and structure. In fact, it brings much to this particular area—communication skills, leadership skills, and ways to clarify your beliefs and values so that you can appreciate yourself and bring more of yourself to your work. Success is about achieving results. The results you get are a reflection of your ability to motivate yourself and others and to work with, or creatively around, the business structure. In any organization, the environment, procedures, organizational values, and identity are as much part of the system as the skills, actions, beliefs, and values of the people within it. One of the great strengths of NLP is the ability to clarify and relate tangible, everyday business procedures with the intangible ideas and values that drive them. NLP is about your unique experience and how you create it.

NLP exercises involve different visual and language exercises to help people change the structure of their experience. For example, people who have problems speaking in public often go through a sequence of mental activity such as:

1. See the audience.
2. Imagine them staring at me.
3. Hear them criticizing me.
4. Feel tense and have butterflies in my stomach.
5. Call this sensation "fear."

NLP has many exercises to help the individual rewrite this script so that it might then read:

1. See the audience.
2. Imagine them smiling at me.
3. Hear them giving me words of encouragement.
4. Feel tense and have butterflies in the stomach.
5. Call this sensation "excitement."

Other NLP exercises can help change limiting beliefs (from "I can't" to "I can"), change the meaning of past events (from "They ruined my life" to "They may have caused me pain in the past, but my future is great"), change future expectations (from "This interview is going to be horrible" to "This interview might be challenging"), and so on.

INDIVIDUAL TASKS AND REFLECTIONS

21.1 Ways of Thinking

The way in which you think will result in your style of speaking. Which of these three different ways of thinking do you experience the most?

◆ **Kinesthetic:** where you experience thoughts as feelings
◆ **Visual:** where you think in pictures
◆ **Auditory:** where you think in words and sounds

If you communicate with someone who thinks in the same way as yourself, understanding will be easily achieved and your relationship will be enhanced. If you are relating to another person, and each of you thinks in a different way, your communication is likely to be more difficult.

21.2 Match/Mismatch

Look at the following boxes. You can approach the business of relating from one of two directions: the match (identifying similar people to yourself or similar situations to your own) or the mismatch (identifying what is dissimilar about people or situations).

What did you notice? The similarities? Or did you notice that two are on their sides and one is upright? Do you look for what was the same (match) or for what was different (mismatch)?

WORKING WITH OTHERS

21.3 Eye Movements

The way in which you think can be revealed in the way you move your eyes. When talking to people, observe whether what they're saying or how they're behaving matches their eye movements. Use the following guide.

◆ Up and right (their right): constructed, visual images
◆ Up and left: visual remembered images
◆ Sideways right: constructed sounds
◆ Sideways left: remembered sounds
◆ Down and right: feelings and internal emotions
◆ Down and left: internal dialogue
◆ Straight ahead: visualization

WORKING WITH A MENTOR

21.4 Internal/External

Which of the following responses would you choose?

I know I've done a good job when:

◆ We get more orders
◆ I can say to myself, "That was a job well done"
◆ I feel good inside
◆ I see people using the results of what I have produced
◆ I know I've met the standards I set for myself

Internally influenced people use internal senses (and are more independent) as proof of fulfillment. Conversely, externally influenced people rely on external sources and other people for the proof. Discuss, with your mentor, your response and more-in-depth definitions of *internal* and *external* (managers are usually internally referenced).

DEVELOPING OTHERS

21.5 The Three Systems

Introduce the subject of NLP. Focus on the three ways of thinking—visual, auditory, and kinesthetic—and brainstorm words for each. Divide the learners into groups of four to explore key expressions for each of the three systems. Ask the learners to decide which system they identify with. Ask how they might communicate with others to ensure that each of the systems are covered in their communication. Organize them into groups of between four and six to discuss. You could put all the visuals into one group, the auditories into another, and kinesthetics into another, or you could mix and match.

21.6 Balanced Approach

Introduce the subject of NLP. This exercise demonstrates finding solutions that enable you to transform your experience of a situation. There are three perceptual positions: the first involves experiencing a situation through your own senses, for which you use the pronoun *I* (good for setting outcomes for yourself). The second involves stepping into the shoes of the other person and experiencing a situation as if you were them (good for understanding the behavior of another). The third position involves standing back from a situation and experiencing it as a detached observer (good for the non-involvement of emotions). Ask the learners to conduct role plays in pairs. Each learner is to use all three positions in turn. The role-play topic is "A colleague fails to understand a point you are making in a meeting. No matter how much you explain, they still don't understand." Reconvene the larger group to share experiences.

22 Listening Skills

Poor listening often results in misunderstandings and time-wasting errors. It leads to lower productivity and lower morale. Most of us think we are good listeners. We spend up to 80 percent of our working hours either listening or acting on what we hear. Untrained listeners lose 75 percent of what they hear in a matter of hours and often capture less than half of the message at the time they receive it.

Do you hear or do you listen? What is the difference? We can all hear, but listening is more sophisticated. You could hear a work colleague say, "I can't complete this project by the deadline." But if you listened to their tone of voice, how they said the words, and their body language, you might pick up how worried they are about not meeting their commitment or that they're not asking for help when they need it. So instead of thinking "Well, here's someone who can't get their act together and finish something on time," you might consider sitting down with them and asking what the problem is or how you could help them.

> Hearing is one-dimensional. Listening is a multifaceted activity.

There can be many sources of interference for you as a listener, such as:

◆ Hearing difficulties
◆ Sight difficulties
◆ Physical distractions
◆ Fatigue or illness
◆ Low attention span
◆ Time pressure
◆ Doubts about the trustworthiness of the speaker
◆ Daydreaming
◆ Perceived lack of relevance
◆ Memory difficulties
◆ Limited vocabulary
◆ Sensitive topic area
◆ Feeling threatened
◆ Anxiety and tension
◆ Selective listening due to a pressing personal need
◆ Areas of prejudice
◆ Dislike of the other person
◆ Persistent thoughts
◆ The needs of another demand your involvement
◆ The appearance of the speaker is extreme
◆ The values you support are under attack
◆ You don't feel accepted by the speaker
◆ An apology from you should be forthcoming
◆ You have to admit an error
◆ You have heard the discourse before
◆ You can't wait to say something
◆ The person speaks with a dialect or accent
◆ Anger and other extreme emotions

Others might find it difficult to listen to you when you:

◆ Ramble and go off the subject
◆ Speak for too long
◆ Exaggerate in your approach or the facts
◆ Make too many points
◆ Do not concentrate on your listener
◆ Become dogmatic
◆ Are not sure of what you are trying to say

Some key points for good listening include the following:

◆ Avoid or ignore distractions.
◆ Maintain eye contact.
◆ Evaluate the message, not the speaker.
◆ Don't interrupt.
◆ Don't dwell on one fragment of a message.
◆ Don't jump to conclusions, but rather hear the person out.
◆ Don't think about things not related to the subject at hand.
◆ Use interjections such as "Yes" or "Go on."
◆ Focus on what is being said.
◆ Don't let your biases prevent you from seeing other points of view.
◆ Ask open-ended questions to expand on information exchange.
◆ Learn the physical and verbal skills that make you look open.
◆ Test your ability to question for the content and intent of the speaker.
◆ Use listening to build relationships and determine the needs of others.
◆ Understand your own listening style and develop an awareness of the listening needs of others.

Active listening skills help you concentrate and become more involved in the conversation. They can be summarized as follows:

◆ Let the other person finish speaking without interruption.
◆ Show interest by inviting the person to share their feelings, beliefs, and values.
◆ Show appreciation for the other person's feelings.
◆ Clarify the meaning of a message by restating and reflecting back what is said.
◆ Be aware of nonverbal and verbal (in terms of tone and pitch) messages.
◆ Avoid judgmental statements.
◆ Create a comfortable place for communicating by eliminating distractions.

INDIVIDUAL TASKS AND REFLECTIONS

22.1 Observing Yourself

Thinking of your particular work situation, which circumstances require a high level of listening—for example, appraisals, meetings, presentations, teamwork, and interviewing? When you next participate in any of the above, monitor your levels of listening and, if possible, make positive changes to your behavior at the time.

22.2 Positive and Negative Listening (A)

Identify one positive experience of being listened to and one negative experience of being listened to. What happened? What did it feel like?

22.3 Positive and Negative Listening (B)

Think of one occasion when you listened well and one occasion when you didn't listen well. What happened? How did you feel about your behavior? What was the result of your behavior? How might you have listened better?

22.4 Role Models

Reflect on examples of good and bad listening. Consider how you were listened to by parents, family members, and teachers. What examples did your role models provide in terms of listening skills? Identify positive role models who can provide you with examples of good listening skills and evaluate why they are good at listening.

22.5 Resolving Argument

When you get into an argument, stop the discussion for a moment and, as an experiment, agree to this rule: "Each person can speak up for themselves only after they have accurately put into their own words the ideas and feelings of the previous speaker, to the satisfaction of the previous speaker."

22.6 Listening to Others

When you are listening to others speaking, do you hear only what is being said or do you also hear the subtleties of tone and pauses and read other nonverbal signals?

22.7 Others Listening to You

When you are speaking, how do you know that the other person is really listening to you? Do you watch them for a nonverbal reaction, wait for a verbal confirmation of what you've said, or assume you're being heard properly?

22.8 Listening Self-Assessment

Complete the following self-assessment and then give it to a colleague to complete about you. Use the following responses: rarely, sometimes, or often.

Levels of Listening	Self	Colleague
1. Diagnostic Listening Questions are asked to encourage the speaker to give more information. Used when a person has something important to say or a problem to work out.		
2. Empathetic Listening The listener shares the speaker's feelings. The speaker needs little response, just indications that you are listening.		
3. Attentive Listening The listener gives the speaker full attention and provides feedback on important points made.		
4. Emotional Listening The speaker arouses a powerful emotion in you and blinds you to what is being said.		
5. Dismissive Listening The listener decides that what the speaker has to say is not worth listening to.		

(continued)

(continued)

Levels of Listening	Self	Colleague
6. Destructive Listening Similar to dismissive listening, but the listener is only intent on putting down the speaker.		
7. Distracted Listening This results from trying to do something at the same time as listening and not giving either activity full attention.		
8. Anxious Listening This occurs when the listener is so awestruck that they submit completely and hear little of what is being said.		
9. Impulsive Listening This happens when the listener is too eager to get going and doesn't listen properly to instructions.		

WORKING WITH A MENTOR

22.9 Personal Disclosure

Discuss with your mentor the range of situations at work and away from work where you use listening skills. Ask your mentor to disclose in which types of situation, and how, they use their listening skills.

22.10 Mentor Feedback

Ask your mentor to observe you using listening skills. Have a feedback session involving active listening and work on ideas to improve your skills. Identify your listening styles and needs and how you can develop listening skills within your holistic learning.

DEVELOPING OTHERS

22.11 Listening Test

Invite the group to use all the resources they can to listen to the instruction you are going to give them. Tell them that afterward, you will ask them six questions. Now relate the following:

> "Please ask your sales rep Mary Smith to meet Alan Ball from our head office at the solicitors at 2:30 p.m. Mr. Johnston from Deerfield Publishers will be waiting for them in the manager's office. Ask Mary to bring Mr. Ball and Mr. Johnston to our shop at 4 Langford Street for a meeting at 4:30 p.m. After this meeting, Mrs. Clevers will decide whether to hold any further talks on the book launch."

The six questions (and answers) are as follows:

- ◆ Who is going to the solicitor's to meet someone? — (Mary Smith)
- ◆ What is the address of Deerfield Publishers? — (Not given)
- ◆ Which company does Mr. Ball work for? — (Only head office given)
- ◆ When does the meeting begin? — (4:30 p.m.)
- ◆ Who is the most senior person mentioned? — (Not enough information)
- ◆ What is the purpose of the meeting? — (Not stated)

When the exercise has been completed, give the answers and discuss.

22.12 Listening Observation

Introduce the importance of feedback. Organize the learners into groups of three with one speaker, one listener, and one observer. The speaker talks for five minutes on a subject of their choice. After five minutes, the observer gives feedback to the listener based on the styles from the listening skills self-assessment (task 8). The speaker also gives feedback to the listener. Reconvene to the larger group and discuss.

22.13 Listening Brainstorm

Ask the group to brainstorm those work-related circumstances that require a high level of listening—for example, appraisals, meetings, presentations, teamwork, and interviewing. Ask the learners to identify one positive and one negative experience of being listened to. What happened? What did it feel like? Now ask the learners to think of one occasion when they listened well and another occasion when they didn't listen well. What happened? How did they feel about their behavior? What was the result of their behavior? How might they have listened better?

22.14 Eye Contact Exercise

Open the session by introducing the importance of eye contact when we talk and listen. Organize the group into pairs. One partner then talks for five minutes on a subject of their choice while the other closes their eyes and listens. They then swap roles. The pairs then take five minutes to discuss how it felt to listen with closed eyes and how it felt to be listened to by someone who had their eyes shut. Reconvene the whole group and discuss.

22.15 True or false?

Ask the participants to consider the following statements, indicating each as true or false:

◆ People are more likely to listen to messages that correspond with their view of themselves than messages that challenge their view.
◆ The amount people reveal about themselves is likely to influence the amount others tell them about themselves.
◆ An important aspect in developing trust is listening and then keeping confidences.
◆ Some people listen too much because they are afraid of revealing themselves.
◆ To be able to listen to others, people need to be able to listen to themselves.

Go through the answers as a group and discuss.

RECOMMENDED HRD PRESS TITLES
....

20 Training Workshops for Listening Skills, 318 pp.
Listening Effectiveness Profile, 16 pp.

INTRODUCTION

Most people's fear of decision making is based on the possibility of one of three outcomes:

1. They make a decision and then are forced to stick to it despite the fact that it is seen to be not working.
2. They make no decision at all and leave things up in the air.
3. They make a group decision that has involved so many compromises that the final results fall well short of the original aim.

There is no such thing as a perfect decision. Any decision is based on the information and resources we have at the time. With the benefit of hindsight, some decisions are seen to be disasters, others prove to be good starting points for improvement, and yet others might exceed our expectations.

There are two key ways of making decisions:

1. The intuitive hunch, taking spontaneous action and then responding to the result (suitable for situations in which little or no information is available)
2. The rational process whereby you specify alternatives, criteria, and outcomes until the right solution presents itself (suitable for well-structured situations)

In uncertain situations, you need to obtain information as soon as possible and be prepared to take rapid action that in itself will generate information.

Problem Solving

Problem solving usually precedes decision making. Its aim is to discover what caused a particular situation so that you can use the knowledge to decide how to handle it. Use the following as guidelines for effective problem solving.

◆ **Step 1.** Once you have identified your problem, gather your data. Decide why you want the facts and the type of data to be collected. Decide on the timescale of the data collection and identify the most appropriate person for the task. Then design an easy-to-use check sheet. Alternatively, you could gather your data in display forms, such as bar charts, spider diagrams, pie charts, or flowcharts.

◆ **Step 2.** Now move on to problem analysis. Two techniques you could use are a relations diagram or a SWOT (Strengths, Weaknesses, Opportunities, and Threats) analysis. A relations diagram is used to relate cause and effects. Define the effect to be analyzed and write this in the middle of a sheet of paper. Keep asking yourself "why?" in order to identify the key factors that caused this effect. Write these as the main spokes radiating from the center. Then consider each cause as an effect in its own right and identify further causes by again asking "why?" Look for cross-links between causes and effects and link them with lines of a different color.

A SWOT analysis is a useful way of summarizing a particular process in terms of its strengths, weaknesses, opportunities, and threats. Identify what is to be analyzed and write it in the center of a sheet of paper. Brainstorm the four areas: strengths, weaknesses, opportunities, and threats. List each in a separate space in your diagram and identify the relative strengths or importance of the factors listed in order to identify priorities of action.

◆ **Step 3.** The generation of ideas and solutions is the next step. The four techniques you could use include: brainstorming, benchmarking, Mind Mapping,* and force field analysis.

—*Brainstorming.* This technique that encourages creative thinking is useful in a group. Appoint a scribe, and agree on a topic to be brainstormed and a timeframe (no more than 20 minutes). Allow no judgment or criticism at this stage. After the initial brainstorming, evaluate the usefulness of the ideas in relation to the original objective.

—*Benchmarking.* This is learning from others as a basis for setting goals toward improvement. Decide what you want to benchmark and who is to do it. Identify your performance standards and processes. Identify whom to benchmark against and collect the data. Observe whom you are benchmarking yourself against if possible. Analyze the data and compare with your own performance. Now set goals using what you have learned, adapting the process to fit in with your goals. Identify how the new process can be improved so that you can exceed, rather than match, the benchmark and integrate the new process with your own processes.

—*Mind Mapping.* This is a good method of generating and collating ideas. Identify the topic and write this in the middle of a sheet of paper. Brainstorm the main elements of the topic and add these as main branches coming from the center. For each branch, brainstorm its separate parts. Draw links between branches if necessary.

—*Force field analysis.* This is a way of identifying the forces that will help or hinder your objective. Define your current situation at the top left-hand side of a sheet of paper. On the right, define your target. Under your left-hand heading, list the forces that will drive you toward achieving your right-hand heading. Under your right-hand heading, list the forces that will restrain you from achieving your target. Decide which forces have the greatest impact (focus on reducing the resisting forces) and which forces you might most easily influence, and develop an action plan tackling the most important, but most easily influenced, forces as a starting point.

◆ **Step 4.** Test out your decision, either mentally or in practice, before committing to it. Look at what can go wrong and assess the risks to make sure that you have covered them.

◆ **Step 5.** The last stage is to implement action. Define the objective, identify the major components, define a goal for each component, attach a completion date to each, and develop an action plan for each goal. Alternatively, do a critical path analysis—that is, organize tasks, according to priorities and time taken. Monitor and follow up the action taken.

---

*Buzan, T. (1974), *Use Your Head,* London: BBC Publications.

Decision Making

The following are the key steps involved in decision making:

1. **Specify the aims.**
   —What are you trying to achieve?
   —What is the purpose of the decision?
   —What is the expected outcome likely to be?

   You need to have motivation to clarify your aims and, in turn, identifying your aims will fuel your motivation. It is useful to externalize your aims by means of a list or chart.

2. **Review the factors.**
   —List the factors that are important in the decision.
   —Determine the impact of each one and rate them in importance.

3. **Determine possible courses.**
   Produce as broad a range as possible through brainstorming.

4. **Make the decision.**
   You now have a broad range of possible courses of action that needs to be analyzed and evaluated against the factors you listed earlier. Part of the decision-making process is that of balancing risk. Consider the risks involved in each possible course of action and then choose an acceptable level of risk. At this stage, you need to use critical thinking: question all the assumptions you have made, evaluate the arguments of others, and appraise the data to make sure of the facts. Then either reject or retain the possible courses of action. A decision is reached when only one course of action remains.

5. **Implement and evaluate the decision.**
   After the decision has been made and action taken, evaluate whether the decision was the most appropriate or whether you need to make adjustments or consider another possibility.

Sourcing information is a core task in decision making. It helps clarify how much you already know, how you can set about finding more information, how to test the validity of what you discover, and who to approach for expert guidance.

Emotions can affect your decision-making process—for example, apprehension and anxiety will make you fear the worst when approaching a decision. Your needs are also part of your decision-making process and, to an extent, your emotions will be driven by your needs. However, your needs change, and it is important to know your different needs in relation to the decision.

◆ A short-term decision is better than no decision.
◆ All decisions have consequences.
◆ Review decisions regularly.

If you find yourself in a situation where someone is demanding an immediate decision from you, you can use a number of techniques based on assertiveness training:

◆ You could acknowledge the request and ask for time.
◆ You could state your interest in the possible outcome of the decision and ask for more information.
◆ You could say "no" and offer an alternative.

**INDIVIDUAL TASKS
AND REFLECTIONS**

23.1 Reviewing Decision-Making Skills

What skills do you think you need to make effective decisions?

23.2 How do you do it?

How do you tend to make decisions? Do you find it easy or difficult to make decisions? Why?

23.3 Good Decision Analysis

Consider a good decision you recently made. What was your decision-making process? Did you involve anyone else? Was the outcome what you expected or better? Have you reviewed your decision since? Is it still working?

23.4 Bad Decision Analysis

Consider a bad decision you recently made. What was your decision-making process? Did you involve anyone else? Why didn't the outcome work? What could you have done differently?

**WORKING
WITH OTHERS**

23.5 SWOT Analysis

Identify a current problem requiring a decision and, with a work colleague, do a SWOT analysis on it.

**WORKING
WITH A MENTOR**

23.6 Problem Solving

Make a statement of goals in relation to a problem. Think of as many different easy ways of attaining the goals as you can. Assess the degree to which any of these courses of action are realistic. Develop, with your mentor, a step-by-step action plan, with a time schedule for attaining the goals.

23.7 Benchmarking

Use the benchmarking technique to generate solutions to a current problem. Discuss with your mentor.

23.8 Force Field Analysis

Use the force field analysis technique to generate solutions to a current problem. Discuss with your mentor.

**DEVELOPING
OTHERS**

23.9 Brainstorming

Introduce the subject of making decisions. Use a problem that the group can identify with and use the brainstorming technique to generate solutions. You could also organize the learners into small groups to use the technique.

23.10 Mind Mapping

Introduce the subject of making decisions. Use a problem that the group can identify with and use the Mind Mapping technique to generate solutions or ask the learners to individually identify a current problem and use the technique. You could also organize the learners into small groups to use the technique.

23.11 Techniques for Making Decisions

Introduce the subject of making decisions. Explain and discuss the following:

◆ Mind Mapping
◆ Brainstorming
◆ SWOT analysis
◆ Benchmarking
◆ Force field analysis

**RECOMMENDED
HRD PRESS TITLES**
....

The Problem Solving and Decision Making Toolkit, 150 pp.
Problem Solving and Decision Making Profile, 16 pp.

24
Managing Change

When we are proactive in initiating change, we feel in control. But sometimes things happen to us that are outside our control, and this can produce difficult feelings that prevent us from moving toward success. In today's world, the speed of change can seem alarming. In order to be able to work with change, we need to be adaptable. Flexibility is a bonus to the art of managing change: the more rigid your attitude, the more you will experience change as a threat. However, there's nothing wrong with feeling anxious when faced by change, and acknowledging your fear is the quickest way through it.

We might have a disproportionate anxiety about change as adults if we have a childhood background of enforced change. We might fear being overwhelmed by change that is externally imposed. We might believe that we don't have the skills to deal with it. We might feel angry at having change forced upon us. Of course, change can bring uncertainty, but it can also bring new opportunities. If you find the word *change* daunting, try using the words *grow, evolve,* or *transform* instead.

> With enforced change, such as being laid off or changing work roles, use the opportunity to change work direction or learn new skills.

You may tend to feel worse about change when you keep your thoughts and feelings to yourself. Expressing these to another person will dilute the negativity, giving you more room for constructive action. Anxieties take up vital energy that could be used to deal with change. Notice how fatigued you became when facing a period of uncertainty. You don't have to like change, but if you can understand it and embrace it, rather than fight it, the quicker the difficult feelings will fade away.

It could be that, as part of your coping strategy with change, you need to allow yourself a period of adjustment. Change takes time to assimilate. If we give ourselves time to consolidate our feelings, we will find ourselves on firmer ground quicker.

It helps to balance the acceptance of change with the security of established safety zones. These are areas of your life that you can rely on—for example, walking the dog, visiting the pub, working out at the gym, or having a meal out. Accepting change becomes easier when there are other points of reference in your life that are under your control.

> Developing self-knowledge is a quality of a change-winner.

Someone who has a strong self-image is better able to cope with change than someone who has not. When you have a good self-image, you know that you can stand as a rock in the midst of change.

When you go through a period of change, you can feel out of control because you do not understand why things have to change, how they might change, and what might happen as a result. So rather than letting the fear of change overwhelm you, gather information to help you feel more in control.

You can choose to:

◆ Fight the change, feel bad, and stay stuck

or

◆ Accept the change and implement a strategy to incorporate it into your life.

In times of change, you need to remain centered on yourself and your own approval. It helps to gather information from others, but not to rely on them to make you feel better in the face of change. It is best to focus internally for your sense of security rather than externally. Self-knowledge, confidence, and self-esteem are the components of this inner security.

Often when change is enforced, people tend to look back with rose-tinted glasses to "the way things were." Maybe things *were* different then, for better or worse. However, *now* is the time you need to be concerned with. Do not become trapped between past glorification and future fear. The past is safe and can be seen as a happy fantasy. The future is unpredictable and therefore unsafe. But that perception is only a reflection of your state of mind.

Taking calculated risks—for example, applying for a promotion—will help you become more receptive to change. In that way, you can get used to being proactive with change and thereby increase your sense of control. Remember, it is the effects of change we fear rather than the actual change itself.

Feel in control of change by:

◆ Adapting yourself
◆ Allowing a period of adjustment
◆ Accepting the change (you don't always have to like it)
◆ Having regular stable reference points in your life—for example, working out at the gym or having a meal in your favorite restaurant
◆ Becoming informed
◆ Managing your time
◆ Setting new goals and working toward them
◆ Managing your stress
◆ Thinking positively
◆ Being proactive
◆ Taking time out to explore and make plans
◆ Developing a core of security within yourself, as opposed to relying on finding it from outside sources
◆ Living in the present
◆ Establishing new routines

Above all, remember that change creates new opportunities.
Change means:

◆ The relocation opportunity—*which you could pick up*
◆ New unmet needs—*which you could meet*
◆ The opening up of gaps—*which you could fill*
◆ Modern technology—*which you could operate*
◆ Development and expansion—*which you could be part of*

"The real voyage of discovering consists not in seeking new landscapes, but in having new eyes."

—Marcel Proust

**INDIVIDUAL TASKS
AND REFLECTIONS**

24.1 Reactions to Change

How do you tend to react to change?

24.2 Fearing Change

What is it about change that makes you fearful?

24.3 Improving Your Attitude

How might you improve your attitude toward change?

24.4 Recent Change

Consider a recent change in your life. How did you react? How did you feel? What was the outcome for you?

**WORKING
WITH OTHERS**

24.5 Change Support

Talking to others when faced by change can be helpful. Identify four people in your personal and professional lives who you could talk to for reassurance and guidance.

24.6 Relationship Change

Identify a personal or professional relationship that has recently changed. Why has it changed? How has it changed? What was your attitude to the change? How were you part of the change? How do you feel about the relationship change now?

**WORKING
WITH A MENTOR**

24.7 Mentor Change

How has the relationship with your mentor changed (for you and for them)? Discuss with them.

24.8 Work Change

Identify a work situation that involves you in change. Discuss what the change would mean for you and how you feel about it. Develop an action plan that will help you deal with the change, both psychologically and practically.

**DEVELOPING
OTHERS**

24.9 In Control of Change

Introduce the subject of managing change. Ask the learners to brainstorm their ideas for coping strategies. Discuss.

24.10 Group Feedback

Introduce the subject of managing change. Ask the learners to select a recent change in their lives that they are willing to talk about. Then ask them to identify a key problem with the change and their ideas for coping with it. Organize them into groups of three to discuss. Each person is to have ten minutes to share the key problem and their coping strategies and five minutes for group feedback.

As a follow-up exercise, each group could write (in bullet-point form on a flipchart sheet) general coping strategies that can be shared with the whole group.

**RECOMMENDED
HRD PRESS TITLES**
....

The Manager's Pocket Guide to Corporate Culture Change, 190 pp.
50 Activities for Achieving Change, 420 pp.
Change Management Effectiveness Profile, 16 pp.

25
Managing Your Anger

INTRODUCTION

Anger is part of our emotional spectrum of self-expression, but is all too often either inappropriately expressed—for example, via aggression, manipulation or blame—or denied altogether and repressed inside ourselves, never to see the light of day.

Repressed anger can make us defensive, resentful, anxious, depressed, sad, shallow, and judgmental. In the long term, it can affect the immune system and make you ill. As with many of our feelings, the way in which we deal with anger derives from our early conditioning. Our childhood observation of our role models, such as our parents, dealing with anger will affect how we deal with anger as adults. Gender also has an effect. For example, it is traditionally acceptable for men to demonstrate anger, and we may expect men to be more aggressive than women. Indeed, many women have a problem with anger, because, traditionally, it hasn't been "proper" for a woman to express this emotion.

Anger can also be a cover-up for fear. A man might believe it is more appropriate to show anger than the fear that he really feels. Anger can also cover up hurt—better to attack or defend than to show vulnerability. Getting angry helps us:

◆ Set limits where appropriate
◆ Grieve hurts and losses
◆ Get our needs met
◆ Get things off our chest
◆ Be assertive
◆ Influence or change others
◆ Discover what lies beneath our anger—for example, hurt
◆ Understand and accept other people's anger

We have choices in how we handle anger. We can:

◆ Deny it and experience numbness
◆ Hold it in as resentment
◆ Repress it and become ill
◆ Anaesthetize the pain with an alternative behavior—for example, heavy drinking or work

How we express anger is affected by the negative beliefs we might have about anger such as:

◆ "I must not make a fool of myself."
◆ "I must always win."
◆ "Others might think I'm pushy if I'm angry."
◆ "Others might not understand my point of view."
◆ "I must be rational all the time."
◆ "I might get out of control if I get angry."
◆ "Others might reject me if I get angry."
◆ "Women shouldn't get angry."
◆ "I must be nice."
◆ "Others might think I'm uptight."
◆ "People won't like me if I get angry."

However, anger must be managed effectively and not denied or projected. You can begin to manage your anger through:

◆ Striving to increase your threshold for getting angry
◆ Examining what has led you to carry around so much frustration
◆ Breaking down the causes of your frustration into smaller pieces
◆ Asking yourself how you could react differently to the issues involved
◆ Making an action plan to change what you can change
◆ Restraining yourself when you feel your anger boiling up
◆ Analyzing the situation to see if there is some other way you could react to it

Other ways in which you could manage your anger include:

◆ Developing an inner arena for expressing anger by having a dialogue with your inner self to find out what hurt lies behind the anger
◆ Separating your projections from the other person's emotions
◆ Expressing anger physically and safely—for example, punching a cushion, tearing up some old magazines or newspapers, doing physical exercise, or having a good shout in private.
◆ Getting your anger out into the open or externalizing it, either directly to the person concerned or by writing down your feelings. Keep on expressing your anger until you reach the underlying feelings or issues.

Developing a task-oriented inner dialogue is an effective tool in managing anger. This means taking control of our thought processes in relation to how we deal with our own and others' behavior. Actually, becoming aware of our thoughts is a little like trying to take hold of air. We tend to be aware of our feelings (vague or intense) and we may be conscious of what causes us to react or behave as we do in response to our feelings. But we can be blissfully ignorant of how our thought processes give rise to our feelings and behaviors—and, more importantly, how we can affect our thought process for good or ill.

<u>E</u>vent   <u>F</u>eelings   <u>T</u>houghts

Until now, you may only have been aware of **E** and **F**. However, what happens at **T** can be critical, not only for how angry you are because of **E**, but also in regard to how rationally you handle the situation. You can influence **F** by learning to think more realistically at **T**.

Task-oriented inner dialogue can be used before, during, and after an event. For example, suppose a work colleague keeps using your work area as a dumping ground for their work even after repeated requests for them not to do so. You are going to raise the issue yet again with the added statement that you will be dumping their work on the floor the next time they put it on your desk. Your inner dialogue might run along the following lines:

◆ **Before:** "Keep calm, remember what I am going to achieve."
◆ **During:** "I am in control. I will stick to what I am going to do."
◆ **After:** "Even though the situation is not completely resolved, I'm glad I'm learning to cope without getting aggressive."

INDIVIDUAL TASKS AND REFLECTIONS

25.1 Reflecting on Anger

Consider the following:

◆ To what extent is your anger a problem for you?
◆ What situations make you feel angry?
◆ What people make you feel angry?
◆ What kinds of physical reaction do you experience when you are angry?

◆ What kinds of thoughts do you have about yourself when you are angry?
◆ How do you behave when you are angry?
◆ How you feel, think, and react when others get angry with you?

25.2 Early Conditioning

It can often be useful to consider how your parents and other childhood role models expressed their anger. How we observed anger being expressed, between others and from others to ourselves, when younger can have a profound effect on how we deal with anger as adults. Consider how your early conditioning and observations of anger management (from others to you or between others) have colored your style of anger management as an adult.

25.3 Helpful Anger

In the past, how has anger been of use to you—for example, acted as a catalyst or helped you move forward?

WORKING

WITH OTHERS

25.4 Harmful Anger

Identify a specific situation in the past where you feel your anger may have been harmful. Reflect on:

◆ The triggering event
◆ Your thoughts (negative/unrealistic inner dialogue)
◆ Your feelings
◆ Negative inner dialogue that preceded or took place during the event

Now change the negative inner dialogue relating to the situation to task-oriented inner dialogue.

25.5 A Current Anger-Provoking Situation

Identify a current anger-provoking situation involving another person. Reflect on:

◆ The triggering event
◆ Your thoughts (negative/unrealistic inner dialogue)
◆ Your feelings
◆ Changing the negative inner dialogue to task-oriented inner dialogue

WORKING

WITH A MENTOR

25.6 Work-Related Anger

Discuss with your mentor a particular anger-evoking situation that you have experienced with a work colleague.

25.7 Mentor-Related Anger

Take a particular anger-evoking situation that you have experienced with your mentor and discuss.

DEVELOPING

OTHERS

25.8 Good and Bad Anger

Introduce the subject of managing anger. Have the group brainstorm what it feels like to be angry. Now ask the learners to identify two situations— one in which they handled the anger well and another when they didn't. Organize them into groups of three to analyze why they handled one situation well and what they could have done to handle the other situation better.

25.9 Ways to Manage Anger

Introduce the subject of managing anger. Have the group brainstorm different ways of negatively handling anger and different ways of effectively managing anger. Organize the learners into groups of four to discuss and identify methods they could use to manage anger. Reconvene the whole group for feedback.

25.10 Task-Oriented Dialogue

Open a general discussion on anger with examples from your own background. Introduce the concept of inner dialogue. Set up role plays in the group in which the learners can practice their task-oriented inner dialogue. Each person is to:

◆ Identify a particular situation involving anger that they feel safe working on
◆ Identify their negative inner dialogue
◆ Develop task-oriented inner dialogue for before, during, and afterward

RECOMMENDED HRD PRESS TITLES
....

Managing Anger in the Workplace, 150 pp.
The Manager's Pocket Guide to Dealing with Conflict, 128 pp.

INTRODUCTION

The concept of mentoring comes from Greek mythology. In Homer's Odyssey, Mentor was the teacher of Telemachus, the son of Odysseus. But Mentor was more than a teacher. Mentor was half-god and half-man, half-male and half-female, believable and yet unreachable. Mentor was the union of both goal and path—wisdom personified (Daloz, 1999). Today, some 3,500 years later, mentoring relationships are still valued. Increasingly, mid-career professionals seek mentors when they wish to develop new levels of expertise and to advance in the profession.

The most effective mentors:

◆ Are confidants, advisors, teachers, guides, coaches, and role models
◆ Want to share their knowledge, skill, and experience with those they mentor in a noncompetitive way
◆ Offer support, challenge, patience, and enthusiasm while they guide others to new levels of competence
◆ Expose the recipients of their mentoring to new ideas, perspectives, and standards, and to the values and norms of the profession
◆ Are more expert in terms of knowledge, but view themselves as equal to those they mentor
◆ Are considered by peers to be experts in the field and demonstrate superior achievement through their work
◆ Are enthusiastic about their field and continue to update their background in the field
◆ Listen to, and communicate effectively with, others
◆ Recognize excellence in others and encourage it
◆ Are able to empathize with others and understand their views
◆ Enjoy intellectual engagement and like to help others
◆ Are sensitive to the needs of others and generally recognize when others require support, direct assistance, or independence
◆ Exercise good judgment in decisions concerning themselves and the welfare of others

Establishing a positive mentoring relationship is very much like establishing other valued human relationships, but has the added dimension of being professional in nature. Both parties need to have a genuine desire to understand the values and expectations of the other, and to respect and become sensitive to each other's feelings and needs. A mentor is responsible for offering support and challenge to the recipient of their mentoring while the recipient strives to fulfill the professional's expectations.

Healthy mentoring relationships are organic, rather than static, in nature. They change because the purpose of the relationship is to enable the recipient to acquire new knowledge, skill, and standards of professional competence. The perceptions of both members of the relationship evolve as the recipient's performance evolves to new levels of competence under the mentor's guidance and support.

One way to view the evolutionary nature of mentoring relationships is to think of them in terms of the following stages of development:

◆ **Stage 1.** The mentor and recipient become acquainted and clarify their common interests, shared values, and professional goals.
◆ **Stage 2.** The mentor and recipient communicate initial expectations and agree on some common procedures and expectations as a starting point.
◆ **Stage 3.** Gradually, needs are fulfilled. Objectives are met. Professional growth takes place. New challenges are presented and achieved. This stage might last for months or years.
◆ **Stage 4.** The mentor and recipient redefine their relationship as colleagues, peers, partners, and/or friends.

In the exploratory stages, individuals who are contemplating a mentoring relationship need to look for:

◆ A degree of enthusiasm for a mentoring relationship
◆ A similarity in personal styles—for example, gregarious, animated, spontaneous versus low-key, retiring, reflective
◆ Similar expected professional assignments and responsibilities
◆ A similar preference for the degree of nurture versus autonomy when establishing expectations for support
◆ Similar professional qualifications route, study history, and previous experience

Mentors need to offer their protégés challenges that stimulate professional growth and new levels of expertise. When the degree of challenge is well matched to the mentee's readiness for growth, the tasks become motivating, whereas challenges that are ill-matched to the individual's level of development can create feelings of being unable to cope. Then, rather than producing growth, the challenge might lead to feelings of failure. It is therefore important for mentors to become sensitive to the growth needs of their mentees and attempt to offer optimal challenges for their protégés' professional development. Some mentors develop a mentoring plan to help maintain optimal levels of challenge for the protégé, the primary function of which is to focus on the developmental nature of becoming a professional and to establish mileposts that will guide and serve as reminders that the recipient is growing in knowledge and skill.

Trust is an important component in the mentoring relationship and includes such qualities as:

assertiveness	reliability
genuineness	dependability
keeping promises	consistency
keeping confidences	trust
loyalty	honesty
fairness	openness
fair behavior	accepting behavior
care	support
cooperation	generosity
kindness	

INDIVIDUAL TASKS AND REFLECTIONS

26.1 Would-be-Mentor Checklist

The checklist below is designed to guide self-reflection for those who are considering becoming mentors. It provides a description of the qualities that are commonly thought to be conducive to successful mentoring.

Mentoring Quality	Agree (✓)	Neutral (✓)	Disagree (✓)
I like and enjoy working with other professionals.			
I am a good listener and respect my colleagues.			
I am sensitive to the needs and feelings of others.			
I recognize when others need support/independence.			
I want to contribute to the professional development of others and to share what I have learned.			
I am willing to find reward in service to someone who needs my assistance.			
I am able to support and help without smothering or taking charge.			
I see myself as willing to adjust my personal schedule to meet the needs of someone else.			
I am usually patient and tolerant when teaching someone.			
I am confident and secure in my knowledge of the field and make an effort to remain up-to-date.			
Overall, I see myself as a competent professional.			
I am able to offer assistance in areas that give others problems.			
I am able to explain things at various levels of complexity and detail.			
Others are interested in my professional ideas.			

26.2 Communications Checklist for Mentors

As a mentor is well placed to help others question themselves, so a good mentor should always be questioning their own motivations, processes, and performance. Using the communications checklist for mentors that follows as a guide, analyze your processes in any current mentoring roles you have:

Communications Checklist for Mentors
◆ How do I perceive myself in the many roles a mentor plays?
◆ How well do I understand the recipient's overall expectations for our mentoring relationship?
◆ In general, is my communication—both verbal and nonverbal—with the recipient effective?
◆ Am I clear in my objectives when communicating?

(continued)

(continued)

Communications Checklist for Mentors
◆ Does my communication method (face-to-face, telephone, written) fit specific mentoring situations?
◆ Am I too formal or informal for the purpose in my communication?
◆ Do I tend to make assumptions in my communication?
◆ What kind of response do I expect from the recipient?
◆ Am I prepared for a very different kind of response?
◆ Have I given them enough time to respond, to ask questions, or to ask for clarification?
◆ If I think I have been misunderstood, can I clarify and paraphrase?
◆ Am I willing to set aside my own communication agenda to listen to theirs at any time?
◆ How should I react to their communication to further our mentoring relationship?

WORKING WITH OTHERS

26.3 Trusting Others

Who do you trust among your personal and professional contacts? Why?

26.4 Others Trusting You

Identify those people in your personal and professional network who confide in you. Why do they confide in you?

WORKING WITH A MENTOR

26.5 Mentor History

What is the history between you and your mentor? Discuss and analyze.

26.6 Personal Qualities

Which of your mentor's personal qualities do you feel comfortable and uncomfortable with? Share and discuss.

26.7 Mentoring Skills

Analyze the mentoring skills of your mentor. Share and discuss.

26.8 You as a Mentor

Analyze your potential for becoming a mentor. What skills and personal qualities do you have that would be of benefit?

26.9 Ready for Mentoring

Identify if this is an appropriate time for you to begin developing your mentoring skills. If it is, how might you make yourself available? Set regular review sessions of your mentoring skills with your mentor.

DEVELOPING

OTHERS

....

26.10 Brainstorming Mentoring

Introduce the subject of mentoring. Ask the group to brainstorm the definitions of mentoring. Then ask the learners to identify one positive and one negative example of being mentored (and the reasons why they were positive or negative experiences). Discuss as a whole group.

26.11 Mentoring Each Other

Introduce the subject of mentoring. Brainstorm mentoring skills and create a checklist from which the learners can assess their mentoring skills. Organize the group into pairs so that each partner can play the role of mentor in turn. The "mentor" is to help their partner work through their mentoring skills checklist to formulate an action plan for development.

RECOMMENDED

HRD PRESS TITLES

....

The Manager's Pocket Guide to Effective Mentoring, 128 pp.
The Step-by-Step Guide to Starting an Effective Mentoring Program,
    100 pp.
50 Activities for Coaching and Mentoring, 306 pp.
Principles of Adult Mentoring Inventory, 16 pp.

INTRODUCTION

What motivates you? Money? Doing a job well? Recognition? Winning? Advancement? Acceptance? Or would you be happy if only you could work in a more pleasant environment? You will work harder only if it gets you what you want. A motivational factor is something you obtain only through your own efforts. Listed below are some thoughts on motivation:

◆ Motivation stems either from satisfaction in doing a good job or from others' recognition of our efforts.
◆ Money can be a motivator, but only if you value more money and perceive a strong relationship between your effort and reward.
◆ The strongest motivators are achieving results; being valued and made to feel important; being included and accepted by an admired group; competing—getting ahead of others; gaining influence and status; earning more money; and gaining opportunities to do things you like doing.
◆ Something can motivate behavior only if that behavior leads to it.
◆ Your power to motivate others will depend, in part, on how much others value recognition from, or inclusion by, you.

Motivation is the driving force that propels us to commit ourselves to a project and see it through to completion. Without motivation, we can feel apathetic, bored, frustrated, and depressed. Motivation provides us with the reasons to keep going. For example, what is your motivation for working? Money, power, and status are the most common reasons. But there are also more subtle reasons such as self-expression or creativity. Or maybe we want the personal challenge of individual freedom. Perhaps we want to help others. It is important that we express as much of our true nature as possible through our work if we are to gain some sense of satisfaction from it. If your work expresses who you are and maybe, to some extent, your value system, the work becomes meaningful to you and you feel motivated.

Motivation comes from inside out, not from the outside in. Motivation can take a knock when life smacks us on the face, but this is when we need to massage our quivering motivation back to life again, albeit possibly in a new direction. Maybe you are ready and willing to be motivated, but lack inspiration. In this case, you could talk things over with someone, read an inspirational book, or take up a new interest. Perhaps you need to clear out your old mind-set before taking on a fresh perspective, in which case you should take time out, do something completely different for a while, or do nothing.

There is a difference between "want" motivation and "need" motivation. A "want" motivation is driven by enjoyment and personal preferences. The trick to staying motivated in work is to identify your "want" drives and use them in the workplace. The way forward is to satisfy the emotional needs those drives represent within your paid work by looking at what you do outside work and identifying what motivates you there.

> Motivation is the provision of incentives to encourage performance.

Abraham Maslow (1987) suggested a hierarchy of needs, which affects people's motivations and decisions. The idea is that people's motivations depend on what position in the hierarchy they currently occupy. For example, someone who is homeless and without an income is not going to be motivated by the project of self-actualization. The hierarchy is illustrated below.

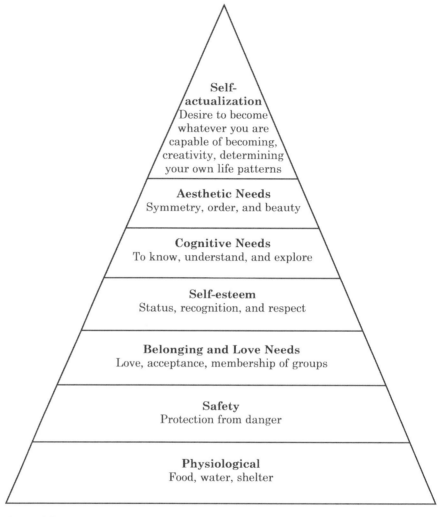

Self-actualization
Desire to become whatever you are capable of becoming, creativity, determining your own life patterns

Aesthetic Needs
Symmetry, order, and beauty

Cognitive Needs
To know, understand, and explore

Self-esteem
Status, recognition, and respect

Belonging and Love Needs
Love, acceptance, membership of groups

Safety
Protection from danger

Physiological
Food, water, shelter

Adapted from Maslow (1987).

Indicators of a lack of motivation in others are as follows:

◆ **Frequent requests for help.** The employee might show a lack of initiative in completing challenging tasks.
◆ **No desire to improve job knowledge.** The employee expresses the attitude: "Why should I learn more? I will still be doing the same old job."
◆ **Little interest in achieving established goals.** The employee will not work to attain work goals, because they do not perceive them as important. They might reject their supervisor's leadership/motivational efforts for personal or other reasons.
◆ **Unsatisfactory output and quality.** The employee will do sloppy work and will not complete tasks adequately.

◆ **Time-killing/clock-watching activities.** The employee might show signs of boredom with the work, but will make no attempt to change employment.

◆ **Absenteeism.** The employee will begin to arrive at work late or not show up at all. Some authorities say that this is the most crucial indicator of employee dissatisfaction.

If you are in a position of motivating others, you can't just plough in there, cheerfully exhorting people to "let's get on with it." If others are demotivated, they won't be receptive to your motivational efforts and are likely to resent you for what they might perceive as a patronizing form of leadership. In order to solve the problem, you need to know the origins and symptoms of the problem—for example, why the lack of motivation is there and what exactly reveals a lack of motivation. Once you have this information, you can create ways to motivate others and overcome behavioral issues.

The following tips will help you motivate others:

◆ Get to know people's individual motivators by asking them—and continuing to ask them.
◆ Help people understand the task, the reason for it, and its value.
◆ Encourage flexibility of roles and responsibilities.
◆ Set clear and achievable targets.
◆ Involve people.
◆ Always look for a positive angle and give praise and acknowledgment where appropriate.

INDIVIDUAL TASKS AND REFLECTIONS

27.1 Immediacy

What is motivating you to do this exercise to understand how to increase your motivation?

27.2 Past Motivations

Consider key accomplishments in your past. What motivated you then to achieve success?

27.3 Key Motivations

In general, what are you motivated by?

27.4 Present Demotivation

Analyze a current situation in which you feel you lack motivation. Ask yourself:

◆ How do I feel about this situation right now?
◆ Have I chosen this situation or am I involved in it at someone else's request?
◆ What would I like to do about this situation to make myself feel better?
◆ Do I have choices in this situation? Can I implement the choice? What do I need to change in order to implement the choice? If I don't have a choice, what can I do about it?
◆ How can I take positive action to get the most out of this situation?

WORKING WITH OTHERS

27.5 Motivating Others

Consider a situation in which you are responsible for motivating others. How do you motivate others? How do they respond? What can you do to improve your motivation skills?

27.6 Increasing Your Motivation

Identify a situation in which someone is responsible for motivating you. Do you feel motivated? If not, why not? Could you discuss your feelings with the other person?

WORKING WITH A MENTOR

27.7 Mentor Motivation

Consider the motivation provided by your mentor. Analyze and discuss it with them.

27.8 Motivating the Mentor

How might you be responsible for motivating your mentor? Discuss.

DEVELOPING OTHERS

27.9 Solutions for Self-Motivation

Ask the learners to identify a situation in which they feel demotivated. Organize them into small groups to discuss. Reconvene the larger group to share experiences and solutions.

27.10 Solutions for Motivating Others

Ask the learners to identify a situation in which they are responsible for motivating others. Organize them into small groups to discuss difficulties of motivation. Reconvene the larger group to share experiences and solutions.

RECOMMENDED HRD PRESS TITLES

The Manager's Pocket Guide to Motivating Employees, 120 pp.
Managing by Motivation Assessment, 16 pp.

INTRODUCTION

Networking brings people together. It builds bridges between what we each know and can share with each other. It is about making contact in order to exchange information. In order to network, we need to feel confident in our skills and our methods of communication. If we don't think positively of ourselves, how can we project a confident self-image? Developing assertiveness can help self-doubt. It doesn't come easily to many people to think well of themselves and to market their skills and strengths in a positive way. But it isn't arrogant to believe in yourself. Arrogance is believing that you possess skills and strengths that you don't have, especially if you put down other people in order to make yourself feel stronger. Putting yourself down doesn't serve any purpose—it helps no one.

Key networking principles include:

◆ **Being seen as a specialist.** To have a single skill, especially a manual one, is no longer enough. You need to be multiskilled and able to transfer your skills across occupations.

◆ **Improving your people skills.** Career networking exists through effective communication. Not only do you need to build interpersonal skills to obtain work, but you also need similar skills to stay in work. You have to refine your communication skills to include informing, listening, supporting, guiding, making requests, and showing appreciation.

◆ **Gathering information.** In order to gain the maximum from career networking, you need to establish objectives, and identify sources of information and ways to gather that information.

◆ **Getting yourself noticed.** Using technology, such as the Internet and fax, is another facet of networking. Other methods such as writing, holding a seminar, issuing a press release, or creating a pressure group might help you become known and gain visibility as an expert.

Today's workplace of today is fast, streamlined, and competitive. The companies for which you work are facing tougher opposition than ever before. They have to cut back their overheads to stay in front. The permanent workforce is shrinking, giving way to part-time, temporary, and contract staff who are flexible. As an employee, you are in competition with other employees. You need to run your working life like a business, identifying and increasing new ways to exploit your skills and knowledge and becoming known to potential employers. You might want to network for promotion, to make a lateral move at work, or to improve your skills base. Use presentations, meetings, and conferences to raise your profile. Show yourself as a team member. Become more actively involved in your appraisal.

Why not start up your own network? Possibilities might include a professional women's network, a particular trade/profession network made up of local members, a mentoring network, or a special interest network. You could use your local Chamber of Commerce or Enterprise Agency for initial publicity. You might have a newsletter, training days, or monthly meetings. Alternatively, join other peoples' networks.

True networking covers the whole of your life: work, play, family, and spirituality. Take time to look at the rest of your life:

◆ **Your domestic network.** Who do you turn to when things go wrong or need doing around the home or in the garden?

◆ **Your health network.** Who forms your basic health network? Do you have complementary therapists you can turn to?

◆ **Your transport network.** Do you have the telephone numbers of public transport contacts? Who do you turn to when something goes wrong with your car?

◆ **Your family network.** Who do you turn to for baby-sitting or daycare? Is there a network in place for dependents or aging parents?

◆ **Your social network.** Who do you socialize with on your own? Who do you meet with your partner? Do you know your partner's network of social contacts?

◆ **Your interest and hobby network.** Do you network with specialist groups? Perhaps through a magazine or the Internet?

◆ **Your educational network.** How are your educational needs met? Do you have college or university contacts?

If we each know 50 people on a professional and personal basis and multiplied each of those 50 people by the 50 people they know, the numbers grow ever larger. A network is any number of people making up any number of groups. Each person you know brings you into their network until your network ties in with many other networks.

> John Naisbett, the networking expert, says he can reach anyone, anywhere in the world, in two contacts!

INDIVIDUAL TASKS AND REFLECTIONS

28.1 Personal Support Networks

Ask yourself:

◆ Who can I rely on in a crisis?
◆ Who can I talk to when I am worried?
◆ Who mentally stimulates me?
◆ Who can I have fun with socially?
◆ Who can I feel close to?
◆ Who values me?
◆ Who challenges me?
◆ Who gives me constructive feedback?

28.2 Professional Support Networks

Ask yourself:

◆ Who can I rely on in a crisis?
◆ Who can I talk to when I am worried?
◆ Who mentally stimulates me?
◆ Who can I have fun with socially?
◆ Who can I feel close to?
◆ Who values me?
◆ Who challenges me?
◆ Who gives me constructive feedback?

28.3 Webworking

Identify ways in which you could use the Internet to network.

28.4 Being Part of Someone Else's Network

Your usefulness to others could link you to those people and place you in a position of power. Consider:

◆ In what ways could you mentor or provide a role model for others?
◆ What useful skills might you use to be of benefit to others?
◆ How can you challenge others to bring out their best?
◆ What kind of people do you attract and why?

28.5 Starting Up a Network

Is there any area of your life or a special interest that would benefit from networking and that has no network in place? Could you start up a network? How might you do this? Who could you network with to help you achieve this?

WORKING
WITH A MENTOR
....
DEVELOPING
OTHERS
....

28.6 Mentor Help

How can your mentor help you network? Discuss.

28.7 Brainstorming Networking

Introduce the subject of networking. Brainstorm the reasons for networking. Brainstorm the ways in which we might network. Brainstorm the skills necessary to network.

28.8 Networking in Action

Introduce the subject of networking. Ask each learner to identify reasons why they should network. Then ask them to identify six people in their personal and professional life who could help them and why they could help them. Organize learners into pairs to compare reasons for networking and to share networking sources if appropriate. Now organize them into groups of four to compare reasons for networking and to share networking sources if appropriate. Keep enlarging the groups until the full group meets up again to discuss the experience.

28.9 Offering Yourself as a Networker

Introduce the subject of networking. Ask each learner to identify a short list of what they can offer to others who are seeking to network. Organize the learners into pairs to share what they have to offer as networkers. Then organize them into groups of four to share what they have to offer as networkers. Keep enlarging the groups until the full group meets up again to discuss the experience.

Networking and Relationship Building Profile, 16 pp.

29 Performance Management

Performance management reminds us that training, strong commitment, and lots of hard work alone are not results. The principal attribute of performance management is its focus on achieving results. Performance management redirects our efforts away from business toward effectiveness.

Increasing competition from businesses worldwide has meant that all organizations need to be more careful about their choice of strategies to remain competitive. This situation has put more focus on effectiveness; systems and processes in the organization must be applied in the right way to the right things in order to achieve results. All the results achieved throughout the organization then must be continuously aligned to achieve the overall outcomes desired by the organization for it to survive and thrive. When this happens, the organization and its various parts are really performing.

Typically when we think of organizational performance, employee performance springs to mind. However, performance management should also be focused on:

◆ The organization
◆ Departments—for example, computer support
◆ Processes—for example, invoicing
◆ Programs—for example, implementing new policies and procedures to ensure a safe workplace
◆ Products or services to internal or external customers
◆ Projects—for example, creating a new corporate Web site
◆ Teams or groups organized to accomplish a result for internal or external customers

Exchanging Ongoing Feedback About Performance

Feedback is information relevant to how well results are being achieved. Useful feedback is timely, feasible, and understood. Ideally, feedback addresses key activities to improve or reinforce performance. Usually, the larger the number of sources giving feedback, the more accurate is the depiction of events. Any ideas that emerge from this to improve or support performance should be implemented as appropriate.

A performance appraisal (or review) includes the documentation of expected results, standards of performance, progress toward achieving results, how well they were achieved, examples indicating achievement, suggestions to improve performance, and how those suggestions can be followed. The performance appraisal should be carried out at regular intervals once performance tracking is underway. From here there are two routes.

First, if someone's performance meets desired performance standards, reward them for their performance. Second, if their performance does not meet standards, implement a performance development plan that clearly conveys: how it was concluded that there was inadequate performance; what actions are to be taken and by whom and when; and when performance will be reviewed again and how. Inadequate performance does not always indicate a problem on the part of the employee: performance standards may be unrealistic or the employee may have insufficient resources. Similarly, the organization's overall strategies may be unrealistic or lack sufficient resources.

A performance development plan for an employee or group of employees can also be initiated in a variety of other situations, such as:

◆ When a performance appraisal indicates that performance improvement is needed
◆ Needing to benchmark the status of improvement so far in a development effort
◆ As part of a professional development for the employee or group of employees
◆ As part of succession planning to help an employee become eligible for a planned change in role in the organization
◆ Piloting the operation of a new performance management system

Improving Employee Performance

Correcting and improving the employees' performance through constructive confrontation is one of the basic duties of any supervisor or manager. Here are some of the more important guidelines to follow:

1. Know the attitudes and personality traits of the individual you are confronting.
2. Make sure that your own attitude is one of genuine helpfulness. If you are criticizing only to show your authority, you will not be successful. Never confront in anger. Always allow yourself time to calm down and think coolly before approaching someone regarding improvement of performance.
3. Gather all the facts first. If possible, find the cause of the behavior or error before you talk with the individual. Do not embarrass yourself by reprimanding an employee before making sure of the facts. Errors are often due to factors beyond the employee's control. Once you have gathered the facts, don't make snap judgments. Give the employee a fair hearing and let them tell their side of the story fully. Most importantly, listen attentively to the story because it might reveal important points that you might otherwise have overlooked.
4. Share the responsibility for an error. A good supervisor/manager tries to let the employee save face. Your job is to correct and improve behavior and performance, not embarrass the employee.
5. Do not belittle the employee. Personal abuse wounds the ego to the extent that it becomes impossible to listen to your suggestions with an open mind, thereby frustrating your purpose. By contrast, constructive suggestions will motivate an employee to improve.
6. Be tactful and unemotional. Have patience. Never use sarcasm or ridicule.
7. People respond much better if they believe that their supervisor/manager has faith in them and thinks they have the ability and intelligence to do the job correctly. Don't seek to establish blame. Seek the cause of the error or action with the employee. Make the cause clear. Show the way to eliminate it and how to substitute the right action. Explain how and why the work must be done in the manner expected.

INDIVIDUAL TASKS AND REFLECTIONS

29.1 Your Most Recent Performance Review

Consider your most recent performance review. How was it conducted? What was your response? How did you feel toward the person conducting the review? How did you feel after the review?

29.2 The Most Recent Review You Gave

Consider the most recent performance review you gave. How did you conduct it? What was the response of the person you were reviewing? How did you feel toward the person? How did you feel after the review? Are you aware of how the other person felt?

29.3 How do you do it?

Consider how you give criticism of performance.

29.4 Skills of a Performance Reviewer

In your opinion, what are the skills necessary for someone giving a performance review?

WORKING

WITH OTHERS

29.5 The Next Performance Review

Consider the next performance review you are to give. Prepare a self-assessment sheet and complete it when you have finished the review. What skills should you improve upon? How are you going to improve on them?

WORKING

WITH A MENTOR

29.6 Review by Your Mentor

Role play a performance review with you in the role of being reviewed by your mentor. Complete an assessment of their skills and discuss it with them.

29.7 Reviewing the Mentor

Role play a performance review with you in the role of reviewing your mentor. Both complete an assessment at the end. Discuss. Work toward an action plan for improving your performance review skills.

DEVELOPING

OTHERS

29.8 Performance Review Analysis

Introduce the subject of performance management. Discuss, as a group, what this means for the person being reviewed and the person doing the review.

29.9 Performance Review Role Play

Introduce the subject of performance management. Brainstorm the skills necessary for a performance review. Divide the learners into groups of three—two to role play, with the third providing feedback. All three should take each role in turn. Reconvene the larger group to discuss.

29.10 Performance Management of the Facilitator

This exercise needs to be done near the end of the session. Ask two volunteers to review your performance—one acting as reviewer and the other as observer, providing feedback. Discuss in the whole group.

RECOMMENDED

HRD PRESS TITLES

Situational Performance Improvement, 200 pp.
50 Activities for Performance Appraisal Training, 350 pp.

INTRODUCTION

Some Physical Symptoms of Stress

- ◆ Headaches
- ◆ Muscular aches and pains
- ◆ Fatigue
- ◆ Breathlessness

- ◆ Frequent infections
- ◆ Muscular twitches
- ◆ Skin irritations
- ◆ Palpitations

Some Behavioral Symptoms of Stress

- ◆ Accident proneness
- ◆ Loss of sex drive
- ◆ Restlessness

- ◆ Increased, or loss of, appetite
- ◆ Increased drinking/smoking
- ◆ Insomnia

Techniques for Managing Physical Stress

◆ **Breathing.** The deeper you breathe, the deeper you relax. Begin by breathing deeply and evenly. Inhale through your nose to a count of eight so that you fill up your lungs to their entire depth with air. Release the breath slowly through the mouth to a slow, deliberate count of twelve. As you breathe out, release the tension and worries that have accumulated. Continue to breathe in and out in this way for at least five minutes.

◆ **Progressive relaxation.** This technique involves tightening and releasing each part of the body by itself on both sides. For example, beginning with your lower body, tense your toes as tightly as possible and hold the tension. Then slowly release the toes. Now, move up to your feet. Tense them, hold the tension, then slowly release them. Continue the tensing and releasing until you reach the top of your head.

◆ **Autogenic relaxation.** This is similar to progressive relaxation in that the whole body is engaged, one part at a time. Rather than tensing the muscles, you say, "My toes are warm" three times and feel the blood moving to that part of the body to warm it. Then you move to the feet: "My feet are warm." You'll find that your muscles are more relaxed when they're warm.

◆ **Meditation.** Many different types can be used for relaxation, including transcendental meditation (TM), Kundalini meditation, and mindfulness meditation. Many forms of meditation require a teacher. However, you can meditate mindfully by following these steps.

1. Close your eyes.
2. Breathe normally and naturally, and gently notice your breathing.
3. Keep your focus on your breathing for the entire time period.

For maximum benefit, practice this meditation technique for 10 minutes.

◆ **Visualization.** Close your eyes and create a relaxing scene (the beach, the countryside, in a woods, by a lake, and so on) in your mind's eye. Create the scene with colors, sounds, aromas, tastes, textures, and emotion—and escape.

◆ **Stretching.** This helps reduce tension in the body's muscles. You can use the stretches you normally use before and after your aerobic or weight workout; however, you need to do them twice as slowly. Breathe deeply during the stretching. Inhale to begin the stretch and slowly exhale as you complete it.

◆ **Physical exercise.** This can help to burn off any excessive negative emotion.

◆ **Homeopathic remedies.** Homeopathic remedies that could help stress include Aconite for panic and Argentum Nit for overwork.

◆ **Herbal remedies.** Kalms is a natural herbal tranquilizer, while fever-few is good for migraines.

◆ **Music.** Listening to music is a great way to relax at any time. Research studies have found that listening to classical music also enhances creativity.

◆ **Nature.** Going out and getting in touch with nature is both enjoyable and refreshing, and the fresh air invigorates the body's cells.

◆ **Yoga.** There are many types of yoga—Hatha, Ivengar, Kundalini, and so on. Hatha is perhaps the most relaxing of them all since the postures are stretches that are held for an extended time and are coordinated with the breathing. Yoga is taught in adult education classes, health clubs, and yoga centers.

◆ **Massage.** This is an excellent way of releasing tension in the muscles and toxins in the body. There are various massage techniques, including sports, deep tissue, and neuromuscular.

Eating Habits

When you are stressed, you will eat on the run or perhaps not at all. Make sure that you make time for food and eat slowly. We are not talking about diet here, but an all-round healthy eating regime which, without you even trying, will be low in fat and high in fiber. Ultimately, a little of what you like does you good. There is no point in eating and drinking all the right things if you die of boredom along the way! A general guide could be as follows:

◆ Limit your intake of salt.
◆ Eat bananas, kiwi fruit, celery, grapes, lettuce, cinnamon, barley, brewer's yeast, oats, and basil, all of which help lower stress levels.
◆ Increase your intake of low-fat foods such as pasta, bread, white meat, vegetables, fruit, and salad.
◆ Minimize your intake of sugar and refined carbohydrates.
◆ If you have low blood sugar, follow a high-protein/low-carbohydrate diet with small, frequent meals.
◆ Avoid, where possible, alcohol, antibiotics, coffee, tea, and sleeping pills, all of which destroy Vitamin B which is vital to the nervous system.
◆ Try garlic, pumpkin seeds, and sunflower seeds for an energy boost.
◆ Eat avocados, lentils, raspberries, and spinach to counteract fatigue.
◆ Take ginseng. Siberian helps focus the mind and Korean boosts physical energy.
◆ Take calcium, magnesium, zinc, and vitamin B and C to help the nervous system.

> Constant work leads to burnout. Give yourself occasional treats, have relaxing interests, and take regular breaks. Plan some idleness every day. Find a private retreat, either in your mind, your home, or at the health club.

INDIVIDUAL TASKS AND REFLECTIONS

30.1 Physical Well-Being Questionnaire

Complete the following questionnaire:

Physical Well-Being	Yes (✓)	No (✓)	Sometimes (✓)
I have a balanced daily diet of proteins and fiber.			
My weight is appropriate for my age and height.			
I drink at least 64 ounces of water per day.			
I drink no more than two bottles of beer or two glasses of liquor/wine daily.			
I take care of my appearance.			
I walk at least one mile a day.			
I take part in non-competitive games or sports on a weekly basis.			
I practice deep breathing.			
I spend time in the fresh air.			
I practice muscular relaxation.			
I practice meditation.			
I take herbal or homeopathic remedies to alleviate stress-related symptoms.			

30.2 Physical and Behavioral Stress Symptoms

Consider your physical and behavioral stress symptoms over the past three months and complete the following.

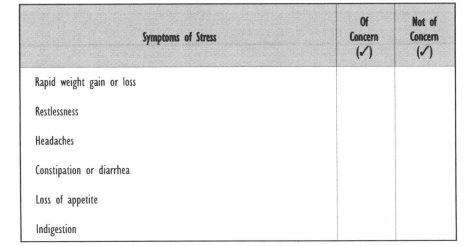

Symptoms of Stress	Of Concern (✓)	Not of Concern (✓)
Rapid weight gain or loss		
Restlessness		
Headaches		
Constipation or diarrhea		
Loss of appetite		
Indigestion		

(continued)

(continued)

Symptoms of Stress	Of Concern (✓)	Not of Concern (✓)
Frequent infections		
Bad driving		
Overeating		
Palpitations		
Voice tremor		
Tight jaw		
Accident-proneness		
Breathlessness		
Excessive sweating		
Increase in smoking		
Muscular twitches		
Loss of or excessive interest in sex		
Skin irritations		
Tiredness		
Increased intake of alcohol		
Vague aches and pains		
Disturbed sleep		

30.3 Relaxation Techniques

Consider the following:

Relaxation Techniques	Enjoy (✓)	Don't Enjoy (✓)	Would Like to Do More Of/Try (✓)
Deep breathing			
Muscular relaxation			
Meditation			

(continued)

(continued)

Relaxation Techniques	Enjoy (✓)	Don't Enjoy (✓)	Would Like to Do More Of/Try (✓)
Exercise			
Taking herbal/homeopathic remedies to alleviate stress-related symptoms			
Listening to music			
Communing with nature			
Yoga			
Massage			
Healthy eating			

WORKING WITH OTHERS

WORKING WITH A MENTOR

DEVELOPING OTHERS

30.4 Stressbuster Group

Get together with a few colleagues and start up a weekly/lunchtime stressbuster group.

30.5 Links in Stress

Consider your physical and behavioral stress symptoms and identify those that give you concern. Discuss with your mentor the situations or times when these symptoms seem worse. Identify links between situations and people and your physical stress responses. Work toward an action plan of dealing with both any identifiable root causes and your physical stress symptoms.

30.6 Stability Zones and Rituals

Introduce the subject of physical stress management. Explain that stability zones are those physical areas where an individual may be able to relax, feel safe, and be able to forget about worries—for example, the beach or the pub. Explain that rituals are enjoyable routines that individuals may have—for example, hobbies, Sunday outings, and so on. Divide the learners into small groups of four to discuss their stability zones and rituals. Reconvene the whole group to brainstorm ideas.

30.7 Forehead Massage

Ask the group to work in pairs. One sits with the other standing behind them. Demonstrate and then take them through the following: "Hold your palms against the other person's forehead for a few moments. Cover the forehead with the hands. Let the fingers spread. Apply no pressure. Pause as long as it seems OK. Let your partner grow used to your touch. Focus on your breathing and make sure you feel relaxed. First, mentally divide the forehead into horizontal strips about half an inch wide. Now begin to massage the center of the forehead just below the hairline with the balls of your thumbs. Glide both thumbs at once in both directions outward along the top-most strip. Continue toward the temples and end there by moving your thumbs in a circle about half an inch wide. Then without taking your hands off the forehead, return to the center of the forehead and begin again—the next strip down. Work progressively downward, ending with a strip just above your partner's eyebrows and a final circle on the temples."

30.8 Foot Massage

Ask the group to work in pairs, sitting opposite each other, with one person's feet resting on the other's lap. (This could be done with one person lying on the floor and the other sitting at their feet or one person lying on the floor with the other sitting on a chair at the feet.) Demonstrate and then take them through the following: "Massage the sole of the foot with tips of thumbs. Press hard as if you were putting a drawing pin into a piece of wood. Press everywhere. Work slowly over the sole. Then lift the foot slightly and work the sides of the heel all the way to the anklebone and around that. You can then work on the toes and the top of the foot. Do the same with the other foot."

RECOMMENDED

HRD PRESS TITLES

······························

50 Activities for Managing Stress, 303 pp.
The Complete Guide to Wellness, 600 pp.
Personal Stress and Well-being Assessment, 16 pp.

INTRODUCTION

Planning is the start of the process by which you turn dreams into achievements. It helps you avoid the trap of working extremely hard, but achieving little. The process helps you to:

◆ Take stock of your current position and identify precisely what is to be achieved
◆ Work out the process of getting there in the most effective, efficient way possible
◆ Detail precisely and price the who, what, when, where, why, and how of achieving your target
◆ Assess the impact of your plan on your organization (or your life)
◆ Evaluate whether the effort, costs, and implications of achieving your plan are worth the achievement
◆ Consider the control mechanisms that are needed to achieve your plan and keep it on course

You may have heard of one interpretation of the Pareto principle: that 80 percent of a job is completed in 20 percent of the effort. By thinking and planning, we can reverse this to 20 percent of the effort achieving 80 percent of the results. When you are about to plan a project, you face problems and risks. These might be:

◆ Risks to status, reputation, your bank balance, career, or a significant other
◆ Problems of lack of resources, with added risks of wasting limited resources, whether money, time, or power
◆ The risk to your self-esteem if you fail

Planning is the process by which you determine whether you should attempt the task, work out the most effective way of reaching your target, and prepare to overcome unexpected difficulties with adequate resources. By applying the planning process effectively, you can:

◆ Avoid wasting effort—it is easy to spend a great deal of time on activities that, in retrospect, prove to be irrelevant to the success of the project
◆ Take into account all factors, and focus on the critical ones, ensuring that you are prepared for all reasonable eventualities
◆ Be aware of all changes that will need to be made—if you know these, then you can assess in advance the likelihood of being able to make those changes, and take action to ensure that they will be successful
◆ Gather the resources needed

There are a number of reasons why planning does not happen:

◆ **Crisis management.** An organization can be so deeply embroiled in crisis management that it does not have the time to plan.
◆ **Apathy.** People may simply not be bothered to devote the time to thinking through a plan.

◆ **Experience.** As people amass experience, they may find that they rely increasingly less on formalized planning—and this may be appropriate. It is easy, however, to overestimate experience.

◆ **Opposition to expense.** Time spent on planning is an investment. Some organizations are culturally opposed to spending resources. Sometimes this may be appropriate, but often it is shortsighted.

◆ **The "get stuck in" culture.** An organization may oppose planning as a waste of time. This may be the case where either the organization is doing a very simple job, or where managers are so experienced in their jobs that they do not recognize that they are planning. This approach cripples inexperienced staff by denying them the benefits of planning, and puts more work on experienced managers.

◆ **Lack of commitment and resistance to change.** People might not see the benefits of the planning process, might believe that there is no need to plan, or might perceive the situation to be satisfactory as it stands.

◆ **Bad planning experience.** People might have had previous bad experiences of plans that have been long, cumbersome, impractical, or inflexible.

◆ **Fear of failure.** Not taking action carries little risk of failure unless a problem is urgent and pressing. Nevertheless, whenever something worthwhile is attempted, there is some risk of failure.

Planning is best thought of as a cycle. Once a plan has been devised, it should be evaluated. This analysis might show that the plan may cause unwanted consequences, may cost too much, or may simply not work. In this case, the planning process will have to loop back to an earlier stage, or even be abandoned altogether—the outcome of the planning may simply be that it is best to do nothing! The stages of the planning cycle are illustrated below:

Analysis of current position

Identify aim

Explore options

Detailed planning

Plan evaluation

Plan implementation

Closure of plan

Feedback

Analysis of current position

Finally, there are several pertinent questions to ask when setting a goal for planning:

◆ Is it measurable and verifiable?
◆ Can those who must implement it easily understand it?
◆ Is the goal a realistic and attainable one that still represents a challenge?
◆ Will the result, when achieved, justify the time and resources required to achieve it?
◆ Is it consistent with the organization's policies and practices?
◆ Can accountability for final results be clearly established?

INDIVIDUAL TASKS AND REFLECTIONS
....

31.1 Planning Skills

In your opinion, what are the necessary skills for effective planning?

31.2 Bad Planning

Consider something that you have planned in the past that went badly. What was your original desired outcome? What was your process for working toward it? What was the final outcome? With hindsight, what could you have done differently?

31.3 Good Planning

Consider something you have planned in the past that went well. What was your original desired outcome? What was your process for working toward it? What was the final outcome?

31.4 Six-Month Action Plan

Develop an action plan for one important objective you could achieve within six months from now. Write your objective at the top of the page and then record your thoughts under the following three headings: action, completion date, review/success measures. Make your actions clearly identifiable and measurable.

WORKING WITH OTHERS
....

31.5 Team Planning

Identify a team/group project that requires you to be involved in planning. Create an assessment sheet and complete it as you go through the planning process. You could share this assessment with the other members.

WORKING WITH A MENTOR
....

31.6 Skills Development

Identify your strong and weak planning skills. Discuss with your mentor and formulate an action plan for skills development. Review.

31.7 Assessing Your Mentor

With your mentor, identify and assess their strong and weak planning skills. What can you learn from them?

DEVELOPING OTHERS
....

31.8 Planning Skills Analysis

Introduce the subject of planning skills. Brainstorm the skills necessary for effective planning. Ask the learners to identify one good and one bad planning experience they have been involved with and to identify the skills used (or not used).

31.9 Rating Planning Skills

Introduce the subject of planning skills. Brainstorm the skills necessary to planning and agree on a group checklist. Ask each learner to write down the list and to rate their planning skills (good, needs improving). Now, ask the learners to form groups of three to focus on two areas that need improvement and to discuss ways of achieving this.

31.10 Paper Plane

Introduce the subject of planning skills. Divide the learners into groups of four and give them the task of making a paper airplane. You could award a prize to the one that has the longest flight. Reconvene the whole group and discuss the planning process that each small group went through to reach their objective.

RECOMMENDED

HRD PRESS TITLES

The Project Manager's Partner, Second Edition; 160 pp.

INTRODUCTION

Flipcharts

Flipcharts are the perfect size for presentations delivered before small groups of 35 people or less. Listed below are some guidelines for using flipcharts to their best advantage:

◆ The best flipchart stands have clamps at the top and will hold most types of flipchart pads. Most allow you to hang your flipcharts, although some stands will only allow you to prop them up. Make sure that the flipcharts you use will fit the flipchart stand you will be using.

◆ Flipchart pads are available either as plain sheets or with preprinted grid lines. Pads with grid lines make it easier to draw straight lines and keep your text aligned. Also, make sure that the pad has perforations at the top to allow for easy removal of sheets.

◆ It is best to initially design your charts on paper before drawing them on the actual flipchart pad. Lightly write out your text in pencil before using flipchart marker pens. This will allow you to make any adjustments to text spacing and to any figures you will be drawing. The chart will be easier to read if you use upper and lower case letters. Have no more than seven words on each line and no more than seven lines to a sheet.

◆ Use flipchart marker pens, rather than regular magic markers, as these will not bleed through the paper. Avoid using yellow, pink, or orange because these are difficult for the audience to see. Also, avoid using too many colors—one dark color and one accent color works best. You can lightly pencil in any notes you need next to key points and perhaps also a note as to what is on the next sheet—the audience won't be able to see them.

> The purpose of using visual aids is to enhance your presentation, not upstage it.

Using Overhead Transparencies

While the current trend in the training industry is heading toward the use of LCD projector technology, the overhead projector is still one of the most popular presentation devices used today. Here are some tips:

◆ Practice giving your presentation using your visual aids to check how well they project.

◆ Standing to one side will allow the audience to see you as the presenter and will prevent you from blocking their view of your visual aid.

◆ Do not face the projected image on the screen. Always face your audience.

◆ Place your overhead projector on a table that is sufficiently low so as not to block you or the screen. Place a small table next to the overhead projector so that you can stack your transparencies before and after you use them.

◆ Place your screen on a diagonal to the room instead of facing straight ahead to ensure that you do not block your audience's view. Also, have the top of the screen tilted forward toward the overhead projector, if possible, to prevent the keystone effect (where the top of the image is larger than the bottom).

Computer LCD Display Projectors

Today's laptop computers coupled with many of the common software packages offer flexibility to the presenter. However, this presentation technique does require the use of a computer and the necessary technical interfaces if it is to work properly. Here are some elements to consider when using LCD display projectors:

◆ Read the LCD projector operating manual. Not all LCD projectors work in the same way and each have their own unique operating requirements. Make sure that your computer can be properly interacted with the LCD projector and familiarize yourself thoroughly with the projector before using it during your actual presentation.
◆ Spend some time making sure that you know how to set up the LCD projector with your computer and other computers. Set up the LCD projector in the presentation environment you will be using, if possible.
◆ Before the presentation, allow yourself plenty of time to set up your computer and the LCD projector.
◆ Check your presentation color combinations. Some colors and color combinations do not project well.
◆ Check the font size you are using. Make sure that you are using the proper text size for the distance you will be projecting your slides.

The Speaker and the Message

One of the principal components of any speech or presentation is the actual speaker. Many presenters today put so much effort into the visual aids that they forget that these are simply that—aids to the speaker.

The presenter's message refers to everything a speaker says or does, both verbally and nonverbally. The verbal component may be analyzed in terms of three basic elements:

1. **Content.** Research your topic thoroughly. Decide on how much to say about each subject. Then decide on the actual sequence you will use. It is important that you consider the audience's needs and time factors as the content of your speech or presentation is prepared and presented.
2. **Style.** The manner in which you present the content of your speech is termed your "style." Most presentations fall between the formal and informal and, in every case, the style should be determined by what is appropriate to the speaker, the audience, as well as to the occasion and setting.
3. **Structure.** The structure of a message is its organization that, in most cases, should comprise:

   —Introduction
   —Body
   —Conclusion

   The introduction should include an opening, such as a quote or shocking statistic; an agenda; and a statement of the purpose or main message of your presentation.

   The body should include your main ideas and points that support your main message.

The conclusion should include a summary of your main points; a closing attention-grabber and time for questions and answers, if appropriate.

When presentations are poorly organized, the impact of the message is reduced and the audience is less likely to accept the speaker or the speaker's ideas.

There are also five important don'ts to observe when making presentations:

1. **Don't** try to fool the audience.
2. **Don't** read the presentation from your text.
3. **Don't** use "inside" stories.
4. **Don't** make your audience the butt of a joke.
5. **Don't** exceed your time limit.

Feedback

Feedback is the process through which the speaker receives information about how their message has been received by the listeners and, in turn, responds to those cues. You can ask your audience questions and even ask them what their understanding is of the point you have just made. Watch for nonverbal clues from your audience and be prepared to respond to your audience's reactions throughout your presentation. It is your responsibility to provide the information that your audience needs to hear.

Room Layout and Strategic Seating

If you are responsible for laying out a room or want to position yourself strategically, the following setups might help:

To promote discussion, you could use a conference-style approach for under 20 people . . .

or a horseshoe for under 30 people.

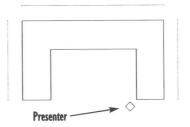

For any size groups, you could use either the theater-style . . .

Presenter ⟶ ◇

or the classroom style.

Presenter ⟶ ◇

INDIVIDUAL TASKS AND REFLECTIONS

32.1 A Good Presentation

Identify a presentation you have attended in the past that you considered to be good. Why was it good? How did the presenter come across? What aids did they use? How did you feel in response to them? What did you gain from the presentation? How did you feel at the end?

32.2 A Bad Presentation

Identify a presentation you have attended in the past that you considered to be bad. Why was it bad? How did the presenter come across? What aids did they use? How did you feel in response to them? What did you gain from the presentation? How did you feel at the end? If you were the presenter, what might you have done differently?

32.3 Given the Best

Identify a presentation that you have given in the past that you considered to be good. Why was it good? How did you come over to the listeners? What aids did you use? How did the audience react? How did you feel in response to the audience? What did you gain from the presentation? What do you think the audience gained from your presentation?

32.4 Given the Worst

Identify a presentation you have given in the past that you considered to be bad. Why was it bad? How did you come over to the listeners? What aids did you use? How did the audience react? How did you feel in response to the audience? What did you gain from the presentation? What do you think the audience gained from your presentation? With hindsight, what might you have done differently?

WORKING

WITH OTHERS

32.5 Presentation Self-Assessment

Identify a situation where you will be giving a presentation to others. Prepare a presentation assessment sheet that you can give to the audience at the end. Analyze the feedback as a self-assessment exercise.

32.6 Assessing Others

Identify a situation where you will be attending a presentation. Prepare a presentation assessment sheet that you can complete as an assessment exercise. If you had given the presentation, what might you have done differently and why? If appropriate, give feedback (other than what you might have done differently) to the person who gave the presentation.

WORKING

WITH A MENTOR

32.7 Presenting Before Your Mentor

Identify a situation where you will be giving a presentation to others. Prepare a presentation assessment sheet that you can complete as a self-assessment exercise. Ask your mentor to attend and give them the sheet to complete. On completion, discuss ways in which you might improve your presentation skills.

32.8 Mentor Presentation

Attend a presentation given by your mentor. Prepare a presentation assessment sheet that you can complete at the end and then discuss.

DEVELOPING

OTHERS

32.9 Five-Minute Presentation

Introduce the subject of presentation skills. Brainstorm basic presentation skills. Brainstorm the content of a simple presentation assessment sheet—for example, was it easy to hear the presenter speak? Have a flipchart handy. Demonstrate how to use a flipchart correctly and how *not* to use a flipchart. Ask each learner to prepare a five-minute presentation (ten minutes if you have more time) on one of their interests. They should use the flipchart at least once during the exercise. As each learner presents, the rest of the group completes the presentation assessment sheet. The group then gives the presenter feedback after each presentation.

32.10 Room Layouts

Introduce the subject of presentation skills and room layouts. Experiment with different layouts and try out mini-presentations to see what the layouts feel like from the perspectives of both the presenters and audience.

RECOMMENDED

HRD PRESS TITLES

The Manager's Pocket Guide to Public Presentations, 128 pp.

33 Psychological Stress Management

INTRODUCTION

A healthy amount of stress can make us perform at optimum efficiency. So how can we thrive on stress in a positive way instead of feeling overwhelmed by it? First, you need to become aware of your own specific stressors and how they make you think, feel, and behave. Then you can do something about it.

Psychological stress management involves:

◆ Setting realistic objectives in your life (and at work)
◆ Learning how to delegate
◆ Time management
◆ Self-organization
◆ Saying "no"
◆ Expressing your feelings
◆ Asking for support
◆ Managing your anger
◆ Developing assertive behavior
◆ Improving your decision-making skills

A stressed out person is usually trying hard to be in control, but does not always succeed. Life will always contain a certain amount of stress. Indeed, a certain amount of stress is healthy because it stimulates adrenaline. However, the trick is to know when stress is taking control of you as opposed to you being in control of stress.

Nowadays, we hear a great deal about burnout—but what exactly is it? In the current working climate, employees either seem to have too much work or not enough. Burnout is a symptom of too much—too much work, too much pressure—resulting in overload. If you feel that you are in a burnout situation, you need to stop and consider what is happening to you and why. Then you need to do something to change the situation—or remove yourself from the situation if it doesn't seem likely to change. We often knee-jerk our way through life, reacting rather than acting. If you are to prevent burnout, make conscious choices and be proactive in managing your life.

Psychological Signs of Stress	
◆ Loss of confidence	◆ Fussiness
◆ Irritability	◆ Depression
◆ Apprehension	◆ Alienation
◆ Apathy	◆ Worrying
◆ Muddled thinking	◆ Impaired judgment
◆ Nightmares	◆ Indecision
◆ Negativity	◆ Hasty decision making

Stress is an individual's response to an external event. It is not the event in itself that causes it. If you can control your levels of response, you can control stress. If you cannot change the circumstances, then you must change yourself and your perception of the event. Psychologists have suggested that there are two types of people in terms of their responses to stress:

◆ **Type A.** Impatient, aggressive, driven, distorted sense of time, fast talker, and mover. High risk of heart problems. The positive interpretation of this type of response could be expressive, in control, and sociable.
◆ **Type B.** Relaxed, unhurried, non-competitive, and non-aggressive. The negative interpretation of this type of response could be overcontrolled and inhibited.

Do you recognize the character called Inner Driver from your subconscious self? Your Inner Driver tells you to "get on; get somewhere; do things; be there; do this; do that; come on."

You have an *active* Inner Driver if you are:

◆ Ambitious
◆ Very busy
◆ Self-assertive
◆ A workaholic
◆ An insomniac
◆ Exhausted

You have an *overdeveloped* Inner Driver if you are:

◆ Anxious to "make it"
◆ Pushy
◆ All work and no play
◆ Lacking in time
◆ Ill
◆ Opposed to making time for recreation

The Inner Driver can fuel unhealthy stress levels by telling us to do more, be more, and have more. The Inner Driver is an inner voice that provides drive, but can also drive us over the edge.

Lines and Pressure Statements

Have you ever found yourself in a situation where you felt pressured to do something you didn't want to do? Lines are the pressure statements that people throw at you when they want you to do something. In some situations—such as when you know there is a safety or health risk—the best response is "no" and you don't have to explain. At other times, it is useful to have a supply of good comebacks to get someone who is pressuring you off your back. The more frequently you use comebacks, the easier it gets. First, you have to recognize when you're being given a line. A line might be:

◆ A statement that seems logical, but your intuition tells you something is not right
◆ A joke that leaves you feeling embarrassed or anxious

In these circumstances, you need a comeback. The following table shows how lines and comebacks work:

Examples of Lines	How the Line Works	Comebacks You Might Use
"You're acting like a scared kid!"	Tries to get you to change your mind by insulting or belittling you.	"I'm an adult, thank you. I can make up my own mind, and this just doesn't work!"
"What are you so worried about? Everyone else is doing it."	Appeals to your pride, sense of adventure, and desire to avoid embarrassment.	"That's great. Then you won't have any problem finding someone else to do it."
"That color suit makes you look like an over-ripe banana."	Makes you feel embarrassed and self-conscious.	"I like this color and I think it suits me. I agree it's not my best color but I think it's OK on me."

If you find yourself without a ready comeback, it's OK to say "no" without explanation.

Further Ways to Manage Your Psychological Stress

◆ Become knowledgeable about stress:
  —Identify your principal sources of stress.
  —Anticipate stressful periods and plan for them.
  —Develop constructive stress-busting strategies and use them.

◆ Come to terms with your feelings:
  —Acknowledge your feelings to yourself and share them with others.
  —Learn to adapt.
  —Let go of perfectionism.

◆ Develop effective behavioral skills:
  —Say "will not" as opposed to "cannot."
  —Acknowledge problems as soon as they appear.
  —Make space for free time.
  —Learn to say "no."
  —Be assertive.
  —Take responsibility for your thoughts, feelings, and behaviors.
  —Become more tolerant.
  —Set realistic goals in your life.
  —Think positively.
  —Become less ambitious.
  —Distance yourself from it—see the situation in two years from now.
  —Delay it—reserve a set worrying time for say 15 minutes every Friday afternoon.

◆ Establish and maintain a strong support network:
  —Rid yourself of damaging relationships.
  —Ask for direct help and be receptive when it is offered.

◆ Develop a lifestyle that will strengthen you against stress:
  —Meditate.
  —Improve your nutrition.
  —Let go of unimportant issues.
  —Learn to physically relax and breathe better.
  —Get into your body and out of your head—take more exercise.
  —Seek out variety in your life.
  —Plan your use of time on a daily and long-term basis.
  —Laugh at life (and yourself) a little more.

◆ Develop a spiritual philosophy of life:
—Maintain a sense of proportion.
—Establish a sense of purpose in your life.
—Have faith in yourself.
—Live in the present.

INDIVIDUAL TASKS AND REFLECTIONS

33.1 Psychological Well-Being

Assess your psychological well-being by completing the following checklist:

Psychological Well-Being	Yes (✔)	No (✔)	Sometimes (✔)
I have close friends.			
I ask for support when I need it.			
I give myself treats.			
I have interests that enable me to learn new skills.			
I have a sense of self-direction.			
I have a good image of myself.			
I can let go appropriately.			
I am emotionally secure.			

33.2 Mental and Emotional Stress Symptoms

Use the following checklist to consider your mental and emotional stress symptoms for the past three months:

Symptoms Experienced in the Past Three Months	Yes (✔)	No (✔)
Feelings of dissatisfaction		
Indecision		
Irritability		
Hasty decisions		
Reduced self-esteem		
Failing memory		
Demotivation		
Impaired judgment		

(continued)

(continued)

Symptoms Experienced in the Past Three Months	Yes (✔)	No (✔)
Depression		
Loss of concentration		
Loss of confidence		
Negative thoughts		
Overfussiness		
Bad dreams		
Tension		
Worry		
Cynicism		
Making more mistakes		
Feeling drained		
Feeling alienated		
Muddled thinking		
Anxiety		
Feeling of pointlessness		

WORKING WITH OTHERS

33.3 Comeback Time

Be aware of how people try to manipulate or control your actions to suit their purposes. Practice using the comeback technique when appropriate.

33.4 Support Network

Consider your personal and professional support network. Are there any damaging relationships you need to shed? Do you know who you can go to for help? Are you able to ask for and make use of help when offered? Identify two people at work and two people outside of work who you could approach.

WORKING WITH A MENTOR

33.5 Inner Driver

Consider the power of your Inner Driver. Discuss with your mentor ways in which you can control it.

33.6 Lifestyle Changes

Consider your lifestyle and how that contributes to your psychological stress. Discuss with your mentor and develop a lifestyle that will strengthen you against stress.

33.7 Feedback on Stress Style

Analyze how you see your psychological stress symptoms (and coping strategies). Ask your mentor to provide you with their perception. Discuss. Work toward creating a plan to develop effective coping strategies.

DEVELOPING
OTHERS
....

33.8 Current Stress Strategies

Introduce the subject of psychological stress management. Brainstorm emotional and mental stress symptoms. Brainstorm possible coping strategies. Ask the learners to identify a current major source of stress and to identify three constructive stress-busting strategies to deal with it. Divide them into groups of four to discuss. Reconvene the whole group and add the contributed strategies to the original list.

33.9 Group Discussion

Introduce the subject of psychological stress management. Discuss either in the whole group or in small groups some or all of the techniques below:

◆ Acknowledging your feelings to yourself and others
◆ Letting go of perfectionism
◆ Learning to say "no"
◆ Being assertive
◆ Taking responsibility for your thoughts, feelings, and behaviors
◆ Becoming more tolerant
◆ Setting realistic goals in your life
◆ Thinking positively
◆ Becoming less ambitious
◆ Maintaining a sense of proportion
◆ Establishing a sense of purpose in your life
◆ Living in the present

33.10 Letting Go of Stress

Introduce the subject of psychological stress management. Open a discussion on what we are trying to protect through our stress reactions. Then pull in other strands, such as how we learn to react to stress, choosing to let go of our mindset, how our defense system creates illusions, and so on.

RECOMMENDED
HRD PRESS TITLES
....

50 Activities for Managing Stress, 303 pp.
The Complete Guide to Wellness, 600 pp.
Personal Stress and Well-being Assessment, 16 pp.

34 Recognizing and Expressing Your Emotions

INTRODUCTION

Your feelings tell you, and others, what you really care about, and there's no right or wrong in how you feel. Events and situations trigger feelings, and it seems that the brain has little control over when a feeling will develop or what it will be. You do, however, have control over what your feelings are telling you. Putting names to your feelings and taking time to reflect on what they mean help you make good decisions. Once you have decided how important a situation is to you, you may have a different feeling about it the next time it occurs.

We need to understand that other people are not responsible for our feelings. Others can say things to us or behave toward us in a particular way that causes us to experience a feeling. But only we are responsible for that feeling. Equally, you're not responsible for other people's feelings either, even though people might try to tell you otherwise—for example, "You make me so angry!" No one can *make* you feel anything.

Denying feelings leads to confusion, resentment, and physical stress. Even intense and uncomfortable feelings are softened when they are acknowledged without self-criticism or self-blame. Allowing yourself to experience uncomfortable emotions means that you are also freer to experience joy and peace. Feelings range from mild to very strong. Consider anger. What irritates you a little? What really makes you mad? It's healthy to feel the whole range of emotions. Each person's emotional responses are unique. And the more you understand, accept, and express your emotions, the easier it is to accept strong emotions in other people, even when you disagree.

Moderate emotion might not call for any action. It might be enough to:

◆ Be aware of the emotion and the circumstances in which it occurred
◆ Label it for yourself
◆ Express your feelings to someone else

> Tuning in to a positive emotion early on can lead you to exciting opportunities.
>
> Tuning in to an uncomfortable emotion before it becomes intense can prevent escalation of both the feeling and concern.

If the same emotion recurs increasingly powerfully with the same situation, it's a stronger signal that something needs your attention. You know when a feeling is really strong because there is usually some kind of physical reaction. When feelings are intense, you need to find a way to step back so that you can work out what your feelings mean and decide what to do. For example:

◆ If you feel sad, what is it that you have lost that means so much to you? How can you comfort yourself through this time? Do you need to ask for help?
◆ If you feel angry, what is it that's bugging you? Is it something you can change or fix? If not, do you need to rethink your view of the situation and how you will respond to it in future?

◆ When you're happy, enjoy it! You deserve good times. Then ask yourself "What is it about this situation that makes me feel so good? How can I recreate that kind of situation?"

◆ If you feel afraid, what do you need to do to feel safe? Could you decrease your worry by planning ahead a little better next time? Do you need to talk positively to yourself to get through a stressful time?

◆ And when you feel guilty, have you done something that you know is wrong? Do you need to apologize or take steps to make amends? If you don't believe what you've done is wrong, what reason have you to feel guilty?

Express the feeling. Tears and laughter are great releases. Music, art, talking things over with a friend, or writing in a journal are other possibilities. Find your own personal ways of working through feelings.

Many people are uncomfortable with, or haven't had the opportunity to learn, positive ways to recognize and manage their emotions. Sometimes they cope by denying their feelings or shutting them down. They might block them with their intellect, with eating disorders, drugs, alcohol, cigarettes, or work. Sometimes they act on their emotions without thinking of the consequences, saying and doing things they later regret. You cannot always control what happens to you, but you can learn to interpret and manage your feelings.

Although psychologists and philosophers still debate which emotions are primary, Paul Ekman (1999) has identified four core emotions recognized in people of many cultures:

◆ **Sadness** helps you reflect on the significance of something you have lost, or something that has disappointed you; when you feel sad, it's natural to need to be alone. Solitude helps you work out the significance of the loss and learn from the experience. Withdrawing when you are sad protects you from further hurt until you feel stronger.

◆ **Anger** motivates you to change a situation or put something right. It may also be a cover for hurt and sadness; if issues are not addressed, unresolved anger may lead to long-term feelings of resentment, hostility, and even depression.

◆ **Joy** represents all the positive feelings that tell you what is working. Pay special attention to these feelings and recreate the circumstances where feelings of contentment, satisfaction, happiness, peace, and joy occur.

◆ **Fear** protects you from unsafe risks and tells you to be cautious or to prepare—it is a normal emotion in unfamiliar situations. However, it doesn't mean that you do not have the ability to do something. Fear may be realistic and appropriate to the risk of the situation at hand *or* it may get out of hand when a situation poses little or no real risk.

You experience the above emotions in varying combinations and intensities, as well as others such as surprise, excitement, love, disgust, and guilt. Problems arise when you use vague words or rely on body language to express feelings. Unclear words such as *upset* are confusing both to yourself and people around you because they can represent so many different feelings and intensities of feelings. Another habit we humans have is saying one thing while our body says another, sending other people conflicting messages.

Recognizing and accepting your emotions are stepping stones toward expressing them appropriately. When we feel comfortable with our own emotions, we will improve our relationships with others because we will be more at ease with their emotions, too.

INDIVIDUAL TASKS

AND REFLECTIONS

34.1 Strong Emotions

When was the last time you experienced a strong emotion? What was it like for you?

34.2 The Body–Mind Link

Notice how your body reacts when you experience a strong feeling. What happens? Where does it happen? How does your body feel?

34.3 Gender Feelings

Traditionally, we're taught that women are over emotional and men don't show their emotions. Reflect on this society-based belief and consider whether you've been gender-influenced with regard to how you express your feelings.

34.4 Early Influences

How might you have been influenced by your childhood role models with regard to expressing your emotions? How did they express emotions to each other and to you? Were you encouraged to express your emotions when younger?

WORKING

WITH OTHERS

34.5 Situations and Feelings

What types of situation evoke strong feelings in you—for example, anxiety or anticipation?

34.6 People and Feelings

What people evoke strong feelings in you? What sort of feelings do you have? Why do you think you have them?

34.7 Act or react?

When you are with others and you experience a strong emotion, what are your thoughts and how do you behave? How in control are you? Do you tend to deal with the situation emotionally or intellectually?

WORKING

WITH A MENTOR

34.8 The Mentor Relationship

How does working with your mentor make you feel? Discuss.

34.9 Daily Feelings

Keep a daily record of your emotional responses to events and people. Notice your emotional reactions and the kinds of people and situation that evoke them. Discuss with your mentor. Focus on and identify the feelings. Talk them through with your mentor so that you can reach some level of self-understanding.

DEVELOPING

OTHERS

34.10 Feeling Cards

Cut up a number of small pieces of card or paper and write an "emotional" word—for example *sad, joyful, depressed, spontaneous*—on each one. Write down as many as you can, using an equal number of challenging and positive emotions. Divide the learners into smaller groups of between four and six and give one person in each group a pile of "emotion cards." Ask them to take a card in turn and, using the word written on it, express the statement "I felt [emotion] when [occurrence]." The objective of the exercise is to share feelings and to create a sense of group acceptance.

34.11 Learning About Feelings

Lead a group discussion on how we learn to identify and express our feelings.

34.12 Gender Differences

Lead a group discussion on the differences between how men and women deal with their feelings.

RECOMMENDED HRD PRESS TITLES

The Manager's Pocket Guide to Emotional Intelligence, 140 pp.
Giving and Receiving Performance Feedback, 200 pp.
Emotional Intelligence Style Profile, 16 pp.

35
Resolving Conflict

The art of resolving conflict is to help both parties win something. The basics of conflict management include:

◆ Acceptance that conflict is inevitable
◆ Knowing that conflict can be a catalyst for better ideas
◆ Digging out hidden agendas
◆ Ensuring that both sides see what they can gain from a compromise
◆ Helping parties in conflict maintain self-esteem

> Don't try to deduce other people's intentions from your own fears.

The first person to experience a rising conflict usually has the greatest opportunity to influence whether or not the conflict will escalate. Much happens in those first few moments when that one person realizes the possibility of loss (and every conflict represents a perceived potential loss of some kind). They can lower their guard in an attempt to foster a positive response to the other person. They can act in an open manner in an effort to find a compromise as events unfold. On the other hand, they can close up and look for more signs of disagreement. The second person in the situation can also use that pivotal point to stay open, even if the first person has already acted, but the second person's actions will have less influence over the situation.

> Connect with others through what they most value.

Suppose you are that first person to experience a rising conflict. You feel vulnerable and instinctively put your guard up. Because you are signaling that your position is weak, you are unwittingly guiding the energy of the ensuing disagreement to your most vulnerable areas. That is why, in that pivotal moment, making a choice to remain open serves not only to move you toward eventual resolution, but also to protect you. Instead of following your natural instinct to look for more adverse signals and prepare to defend yourself or retaliate, stay aware and open. You will then gain more information about the situation and more insight into the motivation and real meaning of the other person's actions.

In conflict, we usually become more intense about what we don't want, rather than what we do want. We simply react; we don't choose how we want to act. By so doing, we give our power away because we let others determine our behavior. It's always more productive to be proactive—to see how you can clear the air. If you steady yourself and decide to be proactive rather than reactive, you will be satisfied with the results and the ensuing relationship. The following is a brief summary of four key steps in resolving conflict:

◆ **Step 1.** In a moment of real or imagined confrontation, we can move into a negative reaction. At such moments, you need to slow down the process and seek clarity by asking yourself what you want. By thinking about your own needs, you blank out the resentment of the other party.

◆ **Step 2.** Ask yourself, "What is the other party's greatest need?" By taking the time for this step, you slow down the pace of the discussion.

◆ **Step 3.** Listen to the other party and demonstrate to them that you have heard their concerns. This is often the most crucial time in a conflict, when your actions can either spark escalation or initiate a cooling-off period.

◆ **Step 4.** When you propose a solution, prove that you are fair by addressing the other person's interests first. Describe, in their language, how they can benefit. Then you can discuss the benefits of such a resolution to yourself as well.

> Because we respond more strongly to the negative actions of people for whom we have strong feelings than to those of strangers, allow yourself more time to get back in balance in these cases.

So far, you have come up with a proposal that you think is fair to all parties. Before speaking about your own needs, you have addressed their needs first and worked through whatever obstacles have surfaced. Now it's time to make a firm offer.

> Everyone needs to feel heard before they'll listen.

Don't talk before you are prepared to reach agreement. If you start talking with the other person before you are ready to reach an agreement, you could end up with less than you want. Make sure that you have obtained what you want out of the situation and that the other person has felt heard. The more opportunities you provide for others to participate in a situation along the way, the more likely they will stay with you to ultimately find a solution.

When presenting your proposal, make sure your initial tone, gestures, and language show that you have good intentions. Don't raise your important points at the beginning of the discussion, nor at the end of the discussion. Waiting until the end can close off some of the best options for trade-offs. Reach agreement on your key items before you make any gesture toward finalizing agreement.

Ask another mutually respected person to mediate if necessary. A fair and neutral witness can make everyone involved in a conflict feel safer and more heard, especially when it's necessary to review items over which you have become deadlocked.

Be flexible in order to maintain the momentum toward a resolution. Observe how the others are reacting to you and your proposal. Stay flexible so that you can correct yourself and shift gears if necessary to make the situation feel safer and more fair. If feelings seem to be escalating or the other person appears to be shutting down, ask for suggestions and express your willingness to look at other options.

It's important to acknowledge the participation of others. Listen and thoroughly consider other people's opinions at the moment they are expressed. If you disagree immediately or counter with another suggestion, reactions will remain hardened long after this particular discussion. Mention that you respect the people who are important to the other side. Praise specific contributions the others have made and let them know you appreciate their efforts.

INDIVIDUAL TASKS AND REFLECTIONS

35.1 Your Behavior in Conflict

How do you tend to react when in conflict with another? How do you behave?

35.2 Others' Reaction to You

How do other people respond to you when in conflict with you?

35.3 True or false?

Consider the following statements. Are they true or false?

◆ It is never helpful to express anger when in conflict with others.
◆ No one individual knows the whole truth.
◆ One of the best ways to resolve conflict is to discuss it with a third party rather than with the person directly involved.
◆ People who try to handle conflicts cooperatively are likely to be taken advantage of.
◆ People can be ruled by their fears when in conflict.

35.4 Role Models and Conflict

How did your parents or other childhood role models deal with conflict? What behaviors and responses have you learned from them?

WORKING WITH OTHERS

WORKING WITH A MENTOR

35.5 Differences in Conflict

How do your conflict management skills differ when relating to a peer, a subordinate, and a superior?

35.6 Editing the Past

Discuss with your mentor a past conflict situation in which you have been involved that didn't have a satisfactory outcome for you. What was the conflict about? How did you react? How did you behave? How did other people react? What was the outcome? How might you have changed your behavior to reach the preferred outcome?

35.7 Skills Development

Identify conflict resolution skills that you need to work on and discuss with your mentor ways you might develop them.

35.8 Current Conflict Resolution

Identify a current relationship involving conflict. Discuss with your mentor what you want from the encounter and how you might work on this in a collaborative manner.

DEVELOPING OTHERS

35.9 Behaviors in Conflict

Introduce the subject of resolving conflict. Organize the learners into smaller groups and ask them to come up with a list of behaviors that are appropriate for resolving conflict and to prioritize them. Reconvene the whole group and discuss.

35.10 Role Play Conflict Resolution

Introduce the subject of resolving conflict. Choose two volunteers to role play their conflicts in front of the groups. Videotape the session. Ask the role-play participants to assess their conflict resolution skills, followed by feedback from you and the other learners. Ask the role-play participants to set goals for themselves for resolving conflicts more effectively.

This exercise can also be run in groups of three—two to role play and the third to provide feedback.

RECOMMENDED HRD PRESS TITLES

....

Dealing with Conflict Instrument, 16 pp.
The Manager's Pocket Guide to Dealing with Conflict, 128 pp.
50 Activities for Conflict Resolution, 163 pp.

36

Responding to Negativity in Others

Being able to respond positively to negativity in others is a crucial part of relationship skills. By understanding some of the ways in which people (including ourselves) express negative behavior, we can change a potentially damaging situation into something much more positive. Some of the ways in which we can show our negativity to others and they to us include:

◆ **Not accepting another's feelings**

For example: "Don't get depressed about it."
Alternative: "I can understand why you feel depressed."

◆ **Faking attention**

For example: "That is interesting."
Alternative: Don't fake it, mean it—or don't say anything at all.

◆ **Imposing time pressures**

For example: "Make it quick—I've got a meeting in five minutes."
Alternative: "I don't have much time right now. I'm off to a meeting. Could we meet later to talk about this?"

◆ **Directing**

For example: "I would like you to talk about your relationship with your line manager."
Alternative: "Is there anything bothering you at the moment?"

◆ **Blaming**

For example: "It's all your fault."
Alternative: "From my perspective, it seems as if both you and Tony may have contributed to what has happened. Maybe we can all have a chat about it."

◆ **Overinterpreting**

For example: "I think you're afraid of having authority and that's why you're not going for that job."
Alternative: "Tell me more about your fears about the new job."

◆ **Labeling**

For example: "You are just being neurotic."
Alternative: "Why do you think you feel like that?"

◆ **Nagging**

For example: "Haven't you done the work I gave you yet?"
Alternative: "When will you complete the work?"

◆ **Preaching**

For example: "Promotion isn't everything in life."
Alternative: "How do you feel about not getting the promotion?"

◆ **Lecturing**

For example: "We should cooperate and then there would be less tension."
Alternative: "What can we do to solve this problem?"

◆ **Aggression**

For example: "Fool!"
Alternative: "I'm angry with what you've done/said. Can we talk?"

◆ **Judging**

For example: "You're not very good at expressing yourself."
Alternative: "How might you be able to improve relations between you
        and Joan?"

◆ **Interrogating**

For example: "Tell me about your weaknesses."
Alternative: "How do you see yourself?"

◆ **Unwanted advice**

For example: "If I were you . . ."
Alternative: "Would you like to talk about this? Maybe I can help."

◆ **Putting on the spot**

For example: "Are you busy on Thursday afternoon?"
Alternative: "I need some extra help on Thursday afternoon. Are you
        free at all?"

What Do You Do when Someone is Angry?

When in an angry situation, it is a good idea to try to reduce the feelings
of anger so that you can begin to solve the problem together. Use the following steps:

◆ Acknowledge the other person's anger—for example, "I can see that you
   are angry about this."
◆ Admit, if appropriate, the possibility that you might have contributed to
   the problem.
◆ Express your desire to solve the problem actively—for example, "Let's
   work this out together."
◆ Help the angry person calm down—for example, "Let's sit down and
   talk about this."
◆ Use listening skills to hear what the other person needs to say before
   moving on to problem solving.

Ask yourself the following questions when coping with negative behavior:

◆ What is my contribution to creating the negative situation?
◆ How defensive am I being?
◆ Is it worth being assertive?
◆ Do I have the requisite skills to cope with another's negative behavior?
◆ Do I need to overcome my mental barrier to other people's negative
   behavior?
◆ Am I managing my anxiety through task-oriented inner dialogue?
◆ Am I clear on what I need to say?
◆ Am I backing up my words with the appropriate verbal and nonverbal
   language?

INDIVIDUAL TASKS AND REFLECTIONS

36.1 Negative Behaviors

Assess your own negative behaviors using the following checklist:

Negative Behaviors	Always (✓)	Sometimes (✓)	Never (✓)
Do you:			
◆ Find it difficult to accept another's feelings?			
◆ Fake attention?			
◆ Place time pressures on others?			
◆ Direct others?			
◆ Blame others?			
◆ Overinterpret another's statements?			
◆ Label others?			
◆ Nag others?			
◆ Preach at others?			
◆ Lecture others?			
◆ Act aggressively toward others?			
◆ Judge others?			
◆ Interrogate others?			
◆ Give unwanted advice to others?			
◆ Put others on the spot?			

36.2 Negative Behavior

How tolerant are you of negative behavior in others (not necessarily toward you)? How tolerant are you of negative behavior in yourself?

WORKING WITH OTHERS

36.3 Others Being Negative to You

How do you feel when others behave in the following negative ways toward you? (You can check more than one column.)

Others' Negative Behaviors	Angry (✓)	Powerless (✓)	Unaffected (✓)
Not accepting your feelings			
Faking attention			

(continued)

(continued)

Others' Negative Behaviors	Angry (✓)	Powerless (✓)	Unaffected (✓)
Placing time pressures on you			
Directing you			
Blaming you			
Overinterpreting your statements			
Labeling you			
Nagging you			
Preaching at you			
Lecturing you			
Being aggressive toward you			
Judging you			
Interrogating you			
Giving unwanted advice to you			
Putting you on the spot			

36.4 Managing Others' Anger

How do you deal with other people's anger? How do you feel? How do you behave?

36.5 Negative Situation Analysis

WORKING
WITH A MENTOR
....

Identify a situation in which you needed to deal with someone else's negative behavior and didn't handle it too well. How did you behave? What did you do? How did you feel? What was the outcome of the situation? How might you have behaved differently? Discuss with your mentor.

36.6 Others' Anger

Identify a situation where someone you were with became angry and you didn't handle it too well. How did they behave? How did you behave? What did you do? How did you feel? What was the outcome of the situation? How might you have behaved differently? Discuss with your mentor.

36.7 Your Negative Behavior

Using the negative behavior checklist (task 1), identify and discuss with your mentor those behaviors that would benefit from some work. Create an action plan detailing how you might do this. Review at a later date.

Developing

Others

....

Recommended

HRD Press Titles

....

36.8 Brainstorming Anger

Introduce the subject of anger management. Brainstorm what it feels like to be angry and the different ways in which we might behave. Brainstorm the skills necessary to deal with anger effectively.

36.9 Changing Behavior

Introduce the subject of responding to negativity. Brainstorm ways in which people show their negativity. Discuss how negativity could affect a situation or another person. Ask the learners to identify how they demonstrate negativity. Organize them into groups of four to work on one area of negativity each and discuss how they might change their behavior.

36.10 Role Play

Introduce the subject of responding to negativity and the different types of behavior. Role play with a volunteer different ways of handling negative behavior. Organize the learners into groups of three—two to role play and the other to provide feedback. Each learner is to take all three roles in turn. Reconvene the whole group for feedback.

Managing Anger in the Workplace, 150 pp.

INTRODUCTION

A value is the worth that you place on something you believe in or consider to be important. Rethinking your values is important to strengthening self-esteem because the process helps you decide what is right for you. Your values help influence your decisions and the goals you set. Values initially develop in response to basic needs—for example, children naturally adopt the values of the people they rely on for love and approval. However, throughout life's stages, and as a result of experiences, values evolve and are modified in response to changing circumstances. A good example of this is the case of someone who is promoted to management and, in order to carry out the job effectively, takes on the values of their new peer group.

If self-esteem is the value you place on yourself, what makes you a worthwhile person? Using criteria such as the size of your social circle, your level of education, or your income to evaluate worthiness means that you have self-esteem only if you earn it. While this perspective of conditional self-esteem may be a powerful motivator to work hard and do your best, what happens when you apply your best effort and still do not reach your goal?

Unconditional self-esteem (as opposed to conditional self-esteem—for example, "I'm OK if I earn over $80,000 a year") is choosing to love and respect yourself simply because you are a human being. This viewpoint reflects an internal value of self that might include such qualities as tolerance and honesty and is supported by the values that you place on areas of your life such as relationships, education, career, self-respect, spirituality, self-expression, self-care and health, community, and financial security.

The emphasis you place on a particular value will depend on what you decide is right for you. Are you spending enough time and energy in the areas you value? Or is your emphasis out of balance? Are you spending too much time on career and too little on family or health? Or too little attention to spirituality and too much to leisure? Consider the following:

◆ When you know what you care deeply about, you are more able to discipline yourself and work hard to apply your strengths and talents in that direction.
◆ Achieving goals that are firmly connected to your personal or professional values strengthens your self-esteem and nourishes your spiritual self.

Beware of values that start out as admirable, but become rigid and life-restricting—for example:

◆ Valuing education so highly that you push yourself (or your children) to pursue areas not suited to personal interests
◆ Buying into the media ideal of the thin, toned body to the extent that your body doesn't get the nourishment it needs

Aim for values that:

◆ Allow you to meet your own basic needs, in balance with the needs of others
◆ Allow you to ask for help when you need it

◆ Are your own and are not just handed down to you by family, society, or culture, and never questioned
◆ Allow you to make mistakes, take responsibility for your mistakes, and learn from them
◆ Enhance your life with expectations that are realistic and achievable

INDIVIDUAL TASKS AND REFLECTIONS

37.1 Adopting Values

What values (and whose) might you have adopted in your early years? Which values have you let go of? Which of those values do you still hold now?

37.2 What You Have and What You Can Do

Is your worth based on:

◆ How many friends you have?
◆ Your level of education?
◆ Your income and material possessions?
◆ Your talents or achievements?

37.3 Conditional Self-Esteem

To what extent do you believe that your self-worth is tied up with conditional self-esteem—for example, if you hold a prestigious position at work you must be an OK person?

37.4 Worth and Society's Views

Is your worth based on society's views of your:

◆ Gender?
◆ Appearance?
◆ Sexual orientation?
◆ Physical or mental abilities?
◆ Religion?
◆ Race, color, or ethnic background?

37.5 Personal Worth

Is your worth based on your:

◆ Generosity?
◆ Tolerance and respect?
◆ View of social justice?
◆ Honesty?

WORKING WITH OTHERS

37.6 Through the Eyes of Others

Do you tend to see your worth objectively through the eyes of others—for example, work colleagues or parents—or subjectively through your own eyes?

37.7 Jeopardizing Values

How much do you jeopardize your own values in order to gain the approval of others?

WORKING

WITH A MENTOR

....

DEVELOPING

OTHERS

....

37.8 Promotion Values

If you have been promoted to management, how might you have taken on the values of the new peer group? Discuss with your mentor.

37.9 Priorities

Consider the following questions and discuss with your mentor:

◆ What's important to you?
◆ What makes your life meaningful?
◆ What are your priorities in the next 2, 5, 10, or 25 years?

37.10 Brainstorming Values

Introduce the subject of values. Brainstorm how we learn values and what influences them. Brainstorm the areas of our life that are affected by values, including relationships, education, career, self-respect, spirituality, self-expression, self-care and health, community, and financial security. Organize the group into pairs to discuss these issues at random or allocate a different subject area to each pair. Reconvene the whole group to discuss conclusions.

37.11 Changing Values

Introduce the subject of values and how values permeate the whole of our lives—for example, how we may take the values we learn as children into our adult working lives and our intimate relationships. Taking the area of work, ask the learners to identify their values with regard to work, career, and money. Then ask them to identify their parents' (and significant others') values with regard to the same areas and note any similarities. Organize the learners into small groups to discuss the following questions:

◆ Do they feel comfortable with these values today?
◆ How do these values affect their performance and career management?
◆ What values might they change and why?

Reconvene the larger group to share and discuss.

Skills and knowledge development has become an essential component of working life because of the increase in technology, the changes in the way businesses are run and commercial competitiveness. Change produces new processes that in turn require new skills. The single-skilled worker is giving rise to the multiskilled worker. Being multiskilled means having a number of transferable skills. In order to maintain appropriate skill levels, you need learning—not just a one-off training course, but a periodic and constant program of learning that ensures your efficiency in your chosen trade or profession. Employers want:

◆ Vocational skills that reflect a specific occupational area
◆ Job-specific skills for the specific tasks that need doing within a job
◆ Interpersonal skills—principally communication skills
◆ Leadership skills—the ability to motivate and inspire others
◆ Customer service skills—sales skills—to deal with customers
◆ Developmental skills—being able to recognize and create opportunities for new business or for increasing productivity

Sources of Education

Adult Education

◆ **Colleges and universities.** These are likely to have an adult education department. Community colleges often run adult education classes as well. Courses are run on a weekly basis and may include Saturday classes. Subjects range from leisure interests through to computer and word-processing skills and go on to give the opportunity to gain qualifications.
◆ **Centers for continuing education.** These centers (often linked to a university) run part-time courses that may or may not be award-bearing. These types of courses provide a good entry point to degree courses.

Further Education

◆ **Public colleges.** Colleges may offer a variety of the following:
— Courses in English as a foreign language
— Adult education courses
— Library and learning resources
— Full and part-time courses geared toward the workplace
— Flexible (open/distance) learning
— Staff development programs catering for business and industry

◆ **Private colleges.** The fees for private schools and colleges are usually quite a bit higher than those of public colleges. If you are considering this option, check the validity of any qualifications.

University Education

Universities offer courses leading to degrees. Mature students are specifically encouraged. Courses might include accounting, chemistry, computing, electronics, and management.

Private Training

There are many commercial training organizations that can help companies get a vocational qualification or learn new job skills. Costs vary enormously, and not all will offer qualifications. Training is usually offered directly to a company or may be offered as "open courses." That means that anyone can join them.

Distance/Open Learning

Open learning is a term used to define methods of learning that allow the learner to take charge of their program of study. The student works at a time, place, and pace suited to them. In order to do this, learners are given a wide variety of material comprising specially prepared information and exercises, and designed to take the tutor's place. In order to support this learning, students should have access to a tutor (via e-mail, online, mail, telephone, or tutorial meetings) and to the option of meeting with other students (for example, through summer schools or drop-in study centers).

Training at Work

Workplace training is on the increase since companies are tending to invest in training programs for their staff more and more. Companies will either have their own trainers situated within their Human Resources department, have a flexible learning center, send employees out to public courses, or buy in specialist training from outside.

Volunteering

Often there is an opportunity for free training when volunteering. Many training courses provide stepping stones toward accredited qualifications.

INDIVIDUAL TASKS AND REFLECTIONS

38.1 Returning to Learning

Why would you like to return to learning?

- ◆ To gain a vocational qualification?
- ◆ To have stimulus in your life?
- ◆ To obtain a qualification to enter a specific career?
- ◆ To look for a new direction in your life?
- ◆ To progress in your existing career?
- ◆ To obtain a higher salary?
- ◆ To obtain a more interesting job?
- ◆ To gain a paper qualification?
- ◆ To do something you have always wanted to do?
- ◆ To increase your confidence?
- ◆ To improve your performance at work?
- ◆ To understand something?
- ◆ To succeed in learning something new?
- ◆ To add a further level of learning to an earlier achievement?

38.2 Ways to Learn

There are many different ways we can learn something new. For most people, the memories of school are enough to put them off learning for life. But whether we are aware of it or not, we are constantly learning, albeit informally. We can teach ourselves (informal learning) or we can have some-one to guide us (formal—for example college or a training course). We can learn through application, reading, or someone showing us. Everyone likes to learn differently. As an adult, there is no reason why you shouldn't enjoy your learning—but you need to find the right way that suits you.

Do you learn best through:

◆ Being challenged?
◆ Having a good reason for taking a course?
◆ Having things organized for you?
◆ Detailed instruction?
◆ Trying things on your own?
◆ Reading around a subject area?
◆ Having some kind of external motivation?
◆ Tutors telling you what to do?
◆ Having your progress checked as you go?
◆ Being regularly prodded into action?
◆ Negotiating what you do with your tutors?
◆ Being allowed to adapt learning material?
◆ Doing one thing at a time?
◆ Having several things on the go at once?
◆ Working with others?
◆ Exams and tests?
◆ Trial and error?
◆ Following your intuition?
◆ A structured course?

38.3 Self-Directed Learning

What have you taught yourself?

WORKING

WITH OTHERS

....

38.4 Formal Group Learning

Identify a situation in which you are learning in a formal situation with colleagues. How do you feel as an adult learner? How do you feel about learning in a group? What are the pros and cons of this type of learning for you?

38.5 Informal Group Learning

Identify a situation in which you are learning in an informal situation with colleagues. What are the pros and cons of this type of learning for you?

WORKING

WITH A MENTOR

....

38.6 Peak Learning

What has been one of your peak learning experiences and why? Discuss with your mentor.

38.7 Worst Learning

What has been one of your worst learning experiences and why? Discuss with your mentor.

DEVELOPING

OTHERS

....

38.8 Adult Learner

Brainstorm on to a whiteboard or flipchart the pros and cons of being an adult learner.

38.9 Immediacy of Learning

Organize the learners into small groups and ask them how it feels to be in a group learning situation as an adult. Use the immediacy of the situation to tease out people's thoughts and feelings about returning to learning.

39
Self-directed Learning in the Workplace

Self-directed learning involves the learner initiating the learning process, making the decisions about what training and development experiences will occur, and how. The learner selects and pursues their own learning goals, objectives, methods, and means to check that the goals have been achieved. Self-directed learning is ideally suited to the workplace and has numerous advantages over traditional forms of classroom instruction for employees. Self-directed learning programs:

◆ Are more effective in development because learning accommodates employees' learning styles and objectives
◆ Save substantial training costs because learners learn to help themselves and each other with practical and timely materials
◆ Achieve increased employee job effectiveness as they learn to learn from their own work experiences and actually apply their learning in their places of work.

> Over the years, it has become increasingly clear that traditional approaches to program design and delivery in the workplace and in associative organizations present some important weaknesses. Problem areas include: coping with the short life span of useful knowledge; passing down acquired competencies to succeeding cohorts; accommodating the demands of productivity while providing for a continuity of learning; [and] enabling learners to pursue activities that correspond to their learning styles and needs. (Bouchard)

After many years of reflection about learning, psychologist Carl Rogers, founder of self-directed therapy, asserted that "anything that can be taught to another is relatively inconsequential, and has little or no significant influence on behavior." He adds, "The only learning which significantly influences behavior is self-discovered, self-appropriated learning" (1995, 276).

Listed below are some suggestions for ways in which managers and learners can turn the workplace into a classroom:

◆ Help learners identify the starting point for a learning project and discern relevant ways of assessing.
◆ Encourage adult learners to view knowledge and truth as contextual—and that they can act on their world individually or collectively to transform it.
◆ Create a partnership with learners by negotiating a learning contract for goals, strategies, and evaluation criteria.
◆ Be a manager of the learning experience rather than an information provider.
◆ Teach inquiry skills, decision making, personal development, and self-evaluation of work.
◆ Help learners develop positive attitudes and feelings of independence relative to learning.
◆ Recognize learners' personality types and learning styles.

◆ Use techniques such as field experience and problem solving that take advantage of adults' rich experience base.
◆ Obtain the necessary tools to assess learners' current performance and to evaluate their expected performance.
◆ Provide opportunities for self-directed learners to reflect on what they are learning.
◆ Promote learning networks and study circles.
◆ Provide staff training on self-directed learning and broaden the opportunities for its implementation.

Employees must take responsibility for their own learning. In the past, many companies could promise a new employee lifelong employment and a predictable career path. Today, very few companies can make that promise. You must take responsibility for your own career path, whether with your current employer or through a series of employers. And the way to build your career is to keep learning throughout your working life. You must be in a continuous learning mode—learning every month, every week, every day. That way you are in control of your working life, because you are continuously reskilling and gaining new knowledge, thereby making yourself a valuable commodity on the job market.

You can plan for your own learning needs by using the "learning contract." The learning contract is negotiated by the employee and their manager (or the employee can create their own mobile learning contract).

It starts with the part of the company's business goals that are affected by the employee's work. Once these goals are understood, ask yourself "How do I need to change my work or my skills and knowledge to help the company achieve these goals?" When you understand the changes you must make to help achieve the goals, then you need to consider what you need to learn in order to make those changes.

The next part of the learning contract deals with how the learning will take place—for example, through a company-sponsored training program, through books, or by getting a mentor. In planning your learning, you need to specify in the learning contract the methods you will use, where you will find the learning resources you need, and a schedule for completion of the specified learning activities. If you cannot find someone to act as a coach, then find someone else who is learning the same skill or studying the same material to be your learning partner. By having a learning partner, you will have support and be able to discuss your experiences as you later try to apply your learning to your jobs. If you cannot find a learning partner in your group or your company, look on the Internet for groups who are interested in the subject.

You also need to specify in the contract how you will demonstrate that the learning has taken place. Will you submit a report on what you have learned? Will you demonstrate the skills for your manager? Next, the learning contract must include a section on how you will apply your learning to your job. The manager must provide the opportunity to make errors and must reinforce the employee's learning with coaching until the new skills are mastered.

Finally, you must specify in the contract what difference in business results are expected once you have applied your learning to your work. This ties back to the first step in the learning contract, where you specified the company business goals to which you contribute. By beginning with the end in mind, all learning activities will be focused on specific, measurable, achievable business results, for the individual, the group/function/department, and the company as a whole.

INDIVIDUAL TASKS

AND REFLECTIONS
·······················

39.1 Company Goals

Identify the company's business goals and how your individual work contributes to their achievement. Specify how you must change your work to help the company achieve its goals. Specify what you need to learn in order to make those changes.

39.2 Career and Life Goals

Identify your career and life goals. Specify what you need to learn or do to help you achieve those goals. Specify what you need to learn in order to make those changes.

WORKING

WITH OTHERS
·······················

39.3 Group Activity

How could you work with others in initiating self-directed learning in the workplace?

WORKING

WITH A MENTOR
·······················

39.4 Learning Plan

Identify a learning goal and develop a learning plan, including:

◆ What you need to learn
◆ What learning resources you will use
◆ A schedule of learning activities
◆ Measures of learning achievement
◆ How you will apply your learning to your job
◆ How you will apply your learning to your career and life goals
◆ What changes in business results are expected from the application of your learning to the job
◆ What changes in your career and life may arise from the application of your learning

Discuss with your mentor.

39.5 Self-Directed Learning for Your People

Reflecting on the people you are responsible for, how might you initiate a workplace self-directed learning program with them? Discuss with your mentor, initiate, and review an action plan.

DEVELOPING

OTHERS
·······················

39.6 The Pros and Cons of Self-Directed Learning

Introduce the subject of self-directed learning in the workplace. Ask the learners to identify current self-directed learning they are undertaking. Brainstorm the pros and cons of self-directed learning, both for the individual and the organization.

39.7 How We Learn

Introduce the subject of self-directed learning in the workplace. Facilitate a discussion on how we learn.

39.8 Facilitating Learning in Others

Introduce the subject of self-directed learning in the workplace. Facilitate a discussion on how learners might facilitate learning in their people.

INTRODUCTION

We develop our skills and knowledge through a variety of channels, including paid and unpaid work. Raising a family, volunteer work, interests, and hobbies add to our skills base. Skills refer to what we can do and what we know. Strengths refer to our positive qualities gained through life experience and through paid and unpaid work. These skills and strengths form a toolbox to which we can add and from which we can use at will. They can increase our confidence as well as provide tools for career and life management.

The following list details the types of skills and strengths that we can all draw upon:

◆ **Core skills.** Core skills are formed by our general education and basic character and include basic literacy, basic numeracy, relationship skills, self-motivation, organization of time, organization of work, and self-management.

◆ **Skills gained via unpaid work.** These might be gained through volunteer or community work or from our home life.

◆ **Vocational skills.** These normally arise from your paid work.

◆ **Transferable skills.** These are the skills that you can take with you between occupations.

◆ **Abstract skills and strengths.** These refer to our attitude toward work, how we conduct ourselves at work, and the personal qualities necessary to deal with today's workplace.

◆ **Leadership skills and strengths.** These are gained through paid or unpaid work.

◆ **Achievements.** Potential employers like to know what you have done in the past (through paid or unpaid work) as it indicates what you might do for them in the future.

INDIVIDUAL TASKS AND REFLECTIONS

40.1 Self-Analysis

Reflect on, and write down, a complete list of your:

◆ Core skills
◆ Skills gained via unpaid work
◆ Vocational skills
◆ Transferable skills
◆ Abstract skills and strengths
◆ Leadership skills and strengths
◆ Achievements

You may use the checklists at the end of this section to help you.

WORKING WITH OTHERS

40.2 Peer Analysis

Identify a work colleague who knows you quite well and who you know as well. Both of you reflect on and write down a list of your:

◆ Core skills
◆ Skills gained via unpaid work
◆ Vocational skills

◆ Transferable skills
◆ Abstract skills and strengths
◆ Leadership skills and strengths
◆ Achievements

On completion, assess each other's analysis.
You may use the checklists at the end of this section to help you.

WORKING

WITH A MENTOR
....

DEVELOPING

OTHERS
....

40.3 A Personal Development Plan

After creating a list of your skills and strengths (see tasks 1 and 2), discuss it with your mentor and work toward a personal development plan for them.

40.4 Job Analysis

Introduce the subject of job analysis using the example given below or one of your own:

Skills of a Bartender	
Tasks	**Skills and Strengths**
Serving drinks	Manual dexterity Products/legislation knowledge
Cellar work/changing bottles/kegs	Fit Health and safety knowledge
Cleaning up	Organized
Handling cash	Honest Knowledge of math
Serving food	Health and hygiene knowledge
Serving people (general)	Friendliness Good listener Outgoing Cheerful Neat and tidy appearance Calm under pressure Good memory Teamworker Communication skills Tolerance Tact

Now organize the learners into two or three small groups, give each group a job title and a sheet of flipchart paper and marker pens, and ask them to produce their own job analyses. When finished, have each group hang their work on the wall. Reconvene the whole group and discuss each group's analysis. Alternatively, you could ask each group to suggest their own job titles—for example, marketing executive, chef de cuisine, or supermarket shelf-stacker.

40.5 Your Job Analysis

On a piece of paper, ask the learners to head one column "Tasks" and the second column "Skills and Strengths." Ask them to think of one job they have had and to list in the Tasks column all the relevant tasks associated with the job. Ask them to write down all the relevant skills and strengths they used in their work in the Skills and Strengths column.

40.6 Strengths and Weaknesses

Ask the learners to think of two strengths and two weaknesses related to skills and personal qualities. Go around the group and write their suggestions under two columns headed "Strengths" and "Weaknesses" on a whiteboard or flipchart, listing two of your own strengths and weaknesses to start them off. List everyone's strengths and weaknesses. Using most of the examples in the weakness column, show how you can turn a weakness into a strength—for example, taking on too much work could be a weakness, but it could also demonstrate enthusiasm.

40.7 Skills and Strengths Analysis

Introduce the concept of skills and strengths analysis. Help the learners brainstorm their own list of:

◆ Core skills
◆ Skills gained via unpaid work
◆ Vocational skills
◆ Transferable skills
◆ Abstract skills and strengths
◆ Leadership skills and strengths
◆ Achievements

You may use the checklists at the end of this section to help you.

TASK CHECKLISTS

Core Skills	Good (✓)	Needs Improving (✓)
Basic letter-writing skills		
Form filling		
Reading skills		
Reading for information		
Basic mathematics		
Initiating/developing relationships with others		
Basic communication skills		
Keeping goal-oriented		
Self-discipline		

(continued)

(continued)

Core Skills	Good (✓)	Needs Improving (✓)
Organizing time		
Looking after yourself		

In the following checklist, check all your unpaid skills. Include all the skills you use at home, in your community, your hobbies, and interests:

Unpaid Skills	
☐ Growing plants	☐ Landscape gardening
☐ Garden maintenance	☐ Growing fruit and vegetables
☐ Putting up sheds/greenhouses	☐ Laying paving slabs
☐ Fence maintenance	☐ Caring for animals
☐ Pet training	☐ Repairing electrical appliances
☐ Do-it-yourself tasks	☐ Internal painting and decorating
☐ Plumbing	☐ Cleaning windows
☐ External painting/decorating/maintenance	☐ Using the Internet
☐ Interior design	☐ Repairing furniture
☐ Making soft furnishings	☐ Restoring furniture
☐ Making or altering clothes	☐ Coordinating clothes
☐ Assisting others with personal care	☐ Giving haircuts
☐ Providing first aid	☐ Organizing a medicine cabinet
☐ Home nursing	☐ Caring for special needs
☐ Planning menus	☐ Gourmet cooking
☐ Entertaining	☐ Preparing food for others
☐ Evaluation and purchase of goods	☐ Managing household expenses
☐ Handling credit/loan applications	☐ Budgeting
☐ Using a home computer	☐ Typing/word processing
☐ Studying	☐ Parenting
☐ Babysitting	☐ Using the telephone
☐ Letter writing	☐ Dealing with "red tape"
☐ Managing your time	☐ Setting priorities

(continued)

(continued)

Unpaid Skills	
☐ Supervising others	☐ Motivating others
☐ Supporting in a crisis	☐ Counseling
☐ Tutoring children	☐ Driving
☐ Route planning	☐ Carrying out routine vehicle repairs
☐ Safety in the home	☐ Organizing tradespeople
☐ Laundry	☐ Housekeeping
☐ Carpet and upholstery cleaning	☐ Booking accommodation
☐ Organizing recreational activities	☐ Arranging events

In the following checklist, check all your transferable skills:

Transferable Skills	
☐ Action planning	☐ Administration
☐ Assembling/repairing things	☐ Being able to improvise
☐ Classifying	☐ Clerical skills
☐ Coaching	☐ Counseling and guidance
☐ Customer care	☐ Decision-making skills
☐ Designing things	☐ Developmental skills
☐ Dissecting information	☐ Facilitation
☐ Financial management	☐ Flexibility
☐ Innovating	☐ Interpersonal skills
☐ IT skills	☐ Leadership skills
☐ Linguistic and cultural skills	☐ Listening skills
☐ Literacy	☐ Managing financial resources
☐ Managing people	☐ Marketing skills
☐ Mediation skills	☐ Motivating people
☐ Negotiation skills	☐ Networking
☐ Accounting	☐ Oral communication skills
☐ Organizational skills	☐ Organizing people

(continued)

(continued)

Transferable Skills		
☐ Problem solving	☐ Project management	
☐ Researching	☐ Selling	
☐ Teaching and training	☐ Teamworking	
☐ Time management	☐ Written communication skills	

In the following checklist, check those qualities that you feel best describe you:

Abstract Skills and Strengths		
☐ Adaptable	☐ Adventurous	☐ Assertive
☐ Calm	☐ Capable	☐ Caring
☐ Cheerful	☐ Confident	☐ Conscientious
☐ Cooperative	☐ Courteous	☐ Creative
☐ Curious	☐ Decisive	☐ Dedicated
☐ Dependable	☐ Determined	☐ Diplomatic
☐ Easy-going	☐ Encouraging	☐ Enterprising
☐ Honest	☐ Impartial	☐ Innovative
☐ Lateral thinker	☐ Logical	☐ Methodical
☐ Observant	☐ Organized	☐ Perceptive
☐ Persistent	☐ Practical	☐ Reliable
☐ Responsible	☐ Sincere	☐ Thorough
☐ Understanding	☐ Discreet	☐ Efficient
☐ Energetic	☐ Enthusiastic	☐ Firm
☐ Hard working	☐ Humorous	☐ Independent
☐ Intuitive	☐ Loyal	☐ Motivated
☐ Openminded	☐ Outgoing	☐ Perfectionist
☐ Persuasive	☐ Proactive	☐ Resilient
☐ Self-reliant	☐ Sympathetic	☐ Tolerant
☐ Versatile	☐ Dynamic	☐ Empathetic
☐ Inquiring	☐ Extroverted	☐ Friendly
☐ Helpful	☐ Imaginative	☐ Vigilant
☐ Inventive	☐ Listener	☐ Mature

(continued)

(continued)

Abstract Skills and Strengths		
☐ Objective	☐ Optimistic	☐ Patient
☐ Persevering	☐ Positive	☐ Reassuring
☐ Resourceful	☐ Sensitive	☐ Tactful
☐ Trustworthy		

For the checklist below, check the skills and strengths that apply to you:

Leadership Skills and Strengths	
☐ A working knowledge of the global market	☐ Ability to administer discipline
☐ Ability to facilitate change	☐ Ability to motivate others
☐ Ability to set objectives	☐ Ability to allow others to develop
☐ Performance appraisal skills	☐ Assessment skills
☐ Coaching skills	☐ Counseling skills
☐ Feedback skills	☐ IT management skills
☐ Innovative stance	☐ Listening skills
☐ Knowledge of languages	☐ Resource management skills
☐ Meeting management skills	☐ Project management skills
☐ Mediation skills	☐ Quality management skills
☐ Direction provision skills	☐ Staff development skills
☐ Selection and recruitment skills	☐ Team leadership skills
☐ Strategic planning skills	☐ Ability to work in consultation
☐ Time management skills	☐ Ability to value others
☐ Customer orientation skills	☐ Stockholder focus
☐ Marketing skills	☐ Report-writing skills
☐ Team-building skills	☐ Problem-solving skills
☐ Long-term goal-setting skills	☐ Good at sharing power
☐ Delegation skills	☐ Financial management skills
☐ Ability to look for challenges	☐ Ability to prioritize
☐ Ability to challenge yourself	☐ Adaptability
☐ Ability to set objectives	☐ Focus
☐ Approachability	☐ Trustworthiness
☐ Being proactive	☐ Creativity

(continued)

(continued)

Leadership Skills and Strengths	
☐ Cooperative stance	☐ Fairness
☐ Decisiveness	☐ Having vision
☐ Objectivity	☐ Loyalty to staff
☐ Resourcefulness	☐ Self-confidence
☐ Good self-expression	☐ Ability to take risks
☐ Ability to acknowledge your own mistakes	☐ Directness

In the following checklist, check off any achievements that apply to you that are listed. Also, add any you have accomplished in work and personal life.

Achievements	
☐ Cutting costs	☐ Improving teamwork
☐ Developing staff performance	☐ Increasing sales
☐ Improving the appearance of something	☐ Meeting deadlines
☐ Turning around a negative situation	☐ Improving the efficiency of something
☐ Providing information	☐ Avoiding potential problems
☐ Introducing something new	

Other _____

_____

_____

_____

_____

_____

_____

_____

_____

_____

_____

_____

41
Speaking Skills

INTRODUCTION

When speaking to groups of people, the rule of thumb is, if you don't have their attention in the first 30 seconds, you never will. Listed below are some guidelines for effective public speaking:

◆ Let your uniqueness and individuality come through when you speak.

◆ Make yourself interesting to others.

◆ Create your own interesting soundbites of wisdom so that your audience quote you.

◆ Mention your own name in your stories to help your audience remember who you are.

◆ Make sure that you know exactly who is going to be in the audience, why they are there, and why they invited you to speak.

◆ Check the setting. Check the microphone, lighting, audiovisual equipment, and any other factors that might affect your performance.

◆ Meet the audience members as they arrive; this is an excellent way to build rapport with a captive audience.

◆ Start with a bang. The first 30 seconds have the most impact. Don't waste these precious seconds; begin with a startling statement, quote, or story.

◆ Use humor with caution. Don't start with a joke unless you are totally confident of your joke, its reception, and your delivery. If the joke fails, you will lose any credibility you have. And if your only humorous material is at the beginning, the audience will be disappointed when you become serious.

◆ Limit your topics. If you're giving a half-hour speech, don't expect to tell the audience everything you know. Pick two or three important points. Embellish your points with story and examples.

◆ Structure your information. You and your audience will remember your points better if you have a clear outline. For example, start by saying, "Here are the five questions I'm asked most frequently."

◆ Use handouts. If your presentation involves statistics and analytical data, put them in a handout that the audience can refer to. Don't bore them by reciting reams of numbers.

◆ Don't read your speech. Look your audience in the eye. Write down key points or statements so that you can refer to them, but deliver the rest of it spontaneously, making eye contact.

◆ End with a bang. Write a strong and memorable closing statement or vivid example. Then memorize it so that, no matter what distractions may occur, you can always "bring it home." When the time comes, deliver your closing line directly to the audience and then accept their applause.

Body Language and Speaking

The most important rule for making your body communicate effectively is to be yourself, but to amplify your movements and expressions just enough for the audience to see them.

> You speak to a single person without any problem. So just think of a large group as lots of single people glued together.

If you are interested in your subject, truly believe what you are saying, and want to share your message with others, your physical movements will come from within you and will be appropriate to what you are saying. By involving yourself in your message, you'll be natural and spontaneous without having to consciously think about what you are doing or saying.

> Speak from the heart and to the soul.

Nothing influences a speaker's mental attitude more than the knowledge that they are thoroughly prepared. This knowledge leads to self-confidence, which is a vital ingredient of effective public speaking. Know your material so well that you don't have to devote your mental energy to the task of remembering the sequence of ideas and words.

Establish a personal bond with listeners. Begin by selecting one person and talking to them personally. Maintain eye contact with that person long enough to establish a visual bond (about 5 to 10 seconds). This is usually the equivalent of a sentence or a thought. Then shift your gaze to another person. In a small group, this is relatively easy to do, but if you're addressing hundreds or thousands of people, it's impossible. In these circumstances, pick out one or two individuals in each section of the room and establish personal bonds with them. Then each listener will get the impression you're talking directly to him or her.

Monitor visual feedback. While you are talking, your listeners are responding with their own nonverbal messages. Keep alert for this valuable feedback. If people aren't looking at you, they may not be listening either. Their reasons for this may include one or more of the following:

◆ They may not be able to hear you.
  Solution: If you are not using a microphone, speak more loudly and note whether this works.

◆ They may be bored.
  Solution: Introduce some humor, vary the tone of your voice, or add some powerful gestures or body movements.

◆ They may be puzzled.
  Solution: Repeat and/or rephrase what you have just said.

◆ They seem to be fidgeting nervously.
  Solution: You may be using distracting mannerisms or have some embarrassing clothing problems—for example, food on your shirt—which you can discreetly rectify or conceal.

Your Appearance

When your actions are wedded to your words, the impact of your speech will be strengthened. If your platform behavior includes mannerisms unrelated to your spoken message, those actions will call attention to themselves and away from your speech. Some common faults of inexperienced or ineffective speakers are:

◆ Gripping or leaning on the lectern
◆ Tapping fingers
◆ Biting or licking lips
◆ Toying with coins or jewelry
◆ Frowning

◆ Adjusting hair or clothing
◆ Shaking head
◆ Staring

When it is time to begin your talk, walk confidently from your seat to the lectern. Pause there for a few seconds, and then move out from behind the lectern. Smile before you say your first words. If you are on the same level as your audience, be careful not to stand too close to, nor move beyond, the people in the front row. Walking can be an effective way to stress an important idea, but your walk must be purposeful and intentional, not just a random shift of position. Also, take care not to walk around too much, because continuous pacing is distracting.

When you speak, your face—more clearly than any other part of your body—communicates to others your attitudes and emotions. Make a conscious effort to avoid inappropriate facial expressions, including distracting mannerisms or unconscious expressions not rooted in your feelings, attitudes, and emotions. In much the same way that some speakers perform random, distracting gestures and body movements, nervous speakers often release excess energy and tension by unconsciously moving their facial muscles (for example, licking lips or tightening the jaw). If you relax and allow yourself to respond naturally to your thoughts, attitudes, and emotions, your facial expressions will be appropriate and will project sincerity, conviction, and credibility.

> Nothing can position you ahead of the crowd like the ability to stand up and speak eloquently, or at least stagger to your feet and say anything at all.

INDIVIDUAL TASKS AND REFLECTIONS

41.1 Presentation Analysis (A)

Consider a presentation for which you did not prepare well and that didn't go well. What happened? How did you come across? What was the listener's reaction? What was the outcome? What could you have done differently?

41.2 Presentation Analysis (B)

Consider a presentation you gave that you had prepared for and that went well. What happened? How did you come across? What was the listener's reaction? What was the outcome?

41.3 Presentation Assessment (A)

Consider a presentation you attended that went badly. What happened? How did the presenter come across? What was the audience's reaction? What was your reaction? What was the outcome? What might you have done differently in the presenter's place?

41.4 Presentation Assessment (B)

Consider a presentation you attended that went well. What happened? How did the presenter come across? What was the audience's reaction? What was your reaction? What was the outcome? What can you learn from the presenter's performance?

41.5 Telephone Presentation

Before calling to request something on the telephone, plan and practice what you are going to say. Even such a simple task as this is essentially a short presentation.

WORKING
WITH OTHERS
....

41.6 Speaking to Others

Whenever you speak to people, make an extra effort to notice how you speak. Observe, too, whether the facial expressions of your listeners indicate that they do or do not understand what you are saying.

41.7 Videotape Yourself

The first step in eliminating any superfluous behavior is to obtain an accurate perception of your body image. This should include posture, gestures, body movement, facial expressions, and eye contact. After you have videotaped yourself speaking, review the tape several times and make a list of all the distracting mannerisms you notice.

WORKING
WITH A MENTOR
....

41.8 The 90-Second Presentation

Prepare a 90-second presentation about yourself. Describe who you are and what you do. Record your presentation in front of your mentor and review it together. Since you are talking about yourself, you don't need to research the topic, but you do need to prepare what you are going to say and how you are going to say it. Plan everything including your gestures and walking patterns.

DEVELOPING
OTHERS
....

41.9 Elements of Speaking

Introduce the subject of speaking skills. Brainstorm the different elements. Ask the group to give good and bad examples of speakers they've heard. Then ask them to give good and bad examples of themselves as speakers.

4.10 Five-Minute Speech

Introduce the subject of speaking skills. Ask each learner to speak for five minutes on any subject that interests them. You can videotape the session. Provide time for feedback between speakers.

The Manager's Pocket Guide to Public Presentations, 128 pp.

RECOMMENDED
HRD PRESS TITLES
....

INTRODUCTION

Downsizing is not necessarily linked to talent—it is usually about cost-effectiveness and the restructuring of the business. But it might not feel like that when it happens to you.

Many of us seek to express our identity through work, and when our work is taken away, we are left floundering and wondering who we are. When we have no work, we might feel lost, without purpose, or not good enough to get by on the merit of our personality alone.

Some companies offer career counseling as part of the layoff package, and if you have been laid off, it is usually wise to take advantage of this option. Alternatively, you may decide to use an external careers counselor whose services may include psychometric testing for assessing your interests, personality, and skills, together with guidance on refocusing your career direction and training opportunities. At the very least, your company should offer you job-hunting time.

> It may be worthwhile negotiating to take a lump sum and leave rather than work out your notice.

Recognizing the Loss

What do we lose when we're laid off?

- ◆ **Self-esteem.** Our sense of who we are, and the security of our position in society, as defined through work, can feel threatened. We may feel insecure about our skills and knowledge. Weren't we good enough for the job? Are we good enough to get another job?
- ◆ **Dignity.** Most of us develop a sense of pride in what we do for a living. There is a sense of ownership and attachment to what we have produced. Losing all this can make us feel stripped of our dignity.
- ◆ **Personal fulfillment.** Work can provide a great deal of satisfaction. It may affirm what we can do and that we are needed.
- ◆ **Status.** Although nowadays there is more sympathy for people who lose their jobs, we may experience feelings of shame about being labeled "redundant" associated with the belief that we are not wanted.
- ◆ **Income.** If we don't have money, how will we pay the bills?
- ◆ **Independence.** For many of us, work represents financial independence. It may also represent independence from the role of parent or caregiver.
- ◆ **Property.** It may be that our home is linked directly with our job—for example, caretaking. Even if our home is not directly linked, there is the threat of our home being taken away if we don't keep up the mortgage payments.

The following factors can complicate the feelings of loss:

◆ **Lack of community support.** One of the first questions we normally ask someone we first meet is, "What do you do?" If at that point in time we are not working, we might feel uncomfortable being asked this question.

◆ **Change.** Part of the human condition is a need to feel safe and secure. We might not mind change if we are in control, but when external circumstances force our hand, we tend to react with hostility and fear.

◆ **Anxiety about making decisions.** When we are laid off, we have to make decisions about ourselves, what we want, and how we are going to get it. Many of us fear making decisions because we don't want to make the wrong ones. This may lead us to not making any and ending up feeling lost and frustrated.

◆ **Inability to share feelings.** Downsizing invariably produces an emotional reaction, and emotions can be difficult to handle—especially if there is a lack of support or acceptance around us.

◆ **Presence of concurrent life crises.** Sometimes life seems to throw everything back at us at once. We may be experiencing problems in other areas of our life and then, to top it all off, we are laid off from work.

Underwriting the Emotions

Any loss triggers grief—and downsizing is no exception. As with any other emotional process, understanding the grieving cycle makes it much easier to deal with.

The Grieving Cycle

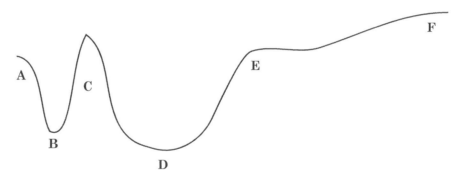

A The pattern of life prior to downsizing.
B The loss and shock due to downsizing.
C The emotional reaction, such as anger, powerlessness, and guilt. Feeling powerless and out of control of our employment is a frightening state. You may feel anger at your boss, at the company, the managing director, God, or the government. Underlying anger that you feel against yourself may be redirected at your family. Anger turned inward against the self can often turn into depression and apathy leading in turn to low self-esteem and lack of confidence. You may experience internal symptoms of nervous anxiety. Psychosomatic ailments such as backache, headache, or an illness may manifest. You may feel a deep self-pity.
D Onset of the grieving process where the reality of being laid off is experienced.
E A change where the loss is accepted and the idea of re-employment becomes a reality.
F Rebuilding a new working life.

Anger is a primary emotion following downsizing. It is fueled by a sense of frustration and powerlessness. It may also be a cover for fear and anxiety about the future. Getting angry helps us to:

◆ Discover what happened and what is happening to us
◆ Set limits where necessary
◆ Grieve our losses
◆ Get our needs met
◆ Discover what is beneath our anger
◆ Be assertive
◆ Get things off our chest

Repressed anger can cause:

◆ Resentment
◆ Self-pity
◆ Stress
◆ Anxiety
◆ Depression
◆ Sadness
◆ Lack of concentration
◆ Physical illness

Fear can be a debilitating emotion as we travel through the trauma of job loss. But it is better to make a friend of fear, and to work with it, than to be afraid of fear itself. We may fear:

◆ The loss of purpose and meaning in our lives
◆ The loss of status
◆ The loss of material possessions
◆ The unknown
◆ Unpredictability
◆ The loss of control
◆ Looking foolish
◆ Change
◆ The loss of financial security
◆ Making decisions
◆ Changing career
◆ Asserting ourselves
◆ Being interviewed
◆ Making a mistake
◆ Rejection
◆ Success
◆ Failure
◆ Being vulnerable
◆ Loss of image
◆ Disapproval
◆ Helplessness
◆ Filling out job application forms
◆ Being unwanted
◆ Being too old
◆ Losing face
◆ Losing our home
◆ Not knowing what to do with ourselves

Facing the Future

If we have lost our job, we can spend a lot of time mentally beating ourselves up. We forget to forgive ourselves or take care of ourselves. If our best friend had lost their job, we would listen to them, be with them, and help cheer them up. So perhaps we need to treat ourselves as our own best friend. Emotional support from our families, partners, and friends is vital for us to feel valued and accepted. Don't be afraid to ask for that support.

Checkpoints for the First Few Weeks after Being Laid Off
◆ Get up at a regular time.
◆ Get yourself out and about.
◆ Do some exercise.
◆ Update your résumé.
◆ Network with colleagues and friends.
◆ Get in touch with recruitment agencies.
◆ Socialize.
◆ Redefine your personal goals.
◆ Improve your image.
◆ Consider going back to school.
◆ Reorganize your finances.
◆ Redefine your career goals.
◆ Do volunteer/community work for a sense of achievement.
◆ See downsizing as a positive opportunity to change.
◆ Allow yourself time to grieve and say goodbye.
◆ Express your anger appropriately.
◆ Write out your feelings.
◆ Put your financial package in a high-interest account.
◆ Organize networking contacts before you leave.
◆ Keep busy.
◆ Look after your health.
◆ Have some fun.

INDIVIDUAL TASKS AND REFLECTIONS

42.1 Getting Hold of the Feelings

Since being told you have been laid off, are you experiencing:

◆ A lack of personal fulfillment?
◆ A loss of status?
◆ Worry about your income?
◆ A loss of independence?
◆ A change in lifestyle?
◆ A lack of community support?
◆ Fear about change?
◆ Anxiety about decision making?
◆ An inability to share feelings?
◆ Family discord?
◆ Presence of concurrent life crises?
◆ Excessive activity?
◆ Depression?
◆ Feelings of alienation?
◆ Anger?
◆ Feelings of powerlessness?
◆ Guilt?
◆ Shame?
◆ Nervous anxiety?
◆ Physical ailments or illness?
◆ Self-pity?
◆ Confusion and mood swings?

42.2 Dealing with Feelings

How are you dealing with your feelings? Who could you to talk to?

42.3 Looking after Yourself

Do you have an outlet for your stress, such as exercise?

42.4 Finances

Do you need to reorganize your finances? Who could help?

42.5 Networking

How are you going to organize a networking strategy?

42.6 Where next?

Do you need to redefine your personal and career goals? Do you need to consider going back to school?

42.7 Résumés

Do you need to update your résumé?

42.8 Job Search

How are you going to organize your job search strategy?

**WORKING
WITH OTHERS**

42.9 The Downsizing Network

Could you network with other colleagues who have been laid off?

42.10 Job Search Network

Who do you know who might be of help in your job search? Who could you talk to about career management?

42.11 Web Working

Have you considered networking with others over the World Wide Web to search for work?

**WORKING
WITH A MENTOR**

42.12 Work Mentor

Have you identified a mentor at your place of work (or out of it) who could guide you in your career management?

**DEVELOPING
OTHERS**

42.13 Surviving Downsizing

Introduce the subject of surviving downsizing. The following questions can either be facilitated in a large group or through smaller groups:

◆ Since being told you have been laid off, are you experiencing:
  —A lack of personal fulfillment?
  —A loss of status?
  —Worry about your income?
  —A loss of independence?
  —A change in lifestyle?

—A lack of community support?
—Fear about change?
—Anxiety about decision making?
—An inability to share feelings?
—Family discord?
—Presence of concurrent life crises?
—Excessive activity?
—Depression?
—Feelings of alienation?
—Anger?
—Feelings of powerlessness?
—Guilt?
—Shame?
—Nervous anxiety?
—Physical ailments or illness?
—Self-pity?
—Confusion and mood swings?

◆ How are you dealing with your feelings? Who could you to talk to?
◆ How are you looking after yourself? Do you have an outlet for stress, such as exercise?
◆ Do you need to reorganize your finances? Who could help?
◆ How are you going to organize a networking strategy?
◆ Do you need to redefine your personal and career goals? Do you need to consider going back to school?
◆ Do you need to update your résumé?
◆ How are you going to organize your job search strategy?
◆ Could you network with other colleagues who have been laid off?
◆ Who do you know who might be of help in your job search? Who could you talk to about career management?
◆ Have you considered networking with others over the World Wide Web to search for work?
◆ Have you identified a mentor at your place of work (or out of it) who could guide you in your career management?

43
Tactics for Negotiation

INTRODUCTION

Negotiation is the process of identifying, arranging, and setting the terms and conditions of an agreement. The basics of effective negotiation are:

◆ Clear communication
◆ Persuasive communication
◆ Give and take
◆ Understanding other people's needs
◆ Decision-making skills
◆ Anticipating responses
◆ Keeping focused
◆ Projecting yourself
◆ Empathy

Negotiation is an interactive skill. All too often, negotiation is seen as an "I win" situation, but true negotiation needs to be an "I win–you win" situation. Those involved in win-win negotiations need to:

◆ Seek common ground
◆ Relate to the other party and their concerns
◆ Be ready to compromise
◆ Facilitate two-way discussions
◆ Use questioning and listening techniques
◆ Disclose appropriate information
◆ Build relationships
◆ Aim for agreement, not stalemate
◆ Seek mutual gains
◆ Yield the highest level of commitment from others
◆ Gain mutual respect and trust
◆ Commit to hard work rather than use force or manipulation
◆ Have full and equal involvement

> Variables are the raw material used in negotiation. They are the "must haves," the ideals, and the loss leaders (a non-profit way of attracting the buyer in). Use them as concessions.

Preparing for Negotiation

◆ Consider the other people involved, their needs, and possible objections; find out their intentions.
◆ Consider your own position.
◆ Set realistic objectives.
◆ Structure the meeting.
◆ Decide how variables can be used for trading purposes.

Conducting the Negotiation

Opening

◆ Summarize contracts and any agreements so far.
◆ Either take the hard approach (indicating that little will be given away) or the soft approach (best for unclear situations).

Main Body

◆ Use specific variables.
◆ Keep looking for additional variables.
◆ Use a promise of reward.
◆ Use a threat of punishment—for example, not giving something.
◆ Use hooks—for example, "My chairman says. . . ."
◆ Build a bridge of rapport through:

  —Discussing a neutral subject, obtaining initial agreement, and getting the other person to talk
  —Presenting options for the other person in your offering (even if you plan to negotiate them out later)
  —Referring back to a past agreement to reinforce persuasion
  —Stating clear objectives

◆ Show confidence.
◆ Ask questions and listen to the answers.
◆ Get the other parties' position firmly in your mind.
◆ Start trading early:

  —Be seen as driving a hard bargain, since the implied value of your concession will bring a relatively more valuable concession from the other party.
  —Optimize your concessions.
  —Minimize their concessions.
  —Play down your gratitude for concessions gained.
  —Build up the value of concessions you make.
  —If you can't optimize or minimize, stay silent.

◆ Put your major issue cards on the table.
◆ Summarize frequently.
◆ Avoid confrontation.
◆ Treat disagreements carefully.
◆ Bide your time.
◆ Make notes.
◆ Leave people feeling that each move forward is a positive one for them.
◆ Read between the lines.
◆ Don't allow yourself to become overemotional.
◆ Maintain neutrality.
◆ Keep your concentration focused.
◆ Don't act precipitately.
◆ Remain professional.
◆ Resolve to lead, albeit in a subtle way.
◆ Use verbal and nonverbal language to your advantage.
◆ Adopt a calm and considered approach.
◆ Don't underestimate the other party.
◆ Don't exaggerate facts.
◆ Don't push too hard.
◆ Don't overreact if responses are negative.
◆ Don't let yourself be affected by psychological warfare—for example, pretended misunderstanding.

◆ Don't push the other party; give them time to react favorably.
◆ Avoid deadlock—always search for variables.
◆ Don't agree to something you don't want.
◆ Aim to end on a pleasant note.

Agreement

◆ Decide on whether a formal or an informal contract is required.
◆ Set the policy and content of any contractual arrangements.

Negotiation is about discussion, not debate.

Influencing

Being able to influence others, in covert or overt ways, is a key factor in negotiating skills. Common influencing tactics include:

◆ Raw emotion (getting angry, making them cringe)
◆ Rational persuasion (presenting facts and logic)
◆ Manipulation (pretending to involve them)
◆ Mental torture (pestering until they give in)
◆ Personal appeal (drawing on loyalty or friendship)
◆ Ingratiation (flattery)
◆ Exchange (doing something for them in return)
◆ Pressure (demanding action, using threats)
◆ Using legitimacy (claiming rights, using authority)
◆ Coalitions (ganging up on them)
◆ Sulking (pretending to be hurt or offended)
◆ Pushing people to settle for short-term gains and long-term losses
◆ Pressurizing to get immediate action
◆ Making people fearful of you

You should be aware of these tactics in case people try to use them on you, but using them is manipulative and unlikely to secure a good long-term relationship once the negotiation is concluded. Also, beware of using "reason" in order to get your way:

◆ Reason can be seen as aggressive—you are trying to change someone else's views.
◆ Reason implies just one way, amounting to "telling" or "selling."
◆ Asking someone to "be reasonable" means asking them to see it your way.

Reasoning becomes involvement only when it stresses the benefits to the other party.

The best influencing skills involve:

◆ Inviting an opinion from someone who has not yet been given an opportunity to contribute
◆ Restoring a sense of proportion and relieving tension
◆ Acknowledging and reconciling others' views
◆ Reminding people of the stage they've reached

INDIVIDUAL TASKS AND REFLECTIONS

43.1 Initiation

Identify a past situation where you initiated a negotiation. How did you handle it? Were the outcomes satisfactory for you and the other person? How might you handle it differently today?

43.2 Negotiating Style

What type of negotiator are you? What are your strengths and weaknesses? Identify the skills you need to develop.

43.3 Past Negotiation

Reflect on a past situation in which you were involved in the negotiation process. How did others handle it? What is your assessment of the process?

43.4 The Power of Influence

What type of influence do you want?

◆ **Interpersonal:** rapport builder, confidant, facilitator, presenter
◆ **Authority:** decision maker, approval giver, supervisor
◆ **Resources:** provider of money, information, promotion, physical resources
◆ **Expertise:** rare or key skills/knowledge specialist, consultant

WORKING WITH OTHERS

43.5 Current Negotiation

Identify a current situation that you could initiate involving negotiation. Work out your game plan. Afterward, assess the outcomes and your performance.

43.6 The Negotiating Process

Identify a current situation in which you are part of the negotiating process. Work out your game plan. Assess the outcomes and your performance.

WORKING WITH A MENTOR

43.7 Shadow Your Mentor

Shadow your mentor in a negotiating situation. Assess their performance. Discuss.

43.8 Videotaping Negotiation

Role play a situation involving negotiation and videotape the session. You might do this with a colleague with your mentor present, or alternatively run the session with your mentor. Assess your own performance, discuss feedback, and identify skills that need improving (and how you're going to improve them).

DEVELOPING OTHERS

43.9 Role Play

Introduce the subject of negotiating skills. Brainstorm the kinds of skills necessary. Have a number of cards ready, loosely detailing role-play situations involving negotiation—for example, negotiating a pay-raise, negotiating a project deadline, negotiating when to enroll in a course, negotiating when to request vacation time, negotiating the need to hire temporary staff, and so on. Organize the learners into groups of four to six and give each group a card. After a few minutes deciding on the specific details of the situation, the groups then perform the role play using some of the skills brainstormed at the beginning, with at least one observer for feedback.

43.10 Lottery Win

Say to the group, "You have won $50,000 in a lottery to spend as you wish. Write down what you would like to do with the money—how you would like to spend it."

Give them time to do this. Then say, "You now need to justify, in six reasons, why you have chosen to spend your winnings as you have. Write them down and then rank them, listing the most important first and the least important last."

When this has been done, say, "The lottery company Winalot has made a mistake. You have to share the winnings with another person. I'm going to tell you who that is . . ."

Select people with different backgrounds and interests to work in pairs and say, "You now have to negotiate how to spend $50,000 between you in a way that is acceptable to you both."

When the negotiations are completed, reconvene the whole group and ask each pair, "What did you first want to spend your money on and what did you end up spending it on?" and "How far did your final choices satisfy the reasons for making your original choices?"

RECOMMENDED HRD PRESS TITLES

Negotiation Style Instrument, 16 pp.
The Everyday Negotiator, 250 pp.
50+ Activities to Teach Negotiation, 300 pp.

44

Tapping Your Personal Power

Power. We've all got it. What is it? How do we use it?

The concept of personal power is based on how we feel about ourselves and is demonstrated by how we communicate and interact with others. When we have a positive understanding of ourselves, we relate to others in a positive way because we have respect for others and ourselves.

We all have personal power because most of us have the ability to understand how we think, feel, react, and act. How we interpret this understanding and how we actively use it vary. A knife may be used to create a delicious casserole or to kill someone. Like using a knife, how personal power is used depends on the individual.

Even when you are affected by circumstances outside your control, you can still use your personal power to make a choice in the way you react. Even not making a choice is making a choice!

> Pleasing others rather than pleasing yourself is sometimes not in your own best interests. OK, so everyone loves you—but does anybody respect you?

Being a "people pleaser" is a key way in which we can give away our personal power. Do you:

◆ Feel guilty when saying "no"?
◆ Avoid asking for what you need?
◆ Tend to have a fixed smile when someone is angry?
◆ Let yourself be manipulated?
◆ Act as a doormat?
◆ Meet other people's expectations most of the time?
◆ Avoid making waves?
◆ Allow other people's needs to be more important than your own?
◆ Keep seeking people's approval?
◆ Persistently think things are your fault?
◆ Feel guilty receiving?
◆ Smile and say "everything's fine" when it isn't?
◆ Identify yourself through the eyes of others?
◆ Avoid voicing your own opinions?

If you answer "yes" to more than 50 percent of the above questions, you are a people pleaser and give away your personal power in order to please others. The beliefs behind being a people pleaser, and the questionable assumptions underlying them, are as follows:

◆ "I'll fulfill an 'obligation.'" To whom?
◆ "People will like me." It's impossible for everyone to like you just as you can't like everyone.
◆ "They'll value me." Therefore I must be OK.
◆ "I'll never be alone." We're all alone—it's how we make use of our contact with another that makes it meaningful.
◆ "They'll notice me." Why do you want to be noticed?

◆ "I'll always be needed." It's natural to want to be needed, but being needed doesn't justify our existence.

◆ "They won't be angry." Does it matter if they are angry? Maybe you need to learn to handle their anger.

◆ "People will think I'm clever." What does being clever equate to? Being noticed?

◆ "I'll always have a role." Therefore you have a right to exist.

You cannot be given power. You can only claim it yourself.

As children, we naturally wanted to receive approval from those around us. If this did not occur to the level we needed, we might tend to seek validation from others today. Not knowing how to approve of ourselves, we seek such validation in order to feel good about ourselves. We look for reaction in others and assume what we need to do in order to please them. When we have a need for approval from others, we may become people pleasers, fear criticism, fear failure, feel unworthy, ignore our own needs, and lack self-esteem. As we begin to rely on our own approval, we come to understand that wanting approval is OK, but we learn to ask for it rather than manipulate others to get it. We can accept compliments from others, and we can say "yes" and "no" when we mean "yes" and "no." As we shed the need for inappropriate approval seeking, we begin to recognize our own needs, be honest about how we feel, and build trust in ourselves and others.

Keeping motivated and positive will help you claim your personal power. It is up to you to take advantage of every opportunity that comes your way. If there are not enough opportunities, you must create them. Other people can contribute to your success and sense of well-being, but, at the end of the day, it's our attitude to life and not necessarily our ability to do that helps us reach our personal potential. In other words, it is your state of mind and creative approach to opportunities that will bring a positive response. No one owes you a living and no one else can give you something that you are not prepared to give yourself. Maintaining this attitude takes determination and discipline and undoubtedly there will be times when you will feel resentful, frustrated, and angry. That's OK. You can cope with these negative feelings—you have a right to feel and express them appropriately. In fact, you will feel better if you *do* express them. However, they will not last, and you will feel hopeful again.

When you take responsibility for your life and what happens to you, you are no longer a victim. Sometimes when you are waiting for that elusive promotion or work opportunity, you might feel as if all the power belongs to "those out there," but it doesn't. You have the power. You have the personal power to feel happy or sad, positive or negative, fearful or excited. You can feel empowered. You are in control. You cannot control other people or their responses, but you can control your own behavior, thoughts, and feelings. Keep yourself proactive and learning. Initiate activities. Take responsibility. Have some fun. Take some risks. While you're busy searching out life's opportunities through tapping your personal power, you'll find that all your positive energy will, in turn, produce unexpected opportunities without you even trying.

Ways to Reclaim Your Power

1. Be aware of the choices you have in any situation that comes your way.
2. Avoid casting blame on an external force for your bad feelings. Nothing outside yourself can control your feeling, thinking, or actions (unless you allow it to).

3. Determine what you want in life and act on it. Stop waiting for someone to give it to you.
4. Be aware of where and when you are playing the victim role—when you are not being responsible for what you are being, having, doing or feeling.
5. Be aware of the pay-offs that keep you bemoaning your fate and not claiming your personal power.

Personal power is also about defining yourself to others and not allowing them to define you to suit their cause. It's about developing a clear and accurate self-image rather than permitting others to label you inaccurately.

INDIVIDUAL TASKS AND REFLECTIONS

44.1 Power Role Models

What role models (alive or dead, fact or fantasy) represent your concept of personal power? Why?

44.2 Another's Personal Power

Consider one professional and one personal situation in which you have experienced another's personal power that affected you directly. What happened? What did you feel like?

44.3 Demonstrating Your Personal Power

Consider one professional and one personal situation where you have demonstrated your personal power to directly affect another. What happened? What did you feel like when using your power? How do you think the other person felt?

44.4 Self-Image

Think of characteristics to describe yourself (as honestly as possible) in each of these four categories:

◆ Personality
◆ Relationships with others
◆ Day-to-day functioning
◆ Appearance

Now rework your own self-image, using the same categories, but celebrating specific strengths.

WORKING WITH OTHERS

44.5 Mentoring Others and Personal Power

If you are in a mentoring role with another, how does this make you feel in terms of personal power? How do you think the other person experiences your power?

44.6 Leading Others and Personal Power

If you are responsible for leading or managing others, how do you demonstrate your personal power through your behaviors? How do you think others experience your power?

WORKING WITH A MENTOR

44.7 Interpretations of Personal Power

Discuss with your mentor your interpretation of personal power.

44.8 Being Mentored

Discuss with your mentor what it feels like to be mentored and how you feel about their levels of expertise and power.

44.9 Action Plan for Increasing Personal Power

Identify an area of your working life in which you feel relatively powerless. Discuss with your mentor the reasons why this might be so and work out an action plan for increasing your power in a positive way. Implement and review.

DEVELOPING

OTHERS

....

44.10 Brainstorming Personal Power

Introduce the topic of personal power and write the words *Personal Power* in the center of a flipchart sheet. Ask the group to brainstorm what they associate with these words.

44.11 Pair Power

Ask the learners to work in pairs to discuss specific areas of power—for example, levels of expertise, physical power, monetary power—for ten minutes. Reconvene the whole group and discuss for a further ten minutes, noting key points on a whiteboard or flipchart.

44.12 Group Power

Organize the learners into small groups. Each person has five minutes to share two key power areas—one in which they feel confident and another that they find difficult. Now double and then triple the size of the groups to continue the discussion until the whole group comes together. The objective of this exercise is for the learners to experience demonstrating personal power (through self-knowledge, disclosure, and discussion) in different sized groups as well as learning about the subject area. To close the exercise, discuss with the group how it felt to do the exercise in relation to using personal power.

This exercise could also be used with small groups to focus on particular issues of power for leaders, supervisors, managers, and directors. The focus could be on identification of power issues and the sharing of solutions, which in turn could lead to discussions about sharing power and the empowerment of others.

INTRODUCTION

The purpose of a team is the creation of synergy. This is where the sum of the whole is larger than the sum of each part (individual). Teams are needed when:

◆ There is a need for people to work together
◆ You are experiencing rapid changes
◆ There is uncertainty about a project and you need to share the problems and solutions
◆ You are dealing with a problem where nobody knows the answer

What motivates each of your team members? A team is motivated by:

◆ Recognition
◆ Responsibility
◆ Reward
◆ Respect

The concept of team roles was "invented" by Meredith Belbin, one of the foremost experts on team dynamics and the visiting Professor at the Centre for Leadership Studies at Exeter University. Team roles fall into two categories: their specialist role or responsibility and their team role.

Team Roles

◆ **Supporter:** team player, concerned with team unit, helpful and supportive to others, mild, diplomatic, dislikes confrontation, adapter rather than changer
◆ **Thinker:** creative, critical, needs acknowledgment
◆ **Organizer:** can turn ideas into workable plans, disciplined, efficient, methodical, slow to adapt
◆ **Implementer:** dutiful, organizer, hard-working, disciplined, resistant to change
◆ **Plant:** unorthodox, serious, imaginative, knowledgeable, problem solver, not too practical
◆ **Specialist:** self-starting, provides key knowledge and skills, can be too focused
◆ **Chair:** calm, self-confident, extrovert, dominant, strong sense of objectives, organizer, non-aggressive, can clarify aims of team, not particularly creative
◆ **Charismatic player:** a salesperson, emotional, insecure, tends to see themselves through the eyes of others
◆ **Shaper:** highly strung, outgoing, dynamic, dominant, lots of drive, prone to irritation and impatience, impulsive, competitive, domineering, concerned with getting things done, intolerant, outgoing, challenging
◆ **Entertainer:** a performer, a clown, someone who is humorous and who always has something to say
◆ **Rescuer:** the person who mediates and balances, caring, nurturing
◆ **Ideas person:** serious-minded, unorthodox, imaginative, inclined to disregard practical details

- ◆ **Investigator:** enthusiastic, communicative, enjoys exploring new potential, responds to challenge, curious, overoptimistic, loses interest quickly
- ◆ **Evaluator:** prudent, unemotional, hard-headed, lacks inspiration, likes to stick to the rules, identifies with facts and figures, objective, analytical, calm, dependable, can be disparaging
- ◆ **Team worker:** social, sensitive, responds to people and situations, promotes team spirit, indecisive at moments of crisis
- ◆ **Traditionalist:** tends to identify with a cause, motivated by insecurity and a need to belong
- ◆ **Completer:** orderly, conscientious, anxious, perfectionist, worrier, reluctant to let go, good at meeting deadlines, analytical, pays attention to detail
- ◆ **Dominator:** leader, competitive, motivated by a need to be in control

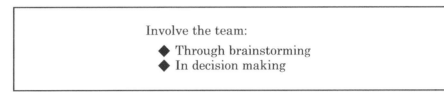

Involve the team:
- ◆ Through brainstorming
- ◆ In decision making

Team Development

Teams go through five natural stages of development in their lifetime:

1. **Forming:** Members explore through the facilitator or leader what benefits and problems are entailed in emotional investment in the team.
2. **Storming:** Members begin to form allegiances and to explore issues of control and power.
3. **Norming:** As the group resolves control and power issues, a sense of equality develops. Members may become involved in emotional attachments to others in the team.
4. **Performing:** The group creates a network of functional roles whereby individuals can use their capabilities and explore their potential.
5. **Mourning:** Endings may be marked by feelings of ambivalence. There may be issues of dependency or flight to avoid the loss of the group.

Team-building Problems

Team Discontent Checklist	
Problem	**Solution**
Your people feel that they are not being led in the manner they need and have become demotivated, leading to internal conflict.	Different team members may require different leadership styles from you. Although you have your own unique interpretation, you need to adapt your style, as appropriate, to different people.
Team discontent due to: ◆ an individual constantly taking the best jobs ◆ an individual antagonizing other team members with their attitude ◆ an individual not pulling their weight ◆ an individual promoting their own interests at the expense of the team	You may need to delegate tasks, rather than leaving the team to organize this themselves. You should objectively observe any discontent between team members before you take action. If you do decide to take action, involve the whole team in discussion first.

(continued)

(continued)

Team Discontent Checklist	
Problem	**Solution**
Team members perceive that there are insufficient or inappropriate resources to do the job.	It is your responsibility to ensure that there are enough resources. Use team contacts to obtain them.
Team members are over- or underworked.	When the team reaches overload, organize a social event to relieve the tension. If the issue is underwork, review the purpose of forming the team in the first place and/or set the team new projects and/or provide them with some training or learning opportunities.
The team lacks the skills or knowledge to complete the job.	Train team members in the required skills or buy them in.
The team is always complaining and grumbling, and lacks a common motivation.	Tolerate the occasional complaining session, but if complaints become disruptive, call a team meeting to establish causes and solutions.
Changes in the team, in objectives, and in working practices are destabilizing the team and affecting morale.	Find and make use of stability zones and rituals. Maintain open communication with all team members in terms of updates, reviews, and reassurance.
A team member lacks team spirit, causing friction.	If someone really does not want to work as part of a team, don't force them to.
The team seems to be out of control.	Make sure that team members know what is expected of them in terms of behavior. Be seen to deal with discipline problems fairly and equally.
The team is stagnating, there are few new ideas, and there is no enthusiasm for new ways of working.	It is your responsibility to encourage creativity and innovation. Try some of the exercises in the sections Critical Thinking or Generating Creative Solutions.
The team leader accepts poor levels of performance and does not encourage and support good performance.	Set standards of quality and behavior, and help those falling below those standards to achieve them through coaching and training.

> Conflict is part of the team-building process.

You know team building is working when:

◆ People work for each other and a higher (company) objective
◆ Good leadership prevails
◆ Information is openly shared
◆ Goals are common to all
◆ Feelings are expressed
◆ Success and failure are shared
◆ Conflict is worked through
◆ Objectives are clear
◆ Trust is shared
◆ People help each other

Leading a Team

There are many facets to team leadership. An effective team leader will use a mixture of the following typical roles:

◆ **Figurehead:** provides a focus for team identity
◆ **Communicator:** provides direction and information and serves as a listener
◆ **Representative:** serves as the interface between the team and the outside world
◆ **Executive:** sets standards and determines objectives
◆ **Controller:** organizes team output using individual strengths
◆ **Coach:** develops individual skills
◆ **Supporter:** provides support and guidance to individuals
◆ **Planner:** decides how the team should reach its goal
◆ **Exemplar:** stands as a model for the team and leads by example
◆ **Recruiter:** selects suitable members for the team
◆ **Involver:** empowers the team to become involved in its processes
◆ **Visionary:** communicates a vision of the future to the team
◆ **Resource manager:** uses all available resources to achieve the team's objectives

Teams led by good leaders:

◆ Have individuals who are allocated tasks they are best suited to
◆ Work to a common objective
◆ Are motivated to do the best they can
◆ Are able to understand its objectives
◆ Are able to understand how the objectives fit in with organizational objectives
◆ Have individuals who know what the team is about and their individual roles within it
◆ Have individuals who support each other
◆ Are prepared to go the extra mile

Develop team spirit through:

◆ Giving the team as much information as possible
◆ Instigating team rewards
◆ Training as a team whenever possible
◆ Thanking them as a team
◆ Ensuring that every team member has a responsibility
◆ Thanking them as individuals
◆ Helping the team help each other
◆ Including everyone in the team

Monitor team performance regularly by:

◆ Assessing the qualitative as well as the quantitative
◆ Involving your team in regular reviews combined with action planning
◆ Involving your team in appraising each other
◆ Involving your team in appraising you

INDIVIDUAL TASKS AND REFLECTIONS

45.1 Your Role

What role do you take in a team?

45.2 You as Leader

What kind of leader are you?

WORKING

WITH OTHERS

································

45.3 Team Roles

What roles can you identify among your team members?

45.4 Motivation of Team Members

What motivates each of your team members?

45.5 Group Dynamics

At the next team meeting you attend, observe the group dynamics. Are they helpful or destructive? If they are destructive, what can you do to remedy the situation?

45.6 Group Development

If you are part of an ongoing group, what stage of group development is the group at?

WORKING

WITH A MENTOR

································

45.7 Mentor Sit-in

Ask your mentor to sit in on a team meeting and to provide you with feedback on your leadership and their observations of the group.

45.8 Team Spirit

Discuss with your mentor how you can develop team spirit.

45.9 Problems and Solutions

Identify key problem areas within your team and discuss solutions with your mentor.

DEVELOPING

OTHERS

································

45.10 Plane Crash

Divide the learners into groups of ten. Tell them that each group has survived from a plane crash in a deserted part of the world. There is plenty of vegetation, birds, fish, and non-dangerous animals. Two people need to go in search of help. The remaining eight may have to form a new community for several months in order to survive. The survivors are: Reverend Mary Lecturn (36), John Gallaway (guitarist, singer, songwriter, also an ex-carpenter, 27), Phil Hert (teacher, 31), Alex White (farmer, 39), Annie Brownlow (doctor, 6 months pregnant, 29), Michael Gretern (teacher, also an ex-athlete, 45), Martin Shaw (engineer, 50) and Laura Hoffman (chef, 33).

  Each group member must put forward an argument for why they should stay. A group decision must be reached as to who goes and who stays. Following the exercise, discuss how the group interacted to reach its decisions and how satisfied or dissatisfied each member was with their role.

RECOMMENDED

HRD PRESS TITLES

································

Teambuilding Effectiveness Profile, 16 pp.
The Manager's Pocket Guide to Team Sponsorship, 128 pp.
50 Activities for Teambuilding: Volume 1, 236 pp.; *Volume 2,* 248 pp.

INTRODUCTION

Good time management involves a shift of focus to concentrate on results—to make time for what is important. Improve your management of time by:

◆ Using an activity log to evaluate your use of time and your energy levels at different times of the day
◆ Knowing how much your time is worth, and hence which tasks should be avoided, dropped, or delegated
◆ Determining and agreeing what is important for success in your job, and what constitutes exceptional performance
◆ Setting the goals and plans that will lead you to that success

Consider using your time more effectively by:

◆ Doing important work when you feel at your best
◆ Eating properly and resting effectively so that you spend more time performing well
◆ Running and attending meetings effectively
◆ Making use of time spent waiting
◆ Making use of traveling time
◆ Improving your reading skills
◆ Dropping unimportant tasks
◆ Making use of delays

> Create more time by delegating effectively and getting up early!

Control the distractions that interfere with your work by:

◆ Getting rid of unwanted jobs
◆ Blocking unwanted visitors
◆ Letting people know when you do not want to be disturbed
◆ Handling telephone calls effectively

By effectively using these basic skills, you can ensure that:

◆ You are successful in your job, because you know exactly what is expected of you and concentrate explicitly on those tasks
◆ You can become more in control of what you do
◆ You are productive and therefore secure in your job
◆ You can plan and move into job areas that you enjoy
◆ You can avoid staying late at work, giving yourself more quality time to relax and enjoy life outside work

The art of time management is the effective organization of the hours available to you. Whether at home, work, or play, it is satisfying to know that you have made the best use of your time. For effective time management, you need to employ the following skills:

◆ **Establishing clear and realistic objectives.** You need to establish what you want and why.

◆ **Planning and prioritizing.** You need to prioritize activities for two reasons: first, to achieve your objectives, and second, to give yourself motivation.

◆ **Decision making.** It's better to make a decision that might be wrong than to do nothing and live to regret it. As the Buddhists say, "Sit or walk, don't wobble." Successful time management involves making decisions, accepting responsibility for them, and seeing them through. We tend to put off making decisions because we are afraid of failing or looking foolish. But if we make a mistake, we learn and if we have self-respect, how can we look foolish? Our own opinion of ourselves is more important than how we believe (often wrongly) we appear to others.

◆ **Problem solving.** In order to plan and prioritize, and make decisions, we need to know the art of effective problem solving.

◆ **Assertiveness.** Managing your time often means saying "no" or maybe "yes" appropriately. Your time is valuable. Other people may intrude upon it, and you need to be assertive about how you want to spend it.

◆ **Letting go.** There are only so many hours in a day to do things, see others, and be with yourself. Sometimes you need to let go of something or someone in order to make room (and time) for new growth.

Major Time Wasters	
Interruptions	Crises
Procrastination	Comfortable jobs
Fatigue	Forgetting
Poor sense of time	Laziness
Addiction to adrenaline	Travel
Lack of planning	Lack of innovation
Not finishing things	Feeling guilty
Lack of confidence	Insecurity
Over-tight schedules	Showing off
Reluctance to confront	Not listening
Needing control	Talking too much
Inability to say "no"	

INDIVIDUAL TASKS AND REFLECTIONS

46.1 Daily Activity Log

Fill in the following activity log for one day and see which activities are useful and which waste time:

Activity Log	
Time	**Activity Description**
6:00	
6:30	
7:00	
7:30	
8:00	
8:30	
9:00	
9:30	
10:00	
10:30	
11:00	
11:30	
Noon	
12:30	
1:00	
1:30	
2:00	
2:30	
3:00	
3:30	
4:00	
4:30	
5:00	
5:30	
6:00	
6:30	

(continued)

(continued)

Time	Activity description
7:00	
7:30	
8:00	
8:30	
9:00	
10:00	
11:00	
12:00	

46.2 Prioritizing Activities

List all the jobs you do at present. You can make this a work-related list or more general. It should contain at least ten items. Work through the following steps:

1. Place an A next to those jobs on your list you consider really important.
2. Place a B next to those jobs you consider not quite so important.
3. Place a C next to those jobs you consider unimportant.

Now go back through the list again and eliminate all the Bs by considering them as either really important (A) or unimportant (C). Now prioritize your As in terms of their importance. Start by identifying the most important and numbering it A1, then work your way through the list until you have numbered each one. You will make best use of your time by concentrating your energy on the A list jobs.

46.3 Waste of Time

How do you think you waste time?

46.4 Administration Time

How do you organize your administration work? Are you at your most effective doing administration tasks or would your time best be used on other things? What could you do to cut down on the time you spend on administration? Could you delegate more?

WORKING

WITH OTHERS
....

46.5 Meeting Time

When you are next in a meeting with someone, observe how the time is used. How much time is wasted? What could have been done differently? Was the meeting necessary at all? Could the outcome of the meeting have been achieved in another way?

46.6 Telephone Time

How much time do you spend on the telephone? Could you handle your telephone calls more effectively? Do you need to take every call?

46.7 Reading Time

How much time do you spend (and waste) reading work-related material? Do you read unnecessary documents? Could you ask someone for a summary? Have you considered learning speed reading?

46.8 Travel Time

How much time do you spend on public transportation? How might you use that time more effectively?

WORKING WITH A MENTOR

46.9 Time and Energy Level Log

Use an activity log to evaluate your use of time and your energy levels at different times of the day. Discuss with your mentor. Identify ways in which you could make better use of your time and energy levels.

46.10 Letting Go of Tasks

Which of your tasks could be avoided, dropped, or delegated? Discuss with your mentor how you are going to achieve this.

46.11 Exceptional Performance

Determine what is important for success in your job, and what constitutes exceptional performance. Set the goals and plans that will lead you to that success.

DEVELOPING OTHERS

46.12 Pie Time

Introduce the subject of time management. Ask the learners to take two typical days in the past week—one working day and one rest day. Ask them to take two sheets of paper and draw a large circle on both, one for each day. They are to divide these circles up into percentages of how they use their time. They can base their use of time on traveling, working, sleeping, domestic tasks, eating, personal hygiene, and any other ways in which they use their time.

46.13 Improving Time Management

Introduce the subject of time management. Brainstorm ways in which we waste time. Then brainstorm ways of improving time management. Ask the learners to take a typical working day from the past week and complete an activity log. Then ask them to consider how they, in general, waste time and how they might have wasted time on the particular day for which they have completed the log. Organize them into small groups of four to six to discuss and work out an action plan on how they could improve their time management. Reconvene the whole group and discuss.

RECOMMENDED HRD PRESS TITLES

Time Management Effectiveness Profile, 16 pp.

47

Using Effective Questioning

If you couldn't ask a question, how would you know an answer when you see it? We ask ourselves questions. We ask questions of others. It's how we find things out. Questioning helps clarify and focus our thoughts and actions.

There are several types of questioning techniques:

◆ **Personal responsibility questions.** These imply that others have the responsibility for owning a problem and for making choices that contribute to solving it. A typical question of this type might be "What skills might you develop in order to help you with this problem?"

◆ **Leading questions.** These are questions that put the answer in the other person's mouth, such as "She really bothers you, doesn't she?"

◆ **Feeling questions.** These questions elicit feelings generated by a problem and might include "How do you feel about that?"

◆ **Closed questions.** Closed questions restrict the response of the other person. For example, "Did you think the report was useful?" is a closed question since it elicits only a "yes" or "no" response.

◆ **Open questions.** These questions invite a detailed or broad response. "What did you think of the report?" is an open question since it invites a wide response.

◆ **Specification questions.** These types of question focus on the details of the problem. An example might be "When you say he keeps badgering you, what exactly do you mean?"

◆ **Elaboration questions.** These give the other person the chance to expand on what they're talking about—for example, "What else would you like to tell me?"

In order to coordinate our life and work with those of other people, we all need to know more of what other people are feeling and thinking, wanting, and planning. But our usual closed questions actually tend to shut people up rather than open them up. You can encourage your conversation partners to share more of their thoughts and feelings by substituting closed questions that encourage only a "yes/no" response, with open-ended questions that allow for a wide range of responses. For example, asking "What did you think of the conference?" will evoke a more detailed response than "Did you like the conference?"

Consider the difference between two versions of the same question, which might be asked during a conversation between two people in a close relationship:

◆ "Do you want to go ahead and buy that house we saw yesterday?"

or

◆ "How do you feel about us buying that house we saw yesterday?"

The first version suggests a "yes" or "no" answer, favors "yes," and does not invite much discussion. A person hearing such a question might feel pressured to reach a decision, and may consequently not make the best one. The second question invites a much wider range of responses.

Even if our goal is to persuade, we can't do it well unless we address our listener's concerns, and we won't understand those concerns unless we ask questions that invite discussion. When you are pressed for time, it is tempting to push people into "yes/no" decisions. Here are some examples of open-ended questions that could help solve problems in a way that better meets everyone's needs:

◆ "How comfortable are you with Plan B?"
◆ "How could I modify this report to meet more of your requirements?"
◆ "What kind of information do you need in order to go forward?"
◆ "What do you think about moving the office to Scarborough?" (rather than "Is it OK with you if we . . . ?")
◆ "How do you feel about all of this?"
◆ "How ready are you to . . . ?" (rather than "Are you ready to . . . ?")

What sorts of question are truly worth asking? When we ask questions, we are using a powerful language tool to focus conversational attention and guide our interaction with others. But many of the questions we have learned to ask are totally pointless and self-defeating (witness the old example of parents asking their pregnant teenage daughter, "Why have you done this to us?"). In general, it is more productive to ask "how" questions about the future rather than "why" questions about the past. Asking questions is one of the principal means by which we try to understand what is going on around us, but we usually pay little heed to the quality of questions we ask. Consider, for example, the difference between "Why are you always such a fool?" and "How could we work together to solve this problem?"

Questions can lead us into the unknown, because they focus our attention and provide a theme for continued exploration. There is no straightforward set of rules about how to ask questions that are more helpful or more tuned to the needs of a particular situation. But you can get an intuitive sense of how to do it by studying a wide range of creative questions. The box below offers you a start:

Examples of Powerful Questions
How important is this?
Where do you feel stuck?
What do you mean by that?
What can we do for you?
What do you think the problem is?
What's your role in this issue?
What have you tried so far? What worked? What didn't?
Have you experienced anything like this before? (If so, what did you do?)
What can you do for yourself?
What do you hope for?
What's preventing you from . . .?
What would you be willing to give up for that?
If you could change one thing, what would it be?
Imagine a point in the future where your issue is resolved. How did you get there?
What would you like us to ask?
What have you learned?

INDIVIDUAL TASKS

AND REFLECTIONS
....

47.1 Being Questioned

How do you feel when you are questioned by others? Curious? Interrogated? Shy? Irritated?

47.2 Yes/No

Translate each of the following "yes/no" questions into an open-ended one. What problems can you imagine arising from each of these closed versions?

◆ Talking with a person who looks disappointed: "So you didn't like that, huh?"
◆ A pilot to a new co-pilot: "Do you know how to fly this thing?"
◆ A nurse to a patient: "Have you been taking your medication?"
◆ A parent to a teenager: "Don't you think it would be better if you did your homework first?"

WORKING

WITH OTHERS
....

47.3 Questioning Others

Monitor yourself for a week and notice how you question others. What types of questions do you tend to use?

47.4 Being Questioned

Take particular notice of when others question you. What types of question do they use? Does your response vary according to how a question is asked?

47.5 Asking Others

Experiment by asking people closed and open-ended questions. Notice their response.

WORKING

WITH A MENTOR
....

DEVELOPING

OTHERS
....

47.6 Developing Your Technique

Use the subject of developing your questioning techniques as a basis for a question-and-answer session between you and your mentor.

47.7 Practice Session

Ask for a volunteer and use them to demonstrate the responses to different types of questions. Organize the learners into pairs and ask them to do the same exercise. Reconvene the whole group to discuss.

47.8 Group Questions

Introduce the subject of using effective questioning. Brainstorm the different types of questioning techniques and when they might be used. Facilitate a group discussion on using questioning techniques.

INTRODUCTION

Valuing diversity is about empowering people. It makes an organization effective by capitalizing on all the strengths of each employee. Valuing diversity involves understanding, appreciating, and using the differences in every person.

Embracing diversity is the first step in building teams. Every team-building theory states that an effective team must contain a diverse group of people—that is, you must avoid only choosing people who are like you. Choosing a team of people like yourself is similar to inbreeding—it multiplies the flaws. By contrast, having a diverse group of people diminishes individual flaws.

Our biases and prejudices are deeply rooted within us. From the moment we are born, we learn about our environment, the world, and ourselves. Families, friends, peers, books, teachers, idols, and others influence us on what is right and what is wrong. These early experiences shape our perceptions and how we respond to them as adults. What we learn and experience gives us our subjective point of view, known as bias. Our biases serve as filtering devices that allow us to make sense of new information and experiences based on what we already know. Many of our biases are beneficial because they allow us to assume that something is true without proof. Otherwise, we would have to learn anew each time we encounter a fresh situation. But if we allow our bias to shade our perceptions of what people are capable of, then it is harmful: we begin to prejudge others on what we *think* they can or cannot do.

Embracing diversity is more than tolerating people who are different. It means actively welcoming and involving them by:

◆ Actively seeking information from people from a variety of backgrounds and cultures
◆ Including everyone in the problem-solving and decision-making process
◆ Creating a team spirit embraced by every member
◆ Encouraging people to ask for support (Because we each have different personal and professional backgrounds, when we are in a group we may feel alienated by our experiences and reluctant to ask for clarification on issues or for support with problems that do not appear to fit in with the "norm.")

Diversity is not only black and white, female and male, homosexual and heterosexual, Jew and Christian, young and old, and so on, but the diversity of every individual—slow learner and fast learner, introvert and extrovert, scholar and sportsperson, liberal and conservative.

Organizations need diverse groups of people on each and every team. For example, having a group of team builders will get you nowhere, because everyone will be out trying to create a team. Likewise, having a group of doers will get you nowhere, because everyone will be trying to accomplish something without a clear goal to guide them.

We all have a natural tendency to categorize people, and perhaps to judge them by the descriptions we assign to them. Below are some of the indicators we sometimes use to "fit" people into categories:

Work Characteristics	
Seniority	Position level
Experience	Union or non-union
Employed or unemployed	Type of education—for example, university, public school
Qualification level	
Personal Characteristics	
Sexual orientation	Physical status
Ethnic background	Religious background
Club associations	Socioeconomic status
Place of birth	Culture
Experiences	Marital status
Home address	Accent
Appearance	Where vacations are taken
Newspaper read	Car driven

However, it is these characteristics and experiences that make a person unique. We value diversity when we see all these unique characteristics and realize that people are more valuable because of their differences.

A realistic ideal of cultural diversity is one of multiculturalism. Multiculturalism is based on the idea that cultural identities should not be discarded but, instead, should be maintained and valued. The importance of cultural diversity has been largely accepted in business. This is illustrated by the increased presence of women and minorities in the business world.

Cultural diversity matters to every single one of us, both professionally and personally. For our businesses and communities to not only survive, but to thrive, each of us needs to be aware and sensitive to all members of the community. When all segments are respected and valued, it benefits everyone involved. Many of us live on the margins of society—in other words, we do fit into the mainstream, popular culture. In the United States, our popular culture, or ideal for business success, favors the white, young, heterosexual male. This means you are on the margins if you:

◆ Are a woman
◆ Have a non-white ethnic background
◆ Are not a heterosexual
◆ Are not between the ages of 21 and 40

If you fit any one of the above criteria, you cannot automatically assume that society's view of you is unobstructed or based solely on your individual character, qualifications, or accomplishments. You will encounter obstacles, prejudices, and stereotyping.

The management of diversity can be considered as a response to the need to recognize, respect, and capitalize on the differences in our society in terms of race, ethnicity, and gender. Different cultural groups have different values, styles, and personalities, each of which may have a substantial effect on the way they do business. Valuing diversity happens from the inside out. When we can embrace our own inner diversities—for example, we like to eat meat but can't bear the thought of blood sports—we are better placed to accept the diversities of those around us. When we can each accept ourselves and the diversities within others, we will find it easier to work together with our differences.

INDIVIDUAL TASKS AND REFLECTIONS

48.1 I Was Called

What labels can you recall from your childhood? Other than the name on your birth certificate, what else were you called?

48.2 Labeling Others

How did you label others when you were younger?

48.3 I See Myself

Complete in as many ways as you like: "I see myself as a . . ."

48.4 Prejudices

Being really honest with yourself, what are your prejudices?

WORKING WITH OTHERS

48.5 I See You—You See You

Choose one personal and one professional relationship where you know the person quite well. Make a list of their characteristics as you see them. Ask them to do the same for themselves. Compare.

48.6 You See Me—I See Me

Choose one personal and one professional relationship where the person knows you quite well. Make a list of your own characteristics as you see them. Ask them to do the same for you. Compare.

WORKING WITH A MENTOR

48.7 Team Diversity

If you are responsible for a team, consider the diversity of personal and professional skills and strengths present. How do you respond to the diversity? How might you improve your ability to make the best use of this diversity? Discuss with your mentor.

DEVELOPING OTHERS

48.8 The Value of Diversity

Introduce the subject of valuing diversity. Brainstorm the types of diversity we can encounter. Discuss what influences our attitudes toward diversity. Discuss why diversity can be valuable.

48.9 My Prejudice

Introduce the subject of valuing diversity. Ask each learner to identify one prejudice they have. Organize the group into small groups of four to six to discuss. Reconvene the whole group for feedback.

48.10 Team Diversity

Introduce the subject of valuing diversity. Brainstorm the types of diversity we can encounter. Discuss why diversity can be valuable in a team. Ask each learner to identify one prejudice they have with regard to teamwork (considering any teams they are part of outside this learning experience). Organize the learners into smaller groups of four to six to discuss their team-related prejudices. The objective of this exercise is to discuss and move toward solutions and also to be aware of any prejudices in the small group with which they are working through this exercise.

Working on the diversity within the small group could further enhance the exercise.

RECOMMENDED HRD PRESS TITLES

....

Diversity and Cultural Awareness Profile, 16 pp.
The Manager's Pocket Guide to Diversity Management, 190 pp.
50 Activities for Diversity Training, 300 pp.

INTRODUCTION

Actions speak louder than words—in other words, the language communicated by our bodies is often in conflict with what we actually say. We give away nonverbal signals through our gestures, facial expression, eyes, body movements, and verbal language. Verbal language, in this context, doesn't so much mean what you say as how you say it and the key phrases you use, such as "You must . . ." as opposed to "I would appreciate it if you could . . ." Which one would you respond to?

Do you give away clues about your feelings via verbal and nonverbal language despite your attempts to control them? These clues may include:

◆ Fiddling—conveying nervousness
◆ Tapping—indicating impatience or anger
◆ Changes in voice pitch and tone—signaling timidity
◆ A clenched jaw—indicating tension or aggression
◆ An automatic or false smile—saying, "Please don't be angry"

> Get to know your own personal space and be sensitive to that of others. Ideally stand or sit directly in front of the other person.

According to a University of Southern California study, up to 55 percent of influence in communication comes from your body language. Let's take a look at how you can control it. First, you must understand that you can control your emotions by controlling your physiology. Try this. Stand up. Smile. Look straight ahead. Put your shoulders back. Take a deep breath. Now, try to feel depressed. If you do this exercise, you'll find that you can't feel miserable when you hold your body this way. Some experts suggest that when you are trying to increase your confidence, you must "fake it till you make it." What they are saying is that if you move your body as though you already know what you are doing, your brain will begin to believe that you do, in fact, know what you are doing.

> Aim for a steady, relaxed eye contact. Avoid intrusive stares or a shifting gaze.

The first person you need to affect with positive body language is not the other person, but yourself. If you cannot affect your own emotional state, how can you influence that of others? Start by controlling your breath. Experiment with taking deep breaths from the diaphragm. The quickest way to change your mental state and body language is to change your breathing.

The Mirroring and Matching Technique

Mirror the physiology of the customer or person you wish to influence. If they are down, go down to their level. If they are up, come up to their level. If they are talking fast, you talk fast. If they are slouching, you slouch. Then, as you talk with them, slowly begin to make small changes in your body language. Your goal is to bring the person you are trying to influence into the physiology that will be most effective for achieving your desired outcome, and you want the other party to feel good about themselves, you, and being with you.

Your mind will follow the lead you dictate for your body and your life. Start by deciding to control your body language in order to feel better about yourself. Over time, others will begin to feel better about themselves while they are around you, because they are unconsciously mirroring or emulating you.

You can't be assertive if you slouch, hunch over, or are off-balance.

INDIVIDUAL TASKS AND REFLECTIONS

49.1 Analysis of Others' Behavior

Which of the following behaviors would you find encouraging and discouraging in a speaker?

Behavior	Encouraging (✓)	Discouraging (✓)
Raising an eyebrow		
Looking anxious		
Leaning far back		
Sitting on the same level as you		
Putting head close to yours		
Whispering		
Leaning slightly toward you		
Bouncing a leg		
Tugging at an ear		
Staring at you		
Waving an arm		
Warmth in voice		
High-pitched voice		
Looking out the window		

(continued)

(continued)

Behavior	Encouraging (✓)	Discouraging (✓)
Vacant look		
Looking toward you		
Comfortable pace of speech		
Shutting eyes		
Sitting higher than you		
Smiling		
Slouching		
Open body posture		
Looking alert		
Shuffling about		

49.2 Observing Others

For one week, observe the body language of those you relate to in your personal and professional life. What do you notice?

49.3 Role Model Analysis

Identify a role model who you admire and analyze how they use verbal and nonverbal language.

WORKING

WITH OTHERS

....

49.4 Reading Behaviors

How do others signify:
◆ Warmth?
◆ Hostility?
◆ Control?
◆ Submissiveness?

49.5 Discouraging Body Language

Assess which aspects of your verbal and nonverbal language discourage others from communicating with you.

49.6 Relating Body Language

Monitor yourself when relating to others. Does what you say correspond to your body language? How do others respond to your body language?

WORKING

WITH A MENTOR

....

49.7 Caught on Camera

Videotape yourself having a session with your mentor. Review and discuss your verbal and nonverbal language. Identify areas that need developing.

49.8 Live Assessment

Arrange for your mentor to be present in two situations where you are relating to others. Assess your own verbal and nonverbal language. Meet and discuss their feedback on your body language and your own assessment. Identify strengths and weaknesses. Formulate a development plan to improve your body language.

DEVELOPING

OTHERS

••••••••••••••••••••

49.9 Aggressive, Passive, and Assertive

Introduce the subject of verbal and nonverbal language. Separate the general styles into aggressive, passive, and assertive. Divide the learners into three groups and ask each to come up with a description of the three general styles on a sheet of flipchart paper. All the groups can describe all three styles or you could ask each group to do one. Each group presents their descriptions. Discuss.

49.10 Verbal and Nonverbal Language Audit

Introduce specifics of verbal and nonverbal language including voice tone and pitch, speech pattern, facial expression, eye contact, body movements, and verbal styles. Give each learner the following template and ask them to provide examples for each box. They can do this exercise alone or in groups. Each group then presents their findings for you to write on to a central flipchart sheet.

Verbal and Nonverbal Language	Aggressive	Passive	Assertive
Voice tone and pitch			
Speech pattern			
Facial expression			
Eye contact			
Body movements			
Verbal styles			

49.11 Observe and Feedback

Introduce the subject of verbal and nonverbal language and divide the learners into groups of three. Two people will discuss related topics of body language while the third person observes and provides feedback on their body language. They then swap roles until each person has had a chance to be the observer. Reconvene the whole group and discuss.

Conversations and Conflict

One of the basic differences between men and women are their reasons for conversing. Women tend to converse to build connections and intimacy. Life is viewed as a community and women have a need to preserve intimacy and avoid isolation. Therefore, women tend to converse about their relationships. Men often perceive this to be gossiping, when in reality it is the way in which women build more connections and create greater levels of intimacy. Men view conversations as negotiations to obtain the upper hand. They tend to see individuals within a hierarchy in which they are either one-up or one-down. Therefore, men converse and compare notes about things such as cars and stereo equipment. The essential element in communication for men is to gain status and independence. Another basic difference is that men give reports when they talk, whereas women try to build rapport. Therefore, men give facts and information, and women are more relationship oriented. For men, talk is information. For women, talk is interaction.

Men and women tend to deal with conflict differently as well. Women are more aware of nonverbal language and can sense when something is wrong. Men, on the other hand, can ignore those same nonverbal signals until the situation escalates. When you have a conflict with a woman, you have broken that important intimacy and it will take time to heal the relationship. Men, on the other hand, can have an argument at 9:00 a.m. and then go out for a beer together that evening. Women have difficulty understanding this. Didn't they just have an argument? Yes. But both men knew which man was up and which man was down, so the conflict was over and they moved on.

Problem Solving

And problem solving? Women like to discuss problems as a way of building intimacy and connection. Men like to solve problems. Remember, men have conversations to obtain the upper hand; therefore, giving advice comes naturally. Women, on the other hand, have conversations to build closeness; therefore, giving empathy comes naturally. Men need to achieve results and like to work out the details of solving a problem alone. To offer a man unsolicited advice is to presume that he doesn't know what to do or that he can't do it on his own. When a woman is asking a man for support, she needs to be direct and brief. She needs to avoid using blame language. She will find that a man wants to make improvements when he feels he is being approached as the solution to a problem rather than as the problem itself.

Men are motivated and empowered when they feel needed and are more willing to say "yes" if they have the freedom to say "no." Men may act out a particular feeling as a cover-up for the real feeling underneath. For example, a man's deepest fear is that he is not good enough, or that he is incompetent, and he may use anger as a way of avoiding sadness, hurt, guilt, and fear, or he may use indifference as a way of avoiding anger.

A woman's sense of self is defined through her feelings and the quality of her relationships. To feel better, women get together and openly talk about their problems. Women talking together doesn't always need to produce solutions. A woman under stress is not immediately concerned with finding solutions to her problems, but rather seeks relief by expressing herself and being understood. She is fulfilled through talking about the details of her problem. Conflicts will tend to escalate when a man begins to invalidate a woman's feelings and she responds to him disapprovingly. Women, too, can cover up their real emotion. For example, they may use concern and worry as a way of avoiding anger, guilt, and fear, or they may use fear as a way of avoiding anger and sadness.

The following are ways in which a man might mistakenly invalidate feelings and perceptions or offer unwanted solutions to a woman:

- ◆ "From now on, I'll handle it."
- ◆ "You shouldn't worry so much."
- ◆ "Why let others treat you that way? Forget them."
- ◆ "Why don't you just do it?"
- ◆ "This is what you should do."

Likewise, a woman might unwittingly annoy a man by offering advice or seemingly harmless criticism:

- ◆ "You're not leaving yourself much time."
- ◆ "You shouldn't work so hard. Take a day off."
- ◆ "Your office is a mess. How can you think in here?"
- ◆ "Don't put it there. It will get lost."

Male/Female Psychology

According to popular psychology, male and female personalities can be further explained by reference to the Anima and Animus.

The **Anima** represents the female qualities within a man as learned through the mother. The positive of the Anima is that it keeps the man attuned to inner values; acts as a guide to his inner self; is intuitive, nurturing, creative; and has feeling. Its negative aspects are irritability, depression, uncertainty, insecurity, or touchiness. If the man's relationship with the mother was too strong, it might make him weak-willed or prone to be victimized by women. The Anima is responsible for a man's image of women.

The **Animus** represents the male qualities within a woman as learned through the father. The positive aspects of the Animus are action, assertiveness, logic, and orientation to goals. The negative aspects are a love of power, coldness, obstinacy, and forcefulness. The Animus is responsible for a woman's image of men.

The Anima and Animus are the underdeveloped sides of the personality attempting to assert themselves for good or bad.

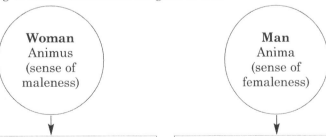

Woman
Animus
(sense of
maleness)

Man
Anima
(sense of
femaleness)

Females learn from the women in their childhood how to be female and how women use their sense of maleness. Females learn from the men in their childhood how to use maleness.	Males learn from the men in their childhood how to be male and how men use their sense of femaleness. Males learn from the women in their childhood how to use femaleness.

A Woman's Guide to Understanding Men

◆ A man's sense of self is defined through his ability to achieve results.
◆ To offer a man unsolicited advice is to presume that he doesn't know what to do or that he can't do it on his own.
◆ A man wants to make improvements when he feels he is being approached as the solution to a problem, rather than as the problem itself.
◆ To feel better, men retreat into themselves to solve problems alone.
◆ A man's deepest fear is that he is not good enough or that he is incompetent.
◆ Men are motivated and empowered when they feel needed.
◆ A man is fulfilled through working out the intricate details of solving a problem.
◆ Men are more willing to say "yes" if they have the freedom to say "no."
◆ When a man is in a negative state, treat him like a storm and lie low.
◆ Men might use anger as a way of avoiding feeling sad, hurt, guilt, and fear.
◆ Men might use indifference and discouragement as a way of avoiding anger.
◆ Men need to receive trust, acceptance, appreciation, admiration, approval, and encouragement.
◆ When a woman is asking a man for support, she needs to be direct and brief, and use "Would you . . .?" and "Will you . . .?" phrases.
◆ Men are prone to argue when they have made a mistake.
◆ The most common way women unknowingly start conflicts with men is by not being direct when they share their feelings.
◆ How women can score with men: Share negative feelings in a centered way without blaming and ask for support without being demanding.

A Man's Guide to Understanding Women

◆ A woman's sense of self is defined through her feelings and the quality of her relationships.
◆ To feel better, women get together and openly talk about their problems.
◆ A woman under stress is not immediately concerned with finding solutions to her problems but rather seeks relief by expressing herself and being understood.
◆ A woman is fulfilled through talking about the details of her problem.
◆ Women are motivated and empowered when they feel respected.
◆ Women need to receive reassurance, validation, respect, and understanding.
◆ Conflicts escalate when a man begins to invalidate a woman's feelings, and she responds to him disapprovingly.
◆ Women might use concern and worry as a way of avoiding anger, guilt, fear, and disappointment.
◆ Women might use fear and uncertainty as a way of avoiding anger, hurt, and sadness.
◆ Women might fall into confusion as a way of avoiding anger, irritation, and frustration.
◆ How men can score with women: Practice listening and asking questions, and validate her feelings when she is upset.

INDIVIDUAL TASKS AND REFLECTIONS

50.1 Gender Characteristics

What of the following gender characteristics (you can apply the words from your own gender or from both) do you associate with?

Male	Female
Competitive	Nurturing
Logical	Emotional
Aggressive	Yielding
Thrusting	Understanding
Protective	Tender
Disciplined	Sympathetic
Rigid	Compassionate
Judgmental	Affectionate
Unemotional	Gentle
Reasoning	Gullible
Dominant	Shy
Forceful	Vulnerable
Independent	Wise
Decisive	Intuitive
Strong	Spontaneous
Self-sufficient	Receptive
Risk taker	Creative
Ambitious	Introverted
Leader	Spatial
Organized	Soft

50.2 Same Gender Parent

What did you learn about your gender from your same gender parent?

50.3 Opposite Gender Parent

What did you learn about your gender from your opposite gender parent?

50.4 Women Together

Observe groups of women together. How do they behave with each other?

50.5 Men Together

Observe groups of men together. How do they behave with each other?

50.6 Mixed Gender Together

Observe mixed gender groups relating to each other. How do they behave with each other?

WORKING WITH OTHERS

50.7 Your Behavior

Observe yourself with your own gender and with the opposite gender. How does your behavior change when relating to each gender (if at all)?

50.8 The Behavior of Others

How does your own gender behave toward you? What are the differences in the way the opposite gender behaves toward you?

WORKING WITH A MENTOR

50.9 Professional Behavior

Discuss with your mentor how men and women behave (and are treated differently if appropriate) in your field of work.

DEVELOPING

OTHERS

....

50.10 Gender Relationship

Discuss how the gender of yourself and your mentor affects your relationship.

50.11 Present Your Observation

Start with one group of men and another of women. Each group has two observers—one man and one woman if possible. If you only use a single observer, use one of the opposite gender to the group. Each group is to discuss a topic related to working with gender differences, resulting in a group presentation. The observers are to provide feedback to the group on how the group related (with reference to traditional gender behavior). Reconvene the whole group for presentation feedback and observation feedback.

You could do a similar exercise with a single large group made up of men and women with perhaps four observers (two men and two women). The conclusion would be feedback from the observers and a key summary of the discussion points.

50.12 Pair Work

Ask the learners to work in pairs—one male and one female. They are to discuss communicating with different genders and any differences that arise for them personally. They then work toward compiling ways of improving communications and understanding with their own and the opposite gender. Reconvene the whole group and discuss key issues, including what the pairs discovered from working with each other.

References and Further Reading

Bandler, Richard, and Grinder, John (1983), *Reframing,* U.S.: Real People Press.

Bandler, Richard, and Grinder, John (1996), *Frogs into Princes,* U.S.: Eden Grove Editions.

Belbin, Meredith (1996), *Management Teams: Why They Succeed or Fail,* London: Butterworth-Heinemann.

Berne, Eric (1996), *Games People Play: The Psychology of Human Relationships* (reissue ed.), London: Ballantine Books.

Bouchard, Paul, "Self-directed Learning in Educational Settings," Montreal: Department of Education, Concordia University at http://artsciccwin.concordia.ca/ education/girat/proposal.html.

Daloz, Laurent A. (1999), *Mentor: Guiding the Journey of Adult Learners,* (2nd ed.), New York: Jossey Bass.

Ekman, Paul (1992), "An Argument for Basic Emotions," *Cognition and Emotion,* 6, pp. 169–200.

Goleman, Daniel (1996), *Emotional Intelligence,* London: Bloomsbury Publishing.

Goleman, Daniel (2000), *Working with Emotional Intelligence,* New York: Bantam Doubleday Dell Publishing.

Littlejohn, Stephen, "Bites of information," *Theories of Human Communication* (5th ed.).

Maslow, Abraham (1987), *Motivation and Personality* (3rd ed.), Wokingham, England: Addison Wesley.

Maslow, Abraham (1993), *Farther Reaches of Human Nature,* Harmondsworth, England: Arkana.

Peters, Tom (1989), *A Passion for Excellence: The Leadership Difference* (reissue ed.), London: Warner Books.

Rehner, Jan (1994), *Practical Strategies for Critical Thinking,* Boston: Houghton-Mifflin Co.

Rogers, Carl (1995), *A Therapist's View of Psychotherapy,* Boston: Houghton-Mifflin Co.

Ruggerio, Vincent (1996), *Becoming a Critical Thinker* (2nd ed.), Boston: Houghton-Mifflin Co.

Tannenbaum, Robert S., and Schmidt, Warren H. (1973), "How to create a Leadership Pattern," *Harvard Business Review,* 51(3).

Made in the USA
Las Vegas, NV
10 December 2021